The Responsible Reporter

"Bruce J. Evensen has put together a masterful book. *The Responsible Reporter* epitomizes what a text on writing and reporting should be. It provides superb insight into the writing and reporting process; offers important historical perspective; and best of all, it's well-written. The fact that so many respected contributing authors are included here—people such as Fred Blevens, Dave Davies, Janice Hume, John Pauly, and Sam Riley—is a reflection of the book's excellence. Students will enjoy and benefit from this book."

Mike Murray, University of Missouri Board of Curators' Distinguished Professor;
Author of Media Law and Ethics

"Media content is created by people who have many professional and practical decisions to make. In examining the ways today's journalists gather and process news, this informative and wide-ranging book illuminates the kinds of thinking and writing reporters must master to do their vitally important work well."

Jeffrey A. Smith, University of Wisconsin-Milwaukee

"Future journalists need the message of this book: keep democracy strong. *The Responsible Reporter* is written with passion, intelligence, and a compelling call to serve public life through accurate, balanced, fair, and thoroughly researched story-telling. Authors model the quality of writing that keeps us wanting more."

Mark Fackler, Professor, Department of Communication Arts and Sciences,
Calvin College, Grand Rapids, Michigan

"Bruce J. Evensen's latest edition of *The Responsible Reporter* is a cure for the benighted who say journalists have lost their sense of true North. The third edition can be subtle but its intellectual undertow will pull readers into greater ethical strength. His collection of some of the finest thinkers on news reporting in the Information Age lead the reader to one conclusion: Journalism is a high calling and more important today than ever. An added bonus is the prose is a joy to read and may help this generation of journalists and the next one write better because they are better for reading mature thoughts from mature models."

Michael R. Smith, Chair, Department of Mass Communication,
Campbell University, Buies Creek, North Carolina

"I recommend this book to anyone who is interested in the key role of journalism in a democratic society. This is a book that focuses—in a very modern way—on key themes of social responsibility, examining the way journalists can—and must—serve society. News is at the center of self-governance; the guiding principle of this wonderful book is the idea that journalists must rise to the challenge of a crowded news/infotainment era by continuing to provide key information to citizens/readers/viewers.

This book reminds us that journalism is central to democratic self-governance, and that journalists have a great opportunity—and responsibility—to make sure we have the news we need. This book reminds us that journalists today need to adapt, and adapt quickly, if they are to continue to be relevant, and if they are to continue to provide news and information so central to democratic self government. Americans today face a dizzying array of news sources (and fake news sources); the burden is on journalists to make sure that the vital news of the day is presented—and is presented in a way that citizens will absorb. Journalists, as the authors point out, need to take seriously their obligation to research and report the news that makes a civil society possible. This is a 'must read' for anyone who values democracy."

Gerald J. Baldasty, Chair, Department of Communication, University of Washington

"At a time when new technologies are transforming the nature of news reporting and the lines separating good journalism from advertising, public relations, entertainment, and propaganda are regularly being blurred, *The Responsible Reporter* offers citizens a clear explanation of the many ways the Fourth Estate is important to our democracy. The editor, Bruce J. Evensen, who is a former reporter and one of the nation's leading journalism historians, is to be commended for assembling a collection of intelligently written essays that explain the principles on which sound journalism should operate. Journalism students and professionals alike will benefit from reading this work."

Stephen Vaughn, Professor, School of Journalism and Mass Communication,
University of Wisconsin-Madison

The Responsible Reporter

PETER LANG
New York • Washington, D.C./Baltimore • Bern
Frankfurt am Main • Berlin • Brussels • Vienna • Oxford

The Responsible Reporter

Journalism in the Information Age
THIRD EDITION

Bruce J. Evensen, Editor

PETER LANG
New York • Washington, D.C./Baltimore • Bern
Frankfurt am Main • Berlin • Brussels • Vienna • Oxford

Library of Congress Cataloging-in-Publication Data

Evensen, Bruce J.
The responsible reporter: Journalism in the information age /
Bruce Evensen.—3d ed.
p. cm.
1. Reporters and reporting. I. Title.
PN4781.R39   070.4'3—dc22   2008009679
ISBN 978-1-4331-0350-6

Bibliographic information published by **Die Deutsche Bibliothek**.
Die Deutsche Bibliothek lists this publication in the "Deutsche
Nationalbibliografie"; detailed bibliographic data is available
on the Internet at http://dnb.ddb.de/.

Cover design by Clear Point Designs

The paper in this book meets the guidelines for permanence and durability
of the Committee on Production Guidelines for Book Longevity
of the Council of Library Resources.

To Scott, my wonderful brother.

First as son and nephew, then as

husband, father, uncle, and worker,

he has always been a faithful friend

and a most responsible man.

Table of Contents

SECTION TWO: WHERE IS THE NEWS AND HOW IS IT GATHERED?

SECTION THREE: HOW IS THE NEWS WRITTEN?

Preface
TO THIRD EDITION

The rise of printing in early modern Europe was a tough time for monks in scriptoria but a terrific time for printers who knew how to handle moveable type. Similarly, the end of the analog era has seen a sea change in the skills that are needed in reporting the news. The digital universe encourages storytelling across multimedia platforms often to targeted readerships. Collaborative newsgathering and dissemination emphasize speed and the ability to think critically as well as visually, often challenging the social responsibility of journalists to give citizens news they need to know.

David Shribman, executive editor of the *Pittsburgh Post-Gazette,* a newspaper now in its 220th year, knows that "newsrooms nowadays don't only produce newspapers." The paper has the nation's forty-fourth-largest circulation, 244,000 daily, but has seen it erode 30,000 in the last nine years. Yet the paper is reaching more readers than ever before in its history through podcasts, studio roundtables, and five-minute video newscasts promoted on the paper's front page.

"Multimedia isn't a trend, it's an explosion," says Allan Walton, an assistant managing editor at the *Post-Gazette.* The paper's webcasts have made it the twenty-fifth most visited among U.S. news sites. It affirms Shribman's certainty that journalists "can succeed more now than ever before" in fulfilling the promise of new technologies. "There were a lot of really good blacksmiths the year the Model T came out," he observes. "I don't want us to be a bunch of blacksmiths."

Time's managing editor, Richard Stengel, is among those who believe journalists need "a point of view" to "get people's attention" and keep themselves and their sites relevant. In April 2008, he told University of Mississippi students, "I don't think people are looking for us to ask questions." Instead, he said, "They're looking for us to answer questions." He was asked what this might mean to traditional journalistic standards of fairness, balance, and impartiality. Stengel answered, "We sort of make [those standards] up as we go along. And I think that will continue to happen."

From the Enlightenment onward, the foundation for liberal democracies has been trusting citizens with useful information to make rational decisions about what's in their interest. Journalism's role, and the reason for its Constitutional protection, is to gather the news of the day, to put it in a context that will give it meaning, and to offer the public a picture of the world upon which they can act. Stengel is among those, however, who have a different model in mind. "You have to have a point of view about things," he explains. "You can't always just say, 'on the one hand this, and on the other hand that.'" Stengel is certain that "people trust us to make decisions." They recognize that "we're experts in what we do."

Poll data does not support Stengel's certainty. In fact, no profession has fallen further faster in public confidence over the past decade than journalism. According to Gallup, journalism now ranks nineteenth of all institutions in American life in terms of its credibility. Three in four people tell Pew researchers that journalism is "vital" to the nation, yet two in three say they're "dissatisfied" with press performance. Citizens cite "lack of objectivity" as their number-one gripe against journalists. They don't want to be patronized by the press. Instead, they demand news worth knowing. And their insistence is a very good thing for democracy.

The third edition of *The Responsible Reporter: Journalism in the Information Age* is intended to ensure that the first generation of digital journalists will not have to make it up as they go along. The technology of newsgathering has radically changed, but the values that undergird socially responsible reporting are more needed now than ever before. In the book's first section, "What's New in the News?," our contributors analyze the collaborative character and changing toolkit of twenty-first-century reporting. A special feature of the book's second section, "Where Is the News and How Is It Gathered?," is an analysis of how online stories are constructed and the niche readerships these stories serve. The book's third and final section examines how news is developed across multiple platforms. "How Is the News Written?" details how the 24/7 news cycle of cable and online is transforming the way print and broadcast stories are assembled.

In the foreword to the second edition of *The Responsible Reporter* we anticipated a period of almost unprecedented opportunity to use new techniques of storytelling in helping reporters and editors create a more civil society. This volume draws together the extraordinary experiences and insights of today's journalists and journalism educators in charting a course for beginning journalists now entering a rapidly changing profession. The digital universe is morphing all it comes in contact with, including journalism. So the future is terrifying and exhilarating for those of us who do this for a living and as a calling. On behalf of my colleagues, we welcome you. Journalism has a proud tradition of serving citizens with news that makes self-actualization and participation in public life possible. With this edition, we affirm journalism's core values while introducing you to new techniques that can be used in support of this important service.

What Is the News?

What's New
in the News?

BRUCE J. EVENSEN

My family has subscribed to the *Chicago Tribune* for more than half of its 160 years. My grandfather was an immigrant Norwegian who worked in a Chicago foundry and bought the *Trib* to learn the language and local customs. His son was a veteran of World War II who found postwar work as an electrician and raised his family in a Chicago suburb, where the *Tribune* appeared each morning on the welcome mat. As young boys my brothers and I started each day with the newspaper opened at the sports page. We first tried reading photo captions. I knew how to spell "shortstop" and "single" and "stolen base" through a world opened to me by staff photographers. We grew up with the *Tribune*, like a lot of kids in my neighborhood. It ended every argument over who had more homers and who hit for a higher average. You could argue Ernie Banks or Hank Aaron or Willie Mays, but the *Tribune* would tell you. It could be trusted. As we grew up, the *Trib* remained authoritative. It could tell you what tomorrow's weather would be. It showed you what Sears was selling. It told you where you could get a used car you could afford. It announced what movies were in town and whether they were any good. Its listings gave you the week in television. Its coupons got you sale prices on Oscar Meyer hot dogs and Swanson TV dinners. You read about highways being built to tie the city to its suburbs, and when you were away at college you missed holding the paper in your hands. You missed its weight and strength and familiar face. **You knew the paper and its sections as well as a member of your own family.** You and the paper had a shared history, and you tried to share it with your son and daughter, but he was much more interested in PlayStation 2 and Sports Center, and she preferred IM'ing when she wasn't playing electronic solitaire. And even for me, drilling online sites, cable, and satellite radio came to occupy the time once devoted to the morning newspaper.

Then, it finally happened. The 104th edition of the *Chicago Tribune,* published in the proud paper's 159th year, on April 14, 2006, featured a two-deck, five-column headline that stated, "Defining a Conflict: On the Ground, It's a Civil War." There was no attribution. It was not a quotation. It was, instead, the paper's opinion that a "civil war" is what the controversial and unpopular war in Iraq had become. Aamer Madhani, a *Tribune* staff reporter, filing from Baghdad, claimed that unnamed Iraqis were telling him that "their country is embroiled in what amounts to a civil war." To substantiate this claim, Madhani cited the words of former prime minister Ayad Allawi, who had told the British Broadcasting Corporation a month before that "if this is not a civil war, then God knows what civil war is." An estimated thirty thousand Iraqis had died violently since a U.S.-led invasion of Iraq in March 2003. And the *Tribune* and its headline writer had come to the conclusion that this amounted to a civil war, despite the denials of the Joint Chiefs, the White House, and the Iraqi government. I would have had no problems with the *Tribune* reporting the competing opinions, but I had a big problem with the paper coming to a conclusion and passing it off as front-page news I needed to know. And so, on that fateful Friday, April 14, 2006, I called the *Tribune*'s business office and, hardly believing my own ears, heard myself canceling the family's subscription to the newspaper. An eighty-one-year-old romance was over.

Twenty months later, the Chicago Tribune Company, saddled with $13 billion in debt, was sold for $8.2 billion to a syndicate headed by Sam Zell, a sixty-six-year-old real estate developer and self-described "professional opportunist." The blunt-speaking billionaire, with no previous experience in journalism, promised that "things will be different" now that there was a "new sheriff in town." The company's new "chairman of everything," steeped in cash borrowed from J. P. Morgan Chase, Merrill Lynch, Citigroup, and Bank of America, promised to "prepare the company for the 21st Century" by auctioning "assets," including the Chicago Cubs and Wrigley Field, long associated with "the Tribune brand." Twenty thousand employees, working at the company's twenty-three television stations and nine dailies, were told that the Tribune would "increase revenue and profitability going forward" by giving readers and viewers "more of what they want." Joseph Medill, who had made the Tribune a household name, by opposing slavery and backing Lincoln, could be heard shuddering in his grave.

"Newspaper boards are in a panic today," says eighty-two-year-old Newton Minow, former chairman of the Federal Communications Commission. They're struggling to find "a successful economic model for newspapers to offer their unique products through the Internet" (the Tribune). Barely two in five Americans read a daily newspaper, according to the Pew Center for the People and the Press, reflecting a continuing twenty-year decline. The Newspaper Association of America reports that circulation declines at major U.S. newspapers were accelerating at rates beyond anything seen since the beginning of the television era. For its part, the nightly network news was fairing hardly better. Gallup was reporting that fewer than half of all Americans were getting all or most of their news that way. The networks were trying to become more interpretative, hoping to win back lost audience share. NBC announced on November 27, 2006, that it too had decided to call the conflict in Iraq a "civil war." The *Los Angeles Times* reported that it would do the same. Nielsen reported that fewer than 10 million Americans regularly watched the NBC Nightly News in November 2006, millions off its previous mark that was set in the 1980s. The Audit of Bureau Circulations announced in the same month that the *Los Angeles Times* circulation decline was the nation's largest—over 8 percent in 2006 alone.

Where have news readers gone? To the Internet. A March 2008 Zogby Poll reports that half of all Americans now go to the web as their primary source for news. Three in ten go to television, one in ten to radio, and an equal number to newspapers. Nine in ten Americans say the World Wide Web is an important source of news. More than half view these sites as "very important." Three in four Americans surveyed said that citizen journalism had a "vital role to play in journalism's future." Three in five said the same about bloggers. Remarkably, Internet sites are now the most trusted sources of news. In fact, one third of all Americans claim that the web is the most trustworthy place to get the day's news. One in five says that about newspapers and television. Fewer than one in six say that about radio.

Beginning reporters need to know that rarely in our nation's history has journalism been seen as more vital, and rarer still has it been more reviled. Seven in ten Americans told Zogby researchers that journalism was "important to the quality of life in their communities." Yet, two-thirds indicated that they were "dissatisfied with the quality of journalism in their communities" and an equal number believe that traditional journalism is "out of touch with what Americans want from their news." That doesn't mean that citizens have given up on the journalism profession. Nearly nine in ten say that professional journalism has a significant role to play in the nation's future. Seven in ten fear that media companies are becoming "too large and too powerful" to serve citizens well. Andrew Nachison from iFOCOS, a Reston, Virginia–based media think tank, observes that "we have a crisis in American journalism" that is perhaps "more serious" than anything the industry has ever faced. It requires, in his view, the training of a new generation of journalists dedicated "to making a difference in people's lives."

Old media are now adapting themselves to the new situation. Net Ratings reports that 57 million Americans visited newspaper sites in 2007, up a quarter from 2005. That figure made up more than one third of all Internet users. Nearly a third of the Americans surveyed by Princeton researchers said they were getting all or most of their news about national or international issues from the Internet. The Pew Internet and American Life Project reports that in 2007, three quarters of all Internet users were fifty or younger. Half of them had college degrees and three in four had some college experience. Two thirds of the total of Internet users were earning $50,000 or more annually. Three quarters of the total of Internet users lived in cities and suburbs. More than four in five had dropped dial-up Internet connections and were getting their news at high speed on broad band. America's middle schoolers are now taking courses in newsgathering and broadcast journalism using iMovie and Garage Band to put together their packages. In February 2008 it was announced that for the first time since Henry Ford began mass producing cars, teens would rather surf the Internet at home than learn to drive and cruise Main Street. Even old-timers are getting in on the fun. A survey by the American Association of Retired Persons states that two-thirds of all Americans over fifty and nearly half of all Americans over sixty-five have gone online.

John Sturm, chief executive officer for the Newspaper Association of America, reports that readership of newspaper websites is increasing 20 percent annually. "The web is making our news brand stronger," he says. Pew Research confirms that in 2007 more than 50 million Americans used the Internet for news every day, double the number of five years before. "The business models for newspapers and websites are increasingly alike," says Sturm. "We don't serve the market alone, but increasingly we are the market nearly everywhere."

Blogs, podcasts, cell phones, text messages, video camera phones, BlackBerries, and commuter newspapers have radically altered the way news is gathered and disseminated. Nic Robertson of CNN News believes that miniature video camera phones "will change the industry" because of their portability and extraordinary ability to discreetly record events with a device smaller than the palm of a hand. The technology is already changing the definition of what it means to be a "citizen reporter." News networks are encouraging "user-generated content" that can be transmitted to network websites at a keystroke. Sharing these narrative and video logs have made Facebook, YouTube, MySpace, Blogger, and Wikipedia some of the go-to sites on the web. This avalanche of news, information, and social networking led *Time* magazine to declare "You" the "Person of the Year" in 2006. "Clearly newspapers aren't the big dog anymore," says Jane Hirt, who became the Tribune's new managing editor in August 2008 because of what editor Gerould Kern called her ability to "understand audiences and how to satisfy them. "We don't have to be a newspaper of record anymore." The *Chicago Sun-Times* followed the lead of other newspapers in November 2007 by becoming a web-first publication. Reporters were advised to break their stories on the paper's website and not wait for the paper's early-morning hard-copy edition. Christine Ledbetter, features editor of the *Sun-Times*, observes, "Increasingly, newspapers are being defined by the word 'news,' not 'paper.'" The web is increasing newspapers' reach. "Twice as many eighteen- to twenty-four-year-olds read blogs about the news than read newspapers," Ledbetter points out.

Lou Rutigliano witnessed the Gannett Publishing push to interactivity as a reporter at the *El Paso Times* and now maps the newly emerging blogosphere from Ft. Myers, Florida, to Oakland, California. The emphasis is on "crowdsourcing," in which news websites draw on citizen networks to conduct investigations in "hyperlocal" news that is "geocoded to your block or apartment complex." Bloggers, who were long disdained by mainstream media, now "network" with professional counterparts in creating "working relationships unimaginable a few years ago." News increasingly becomes "having audiences producing more of its content." Supporters suggest that these new news networks "break down barriers between reporters and citizens," (Rutigliano) while critics claim that this further erodes the gatekeeping responsibility of reporters and editors to give citizens needed news. "News doesn't have to be told by someone behind a desk," says Spike Jonze, creative director for VBS-TV, a web-based channel financed through Viacom and MTV.

"Our ethos is subjectivity," says Suroosh Alvi, the network's executive producer. "Our aesthetic is raw," says Bernardo Loyola, a VBS editor. Alvi and his two partners, Eddy Moretti and Shane Smith, haven't had training in journalism, but that doesn't stop their advertising arm from calling their stories on extreme sports, independent music, date rape, and environmental abuse "a kind of '60 Minutes' meets 'Jackass.'" They are the advancing arm of the venture capitalists producing web videos through content partners who have more hits than major players in the establishment press.

Monthly advertising revenues on the Internet surpassed radio advertising in December 2007, at a time in which leading newsgathering organizations were reorganizing their newsrooms to take advantage of new storytelling opportunities. Gannett in February 2008 announced plans to reengineer its television stations. Gannett broadcasting chief David Lougee called local television's model of having 10 of 150 employees out gathering news and generating income "anachronistic." Lougee sees closer cooperation between Gannett's television stations and local newspapers. Critics are concerned that local news producers and sales representatives will be assigned overlapping roles to generate content and revenue. A similar strategy to increase the number of places where an organization's news can be read is being tried at the *Chicago Tribune*. A record 5.5 million page views greeted the paper's coverage on February 14, 2008, of a shooting at Northern Illinois University that left six dead. Web-friendly headlines and slugs attracted extra traffic that day from Yahoo and a tenfold increase in Facebook readership, pegged at offering tributes to the students who were killed. Newspapers have followed these success stories by mandating that their reporters join Facebook as a proactive way of seeking out readers for newspaper journalism.

Whether Americans turn to newspapers, the Internet, web logs, satellite radio, or cable to get their news, Minow is among those certain that "there will always be a need and a market for credible, trustworthy information and opinions." Yet, no profession has fallen further faster in the public's estimation than journalism. In the first and second editions of *The Responsible Reporter*, we reported Gallup findings that "the field of journalism is experiencing a crisis in public confidence." At the height of press reporting on the war in Vietnam and the Watergate investigation, Walter Cronkite, the anchor on the CBS Evening News, was "the most trusted man in America." Half of all Americans said they had confidence in what the press reported at the end of the 1970s and nearly half felt that journalists had high ethical standards. By the mid-'90s, on the eve of the Internet era, only one in five Americans believed that journalists were "ethical and honest." Respondents told Pew researchers that a "lack of objectivity" was the number-one frustration they had with the press. In the beginning of 2008, public confidence in journalists continued to languish. Journalists rated well below health-care professionals, military officers, police, clergy, and judges in public regard. In fact, daycare providers, bankers, auto mechanics, and nursing-home operators were more highly regarded than reporters. The public has no greater regard for its journalists, Gallup reports, than its politicians, business executives, lawyers, and funeral directors. Used-car salesmen and advertisers were among the few professionals who regularly rated lower. Only one in five Americans have a "high" regard for the honesty and integrity of journalists.

At times of national emergency the public is particularly attentive to the press and appreciate its service to the country. In the aftermath of the terrorist attacks on September 11, 2001, 90 percent of all Americans reported that they were watching press coverage closely. Seven in ten praised the press for "standing up for America" in reporting the "War on Terror," and six in ten believed that this reporting was critical to "protecting democracy." Throughout 2002, two-thirds of all Americans claimed they were following the news, particularly international reporting, closely. Two years later, however, two thirds of journalist respondents were telling the Project for Excellence in Journalism that the effect of bottom-line pressures on news coverage was "hurting the press in doing its job." Half of all reporters believe that the "race to be first" with Internet deadlines every second of every day is making "reporting increasingly sloppy and error prone."

Beginning reporters need to know that the habits and demographics of citizens who use the news are also changing. Barely half of all Americans now get their news at regular times of the day. Nearly as many are "news grazers" who check in on the news from time to time. Pew reports that grazers are "younger, less dedicated to the news, and have an eclectic news diet." While three in five Americans over sixty-five read a daily newspaper, fewer than one in four over thirty do. More than half of all Americans eighteen to thirty-four "don't trust what news organizations are saying" and believe that "people who decide on news content are out of touch." Younger Americans tend to cruise to multiple sites, checking out news and opinions on events of the day. Nearly half of all web-newspaper readers have college degrees, compared to a quarter of those who rely on print. Three quarters of those who read newspapers online say it is more "convenient" for them to do so. One in ten gets news online because it's "free." Readers young and old are increasingly distrustful of the news. By 2007, barely half of all people polled found daily newspapers "believable." Only twenty years before, more than four in five had a "favorable" attitude toward the daily press and found it "credible." Now, fewer than two in five Americans read a daily newspaper, and nearly half of these do so online. Nearly two thirds of all Internet users say they read the websites of local or national newspapers.

A generation ago, journalism was essentially the lone institution in American life that connected citizens to the news of public life. Today, blogs, talk shows, text messages, corporate websites, cablecasts, and government postings communicate claims to a vast and growing citizen network. That competition is having its consequences. Declines in market shares have pressured news organizations to improve their stock performance for corporate stakeholders less interested in the social responsibility of the press than turning a profit. The Project for Excellence in Journalism observes that "the challenge for traditional journalism is whether it can reassert its position as the provider of something distinctive and valuable—both for citizens and advertisers." Gary Meo, senior vice president of print and Internet services at Scarborough Research, told a colloquium at DePaul University that news now needs to be "portable," making news organizations "more like a Rolodex." This means that beginning journalists need to know the "how" and "why" of stories and how to communicate that quickly to audiences. Ken Doctor, a market analyst in the information industry, says that news organizations need to consider themselves "content companies" who "publish once and distribute across the information spectrum."

Hirt calls it "giving people what they're interested in." Sturm warns that news organizations that don't meet the needs of "news consumers" will be in trouble. "It's hard being successful," he says, "telling people what they should want."

For beginning reporters and for seasoned journalists there is always the challenge of giving citizens the information they need or think they'll like. The first is news that makes democracy and self-governance possible. The second may not be. Laura Washington, an award-winning journalist who teaches at DePaul University, says the balancing act should never lead reporters to "patronize" their readers. There is also the growing problem of getting good information from sources hiding behind computers. Veteran legal affairs reporter Janan Hanna warns that electronic newsgathering makes reporters more subject to spin. "Reporters have totally lost control of the game," she says. "Some sources won't accept interviews except through e-mail. This is making information more and more centralized for newsmakers who do not have to look reporters in the eye." Polling seems to support these concerns. Three in five Americans interviewed told Pew researchers that "news organizations don't get their facts straight," and seven in ten were certain that news organizations "do not deal fairly with all sides of an issue." In more than twenty years of polling, twice as many Americans have consistently said they rely on their news media and not the government to give them a picture of the world on which to act. Three in four, regardless of their political affiliation, continue to believe that a free press is crucial to preserving a democratic form of government. Yet, nearly nine in ten think that "members of the news media let their own political preferences influence the way they report the news." The 2006 study "State of the News Media" demonstrates that reporters have a long way to go in living up to their social responsibility. The study concludes that "Americans since the 1980s have come to view the press as less professional, less accurate, less caring, and less moral." Pollster Andrew Kohut writes that Americans have increasingly come to the conclusion that "news organizations act out of their own economic self-interest and journalists themselves act to advance their own careers."

The public's increasing need for information worth knowing post-9/11 and the widening perception that the press in its pursuit of profits is failing its public calling has put journalism students in an extraordinary position. Rarely has the need for social responsibility in reporting been greater and rarer still have there been moments like this one—where digital technologies make information available at extraordinary speed to an overwhelming number of people. These dynamics make it all the more essential that the next generation of journalists take seriously their obligation to research and report the news that makes self-actualization and community building in a civil society possible.

2

A History of Responsible Reporting

BRUCE J. EVENSEN

The famous First Amendment, which prohibits Congress from abridging the freedom of the press, was originally the Third Amendment and not the First, and the press was not originally mentioned in it. James Madison, one of the architects of the U.S. Constitution, had successfully run for the First Congress on the pledge that he would work for a bill of rights that could be added to the Constitution. Five of the states that ratified the Constitution, including Madison's Virginia and New York State, did so on the condition that a bill of rights would protect civil liberties from the encroachments of the federal government. In all, 210 amendments were proposed. On May 4, 1789, Madison announced that he would introduce a bill of rights that could be debated in Congress. It wasn't until June 8 that he had his say. Seventeen amendments were proposed, including two on the press, neither of which was passed. One amendment stated, "The people shall not be deprived or abridged of their right to speak, to write, or to publish their sentiments; and the freedom of the press, one of the great bulwarks of liberty, shall be inviolable." The other proposed amendment by Madison on the press stated, "No state shall violate the equal rights of conscience, or of the press."

Madison's language was lifted almost directly from the Virginia Bill of Rights, which in 1776 had stated that the "freedom of the press is one of the great bulwarks of liberty, and can never be restrained but by despotic governments." Nine of the thirteen states already had statutes protecting press freedom by 1787, which was the reason why a conference committee rejected Madison's proposed amendment, despite his plea that it was "the most valuable amendment on the whole list." Madison's arguments in behalf of a free press are recorded in *The Annals of Congress* and are a window into the critical role the founding fathers saw a responsible press playing in the life of the nation. Taken together, Madison argued, the amendments ensured "the liberty for which many valiantly fought and honorably bled." The rights would help create a country "devoted to liberty and a Republican Government" as opposed to one founded on "an aristocracy or despotism."

Opponents of an amendment expressly supporting press freedom charged that English Common Law had long protected the press from incursions by the crown. William Blackstone summarized these protections in his *Commentaries on the Laws of England*, stating in 1769 that press liberty meant "laying no previous restraints upon publication," while punishing "criminal matter when published." Madison considered the safeguard insufficient. "The freedom of the press," which Madison likened to "the rights of conscience," were "the choicest privileges of the people" and remained "unguarded in the British constitution." That is why Madison was certain he spoke for "the people of many States who have thought it necessary to raise barriers against power in all its forms." Such an amendment would be a "restraint" against "the abuse of the executive power, sometimes against the legislative, and in some cases, against the community itself; or, in other words, against the majority in favor of the minority." Madison argued that an amendment to the federal Constitution was necessary so that **"no State shall violate the equal right of conscience and freedom of the press** because it is proper that every Government should be disarmed of powers which trench upon those rights."

By September 25, 1789, two-thirds of the House of Representatives and the U.S. Senate had approved twelve amendments to the Constitution and submitted them to the states for ratification. On December 15, 1791, three quarters of all states approved ten of those twelve amendments. The First Amendment, proposing the number of constituents for each representative, and a Second Amendment, on legislative pay, were not supported. This elevated the Third Amendment to first spot. It simply stated, "Congress shall make no law respecting an establishment of religion, or prohibiting the free exercise thereof; or abridging the freedom of speech, or of the press; or the right of the people peaceably to assemble, and to petition the Government for a redress of grievances." This put the country on record as keeping the government off the back of its press so that institution could fulfill its republican obligation to give citizens the news they need to know to make democracy and self-governance possible. This is not to imply that women, and people of color, and non-land-holding whites saw the early Republican press as their ally and advocate in the long fight to expand their rights. The press in the early republic was a kept press. It served as an extension of two competing political parties that paid its bills and appointed its editors. The intense political partisanship of this press would lead to a Constitutional crisis over whether the press could be both partisan and free.

The Early Republican Press

In 1798, Federalist president John Adams attempted to silence opposition in the Democratic-Republican press through passage of the **Alien and Sedition Acts**, which made it a crime to "print, utter, or publish…any false, scandalous, and malicious writing about the government." The Federalists brought fourteen indictments, largely against Republican editors. Eleven trials followed and ten convictions. Vermont representative Matthew Lyon was jailed for four months and fined $1,000 for writing that Adams had "an unbounded thirst for ridiculous pomp and foolish adulation" and that his Federalist cronies were guilty of a "selfish continual grasp for power." When Anthony Haswell, the Republican editor of the *Vermont Gazette* defended Lyon as "a victim of the oppressive hand of usurped power," he was imprisoned for two months and fined $200. James Callender, editor of the *Richmond Examiner,* was sentenced to serve nine months. Luther Baldwin of Newark, New Jersey, was fined $150 for observing that cannons firing a salute to President Adams would be better served targeting the president's very substantial behind. Alexander Addison argued the administration's case before grand juries in Pennsylvania. "Liberty without limit is licentiousness," he claimed. "It is the worst kind of tyranny. The principle of liberty, therefore the rights of men require that our right of communicating information, as to facts and opinions, be so restrained, as not to infringe the right of reputation."

If the Adams administration and its defenders had hoped that fining and jailing journalists would silence critics, it was mistaken. Thomas and Abijah Adams used front-page bold type in the *Boston Independent Chronicle* to announce that their paper would "stand or fall with the liberties of America, and nothing shall silence its clarion but the extinction of every principle which leads to the achievement of our independence." Thomas Jefferson found himself in the unique position of being the nation's vice president, while serving as leader of the political opposition. He summoned Madison and other Republican leaders to his home at Monticello to plot their campaign to win the presidency from Adams in 1800. They would use the muzzling of free speech and the press under the Alien and Sedition Acts as a cornerstone of their campaign. "These and successive acts of the same character," Jefferson wrote, "unless arrested on the threshold may tend to drive these states into revolution and blood and will furnish new pretexts for those who wish it to be believed that men cannot be governed but by a rod of iron." Since the states had created the federal government, Jefferson argued in the Kentucky Resolutions of 1798, the states reserved "the right of judging how far the licentiousness of speech and press may be abridged without lessening their useful freedom." Madison, writing in the Virginia Resolutions of 1798, was more direct. The Alien and Sedition Acts, he argued, were an affront to the Constitution because they were "leveled against the right of freely examining public characters and measures." That "free communication among the people" carried on by the press was, in his view, "the only effectual guardian of every other right."

The arguments of Jefferson and Madison won the day. Jefferson defeated Adams in the presidential election of 1800, and the Federalists never again won the presidency. The Alien and Sedition Acts were allowed to lapse, and although Jefferson tacitly sanctioned isolated prosecution of opposition editors at the state level, he was generally sympathetic to the proposition that his presidency was "a great experiment" that would demonstrate that "freedom of the press" was not "incompatible with orderly government." Jefferson was more sanguine about the therapeutic role of the press in a democracy before becoming president than after. A year before George Washington took the oath of office, Jefferson had written a friend that what the nation most needed were "newspapers that penetrate to the whole mass of the people. The basis of our government being the opinion of the people, the very first object should be to keep that right; and were it left to me to decide whether we should have a government without newspapers, or newspapers without a government, I should not hesitate a moment to prefer the latter." Reeling under withering personal attacks during his presidency, he remarked, "The newspapers of our country by their abandoned spirit of falsehood have more effectively destroyed the utility of the press than all the shackles devised by Bonaparte." At the close of his two terms in office he discouraged a young man who had written to him asking what he thought of those who made journalism their career. "Nothing can now be believed which is seen in a newspaper," Jefferson wrote to him. "Truth itself becomes suspicious by being put into that polluted vehicle." Later in life, the sting of an irresponsible press having diminished, Jefferson wrote to the Marquis de Lafayette, who had helped Americans win their freedom, that the press with all its faults was critical to preserving that freedom. "The only security of all," Jefferson believed, "is in a free press. The force of public opinion cannot be resisted, when permitted freely to be expressed. The agitation it produces must be submitted to. It is necessary, to keep the waters pure."

One of the newspapers of Jefferson and Madison's day that pointed to the future, when a responsible press would play a central role in giving citizens the news they needed to know, was *Niles' Weekly Register*, published from Baltimore starting in 1811 by Hezekiah Niles. By the 1820s, the *Register* was established as America's national news magazine of record with a circulation in each of the twenty-four states and abroad. Members of Congress could be seen reading the *Register* for its verbatim reporting of key House and Senate speeches and its publication of important documents that became part of the public record. This is how many Americans became aware of the Missouri Compromise of 1820, which extended an imaginary line from the southern border of that state to the western extremity of the Louisiana Purchase. All states entering the Union north of that line would be free; all states south of the line would be slave-owning. Niles's expanded coverage included speeches on both sides of the issue, reports from Congressional committees, and news articles and editorials appearing in newspapers across the country. It was Niles's hope that "by the insertion of original and selected essays on both sides of great national questions" the American people would have enough information to make up their minds on critical issues of the day. Niles considered it the "duty" of the press to "be open to all parties" so long as their views were expressed with "moderation" and "dignified restraint." The role of the press was to "be devoted to no party or partisan," but instead to be "an honest chronicler" to report "with impartiality" all sides of the news of the day "so that the public reason may fairly discern the merit of a case in controversy." In the case of the Missouri Compromise that had meant "the presentation of a full view of the subject, on both sides of the question. How far we have succeeded in this, our readers will determine."

Niles' Weekly Register would become a template for an emerging generation of editors who were weaning themselves from dependence on political party financing. Reduced printing costs and the rise of a democratic marketplace in industrializing America were creating vast urban landscapes teaming with newly arrived, semiliterate immigrants eager to find their place in the New World and to build a better future for their families. Throughout the 1820s and 1830s, state land-holding requirements for voting were disappearing. The franchise would soon be extended to all adult white males. Niles urged them to "go to the polls with the same deliberation that you go to church, with hearts devoted to good purposes." It was his view that the social responsibility of the press was to trust an informed citizenry to make the decisions that made democracy possible. He was an optimist. He believed in the Enlightenment principle that suggests that human beings will act rationally if given enough information to decide their futures. Citizens knew best, Niles and responsible journalists since have believed, "to act in the interest of the nation, and by all that is beneficial to themselves in the preservation of an American system that is the fountain of public wealth and the guarantee of private liberty."

The Penny Press and Social Responsibility

The **penny press**, which emerged in the 1830s, mainly marketed news, not views, claiming that it was independent of political control, while relying on advertising revenue stimulated by circulation. Editors claimed that they represented "the people" and not the "interests." In some cases it was true and in all cases it was good business. James Gordon Bennett immodestly claimed in the inaugural edition of the *New York Herald* on May 6, 1835, that the paper would become "the great organ of social life and the prime element of civilization, mixing together commerce and business, pure religion and morals, literature and poetry, the drama and dramatic purity." Bennett said in August 1836 that the *Herald*'s "spirit" of public service was behind its "success" and soon its record-setting circulation of forty thousand. Critics claimed that Bennett's reliance on sentiment and sensation made the *Herald* a "ribald vehicle" of "moral leprosy," but that did not stop them from copying his pattern of sending reporters to cover stories. Journalism made by men on their feet took readers to police court, city hall, the schools, the neighborhoods, and theaters to report the public world of New York's competing communities. The *New York Sun*, published by Benjamin Day, developed the **"human-interest" story**, showing readers "a picture of the world" that would alert the community to problems it had the power to solve. This early sense of social responsibility, however, did not stop the paper from publishing reports in 1835 of four-foot-tall bat-men and blue unicorns that had been spotted on the moon. The pseudo-scientific story was a crowd-pleaser, boosting readership fivefold. Competing papers, claiming the same social responsibility, strangely and suddenly saw bat-men and unicorns of their own. Their example has been often repeated ever since, a faith in facts and excursions into fiction being used to win readers, and all in the name of giving citizens the news they need to know.

Ever since the rise of the penny press, editors have claimed to be doing the people's business, even if some supposed their real business was money-making. Russell Jarvis, who started the *Philadelphia Public Ledger*, spoke for many when he observed that the job of a newspaper editor was a calling of "high responsibility…to instruct, to improve the world" by exposing "folly and vice." Henry J. Raymond launched the *New York Times* on September 18, 1851, promising to be "a public instructor in all departments of action and thought. What is good we desire to preserve and improve," Raymond told his readers, "and what is evil to exterminate or reform." Raymond respected the seriousness of his readers and denigrated competing papers that did not take the readers seriously. "We do not mean to write as if we were in a passion," he pledged, "unless that shall really be the case, and we shall make it a point to get into a passion as rarely as possible. There are few things in the world which it is worthwhile to get angry about, and they are just the things anger will not improve." Raymond's mentor Horace Greeley, publisher of the *New York Tribune*, believed that editors of his era were increasingly "guided by a larger wisdom," often "at personal cost," to try and "discern the right and defend it."

Greeley argued aggressively to prohibit slavery in states coming into the Union. In this he was joined by Joseph Medill, publisher of the *Chicago Tribune*, who bitterly opposed fugitive slave laws that required citizens in the North to return runaway slaves to their masters in the South. "Involuntary servitude," Medill wrote, "is inconsistent with all principles civil or religious. Slavery is a national shame and scandal" in a country that claimed that "all men are created equal." Medill and Greeley helped organize the Republican Party, which opposed the extension of slavery, and helped elect Abraham Lincoln president. Their efforts were greatly aided by abolitionist editors, who published their opinions at considerable risk. Elijah Lovejoy was killed on November 7, 1837, when his anti-slavery newspaper office in Alton, Illinois, was attacked by a mob. William Lloyd Garrison, publishing *The Liberator* in Boston, was twice badly beaten up for demanding the immediate abolition of slavery. It was a sin, he argued, to subjugate a class of people created in the image of God. Even after a jailing, Garrison was undeterred. "I am in earnest," he told those who threatened him. "I will not equivocate. I will not excuse. I will not retreat a single inch. And I will be heard." James Gillespie Birney was run out of Cincinnati, his life and family threatened, when his *Philanthropist* urged the end to slavery. Editors try "to persuade our fellow countrymen to do justice and to show mercy to the poor. That is the head and front of our offending," he wrote, "no more." Frederick Douglass, an abolitionist editor whose mother was a slave and whose father was a white man, predicted that slavery would end only through bloodshed. "Slavery is a system of brute force," he wrote in *Frederick Douglass' Paper*, and it "must be met with its own weapons."

The Civil War and Eyewitness Reporting

During the Civil War, Greeley continued to pressure President Lincoln to free the slaves. His open letter to the president, published as a "Prayer of Twenty Millions," insisted on August 20, 1862, that Lincoln recognize that the controversy over ending slavery had caused Southern secession and that unity after the war required it. Lincoln answered Greeley in print, stating that "saving the union" and not "freeing slaves" had been his "paramount" objective. A year later, however, when Lincoln dedicated a national cemetery in Gettysburg, Pennsylvania, he accepted the argument of Greeley and other abolitionists, and pledged the nation "to a new birth of freedom" in which the country would live up to its Constitutional obligation. It was at the battle of Gettysburg on July 4, 1863, that *New York Times* correspondent Dan Wilkeson reported the costly victory of Northern forces and the death of his nineteen-year-old son Bayard. Whitelaw Reid's fourteen-column account of the Gettysburg fighting for the *Cincinnati Gazette* set a standard for eyewitness reporting. The reporting of George Alfred Townsend of the *New York Herald* and that of Charles Anderson Page of Greeley's *New York Tribune* were widely circulated from the Peninsula Campaign through the Battle of the Wilderness. The Civil War stimulated the appetite for information and the national syndication of news. Ansell Kellogg, based in Chicago, syndicated stories to fifty-three newspapers in ready-to-print pages. Battlefield reports, filed by telegraph, became the way most Americans, including the president, kept up with daily battle accounts. Throngs of citizens gathered before newspaper offices all across the country during active campaigns, anxiously awaiting word of those killed and wounded in action. Battlefield photographs, taken by Alexander Gardner, who began his career at the studio of Matthew Brady, gave illustrators and readers a vivid picture of the dead and dying. At Antietam, Gardner and his colleagues photographed only what they saw. At Gettysburg, they manipulated bodies and body parts to compose their pictures and "tell the story of the fighting."

Gardner was not alone in his spirit of invention. Civil War reporters called themselves the "Bohemian Brigade" because of their rakish tendency to rely on hyperbole rather than fact gathering in writing on the war. Some had little regard for accuracy and faked or slanted quotes to make their stories more compelling. The Confederate Press Association exerted close control over all forty-three newspapers published in the South, ensuring "accurate accounts for the good of the public, consistent with military security." No such arrangements were made in the North. General Ulysses S. Grant had a handful of reporters he trusted "to give no information of value to the enemy." The irascible general William Tecumseh Sherman did not share Grant's civility. Sherman threatened to "shoot on sight" reporters he found "lurking about the camp." He considered them "spies" because of their undisciplined reporting of military secrets. Twenty-two newspapers were suppressed during the Civil War for what local military commanders considered conduct harmful to the war effort. Several editors were briefly jailed. War Secretary Edwin Stanton took over the telegraph office in Washington, D.C., hoping to control the flow of information on the war. He preferred his own page-one "War Diaries" to what correspondents at the front were reporting.

At the close of the Civil War, the Associated Press had established itself as a major source of responsible reporting. The organization had been in existence since 1846, when New York's leading newspapers initiated cooperative newsgathering to keep costs down and quality up. On the eve of the fighting, the Associated Press was able to transmit messages received by transoceanic cable. Its reporters traveled with the Army of the Potomac and reported General Robert E. Lee's surrender in Appomattox, Virginia, on April 9, 1865. Six days later, the AP's Washington correspondent Lawrence Gobright reported President Lincoln's assassination at Ford's Theater. After the war, the AP rapidly processed news through a 226-mile-long leased wire that connected New York, Philadelphia, Baltimore, and Washington. The AP served newspapers all over the country. This had a profound impact on the history of responsible reporting. Its stories would be published in communities with a wide range of political affiliations. The AP's bottom line was enhanced if it played stories straight, maintaining a neutrality designed to alienate no one. As a result, reporters' opinions were kept out of stories. Their charge was to gather and carefully arrange the opinions of others. The AP's general manager, Melville Stone, understood that fairness, balance, and impartiality was not only good journalism, it was even better business. During Stone's twenty-eight years of stewardship, the AP became a highly professional, nonpartisan news service to twelve hundred newspapers. This led to increasing standardization of reporting practices, when the affordability of AP stories made them a favorite of weekly and small-town editors, who wanted to offer readers a picture of regional or national coverage they could not have afforded on their own. Reuters, United Press, and International News Service became major news services designed to serve readers by cashing in on the growing appetite for professionally turned copy.

The social responsibility of the press during the second half of the nineteenth century focused on serving the needs of increasingly diverse communities drawn to industrializing America and its rapidly expanding cities in the Northeast and the Midwest. There were nearly five thousand newspapers in the United States at the end of the war and more than twice that many a decade later. The *Chicago Daily News*, started in December 1875 by Stone and publisher Victor Lawson, was a template for many of the successful papers that emerged during America's Gilded Age. Stone saw the paper as "more than a mere business enterprise." The two men produced a paper with a communitarian vision of the city it served. Stone sought to daily offer "a true perspective of the world's developing history that a woman can read alone in mixed company." In ten years its circulation soared from 14,000 to 100,000. When Stone left the paper in 1888, its circulation had grown to 200,000, second largest in the nation. At Lawson's death in 1925, a half million of Chicago's 3 million residents read the paper. A newspaper that struggled to pay its $50 wire service bill in its first year was now worth $13.5 million.

Pulitzer's Investigative Journalism

German immigrant Joseph Pulitzer had begun the *St. Louis Post-Dispatch* on December 12, 1878, promising that the paper "will serve no party but the people," while pledging itself "an enemy of all frauds and shams" and a proponent of "the principles upon which our government was originally founded." To Pulitzer and his direct descendents who controlled the paper over 127 years, that meant "opposition to all special interests." On December 30, 1878, Pulitzer wrote, "If it is a crime to sympathize with the struggle of the poor, we plead guilty." His paper published the tax returns of local business leaders and editorially attacked those who hadn't paid their "fair share. Democracy means opposition to special privilege," he told his readers, in printing exposés on pricing schemes of insurance and gas companies and insider deals struck by bankers and street car monopolists. In four and a half years Pulitzer created a municipal legend in St. Louis. In May 1883 he took over the cash-strapped *New York World* and made it the nation's leading newspaper. "There is room in this great and growing city," Pulitzer told his 22,000 readers, "for a journal dedicated to the cause of the people rather than the purse of the potentates that will serve and battle for the people with earnest sincerity." Pulitzer's paper took a deep interest in the struggles of the urban underclass and the frightful living conditions of the immigrant poor. On June 23, 1883, the paper published a page-one story describing how Kate Sweeny, a young immigrant girl, had suffocated in raw sewage that had flooded her basement apartment on Mulberry Street. The World launched an investigation when a young boy was beaten to death by guards in the Elmira Prison for Boys. Inside pages and special sections helped new Americans assimilate to their adopted homeland. Readers responded, pushing the paper's circulation to 56,960 in 1884, 123,295 in 1885, and 217,769 by September 1887.

It was on October 9, 1887, that Pulitzer helped to invent investigative journalism when Nellie Bly went undercover to report appalling conditions at an insane asylum for indigent women on Blackwell's Island. *Harper's Weekly* had probed allegations that women inside the center were being mistreated. A reporter met with officials and took a guided tour of the center, leading the magazine to tell its readers that care was "kindly." Pulitzer's purpose was to find out what conditions were really like for women sent to the center, so Bly feigned insanity and was sent there. She found that sane women were made sick by cruel mistreatment. Women were forced to sit unattended for hours at a time. If they tried to get up they'd be punished. Patients were forced to choke down stale bread and rancid butter. If they objected they'd be beaten. Freezing cold baths were a "terror" in which patients feared they were drowning. Bly's reporting for the *World* revealed that many of the women sent to the asylum were poor immigrants who didn't speak English and couldn't defend themselves. Her revelations mobilized public opinion and forced city officials to fire those responsible for the abuse and to spend $1 million to improve the care of impoverished women.

Reporting that takes its social responsibility seriously has long struggled with sensationalism. In Pulitzer's case, the crisis came when William Randolph Hearst arrived in New

York in 1895. The heir to a silver fortune wanted to out-Pulitzer Pulitzer. He doubled the salary of many of Pulitzer's key staff members and set them to work on the *New York Journal*. The competition for readers reached a shrieking crescendo on February 15, 1898, when the U.S.S. Maine blew up in Havana harbor, killing 260 sailors. Hearst's front-page pitch in the *Journal* offered a $50,000 reward "for the detection of the perpetrator of this outrage!" Pulitzer promised that the *World* would "send a special tug with submarine divers to Havana to find out" who was responsible. The front page of both papers blamed the explosion on the Spanish, although the exact cause of the blast was never known. The *Journal's* banner headline on February 17 charged "Destruction of the War Ship Was the Work of an Enemy." The *World* offered a front-page four-column illustration of the frigate blowing up below the headline "Maine Explosion Caused by Bomb or Torpedo?" Each paper attempted to surpass the other in reporting Spanish atrocities. When famed illustrator Frederic Remington tired of the game, he reportedly wired Hearst from Havana, asking to be relieved of the assignment. A Hearst insider charged that the imperious editor had wired the warning, "You furnish the pictures, and I'll furnish the war." The *World* would not be outdone; its reporters claimed to have witnessed "skulls slit to the eyes," "ears cut off as trophies," and "mouths gashed to the angle of the jaw to give each face a ghastly grin." The stories sent the *World's* circulation soaring to near the 1 million mark and helped mobilize public opinion against the Spanish, eventually leading to the short-lived Spanish-American War.

Pulitzer later regretted that he had relied on the lurid in an effort to out-Hearst Hearst. In failing health, his will created the Pulitzer Prize to annually reward, beginning in 1917, excellence in journalism. A separate endowment to Columbia University set up its journalism school, designed to promote professionalism in journalism training. Medill's estate left money to Northwestern University to launch a journalism school in his name. Walter Williams became dean of journalism education at the University of Missouri. Allen S. Will led journalism education at Rutgers. Willard G. Bleyer headed the University of Wisconsin's initiative in journalism instruction that emphasized "a journalist's responsibility to the community." Bleyer and Leon N. Flint, who headed journalism training at the University of Kansas, produced early textbooks that guided journalism students in producing professional stories. Flint urged a code of conduct with "enforceable standards" that would force journalists to take their social responsibility seriously. By 1925, leading journalism educators had formed the Council for Education for Journalism, which established professional standards for instruction in journalism, hoping to elevate reporters to the status enjoyed by doctors and lawyers. Their intention was the creation of qualifying standards for journalists and a mechanism to expel journalists who violated ethical codes. By June 1926, *The Journalism Bulletin* was reporting that more than fifty schools offered journalism instruction to a student population of 5,500.

Responsible Reporting and Money-Making

The early twentieth century saw the start of a century-long struggle between two competing paradigms in the press. One emphasized the social responsibility of the press. The other focused on its obligation to make money. Each recognized that publishing was now a multimillion-dollar business with a division of labor that situated circulation managers and the business office at the center of acquiring the advertising revenue necessary for continued operation. The editorial office had the obligation of producing a product that sustained a readership that could be delivered to advertisers. The *Chicago Daily Socialist* refused advertising from "predatory capitalists" when it mass marketed a forty-page news-paper to 300,000 readers in the summer of 1912. The result was bankruptcy. The newspaper business took money and lots of it. Press critic Nelson Crawford charged that newspapers were becoming "giant commercial operations" that compelled publishers "to appeal to larger and larger masses of undifferentiated readers." H. L. Mencken put it more colorfully. Newspapers were being overrun, he wrote, by "ham-minded men who are forcing news-papers to be ham hooks with which to get their ham."

Adolph Ochs was a successful businessmen with a strong sense of civic responsibility. When he bought a controlling interest in the *New York Times* in August 1896 its circula-tion had sunk to nine thousand. In his inaugural issue he pledged, "It will be my earnest aim that the *New York Times* give the news, all the news impartially, without fear or favor, regardless of sect, party, or interest," in a "clean, dignified, and trustworthy" manner, so that the *New York Times* would become known for its "honesty, watchfulness, earnestness, industry, and common sense." One week later the paper committed to report "all the news that's fit to print," becoming America's newspaper of record, while boosting its circulation under Ochs's watch to a quarter million daily and three quarters of a million on Sunday. Ochs heartily believed "in the educational value of a newspaper to give complete, accurate, non-partisan news of events of interest to intelligent readers." Under publisher Charles Taylor the *Boston Globe* became a champion of Irish immigrant interests in its editorial support for higher worker wages, an eight-hour day, and the right of priests to administer last rites to dying patients in local hospitals. William Rockhill Nelson's leadership at the *Kansas City Star*, Eugene C. Pulliam's work at the *Indianapolis Star*, and Lucius W. Nieman's stewardship of the *Milwaukee Journal* reflected newspapers that boosted their cities and held public officials accountable for the problems of the community.

A national magazine-reading culture emerged during the progressive period filled with investigative reporting that exposed wrongdoing and urged remedies designed to create a more civil society. These journalists had a faith in facts and a confidence that citizens would do the right thing when given enough information to act. "Capitalists, workingmen, politi-cians, citizens—all breaking the law, or letting it be broken," wrote S. S. McClure in introducing the January 1903 edition of the muckraking magazine that bore his name. "Who is left to uphold the law?" he asked. "There is no one left; none but all of us." That issue of *McClure's Magazine* contained Ida Tarbell's seminal work on the Standard Oil Trust that would later lead to an order of the U.S. Supreme Court to break up the illegal monopoly; an installment of Lincoln Steffens's series exposing municipal mismanagement; and Ray Stannard Baker's investigation of unfair labor practices directed at coal miners. Baker went on to do investigative pieces in *McClure's* attacking racism, mob violence, and lynching. Burton Kendrick exposed fraud in the life insurance industry. George Kibbe Turner chronicled the links between political corruption, organized crime, and prostitution. Other articles advocated conservation, penal reform, and public health.

The enthusiasm displayed by *McClure's* was embraced by other monthly magazines, including *Harper's, Century, Scribner's, Collier's, Everybody's, and Hampton's. The excitement spread to Atlantic Monthly, Cosmopolitan, Ladies Home Journal, Munsey's, Godey's,* and *Peterson's.* Baker called the contagion "an awakening sympathy for the world's downtrodden and oppressed." Samuel Hopkins Adams exposed the patent medicine industry. Upton Sinclair's scathing summary of working conditions in Chicago's stockyards led to the creation of the Food and Drug Administration. Charles Edward Russell muckraked slum landlords, election graft, railroad fraud, and race relations. Russell's charge to other investigators was to marshal facts and "discover the innumerable and indispensable details" that laid problems bare before readers. This was the plan taken by Edwin Markham's powerful indictment of child labor. The reporting of Mary Alden Hopkins and Rheta Childe Dorr brought labor protection to women workers. Thomas Lawson chronicled stock market fraud. Ernest Crosby exposed machine politics.

William Kittle observed that because journalism was a big business with a wide following it could exercise its influence to police special interests and widely ignored abuses to "better serve the public good." William Allen White, a small-town editor from Emporia, Kansas, believed that journalism's greatest achievement was "to widen the public sense of evil-doing" as a means of empowering reformers. In Osceola, Wisconsin, that meant Alfred Roese's stand against the extractive policies of Weyerhauser. In New York City, it meant Jacob Riis's photojournalism that captured the plight of street children. For Abraham Cahan, it meant agitation in behalf of garment workers and pushcart peddlers on the city's Lower East Side. Will Irwin, looking back on the role of muckraking in fulfilling the social responsibility of the press, described the period as one in which reporters and editors "were on the lookout for stories that had human values" and "wrote lucidly with unity and individuality" stories that their fellow citizens needed to know.

World War I brought an abrupt end to America's appetite for a journalism that powered social change. The "war to end war" didn't end war. The public was mobilized for battle through recruiting billboards, newspapers, films, magazines, and an advertising industry that urged "halting the Hun." Book burnings and vigilante action against foreign "radicals" followed. Passage of the Espionage and Sedition Acts criminalized criticism of the government that "aided the enemy." "The sewage of the war spirit," wrote Randolph Silliman Bourne, who had helped launch the *New Republic,* "left one with a sense of having come to a sudden, short stop at the end of an intellectual era." On the other side of the war was the Jazz Age. Walter Winchell became one of the era's highest-paid journalists. He made an industry of social gossip and the wisecrack. The seduction of Jazz Age journalism was that it appeared to let you in on everything. It had its own language for those "in the know." It romanticized public enemies who liked to "bump off" the competition.

The social scene of "speakeasies" flouted Prohibition with "giggle water" sipped by "Dumb Doras" who were stalked by "Drugstore Cowboys." A parent's worst nightmare was a "struggle buggy," the backseat of a car. For the tabloids, city life was transformed into a circulation-stimulating spectacle of romance, danger, leisure, and, "if you played your cards right," opportunity.

Jazz Journalism

No newspaper followed the tracks of "men on the make" and the "new woman" more successfully than the *New York Daily News*. The paper was the brainchild of Joseph Medill Patterson, who inherited his grandfather's name if not his manner in reporting news. Patterson's "new kind of newspaper" first appeared on June 26, 1919, and from the first "thought visually" in reporting "the rush of big city living" that "tells each story in a flash." Patterson insisted that his editors inject "romance and drama" into the stories they assigned. Reporters were reminded to "make it snappy, make it local, make it news." The paper's circulation surged to 100,000 in its first year and nearly tripled that six months later. By 1924, the paper's heavily illustrated Sunday edition shot to a million circulation, the nation's largest. Patterson advertised the *Daily News* as a "people's paper," and saw himself as a defender of the public interest even if it meant publishing a page-one stealth photo of a Sing Sing electrocution under the big, bold headline "Dead!" On the eve of World War II the paper's daily circulation of 2.4 million and Sunday circulation of 4.5 million were twice the totals of any other newspaper.

The astonishing success of the *New York Daily News* spawned many tabloid imitators. *The New York Daily Graphic*, nicknamed "the Pornographic" by its critics, focused on young girls in short skirts and "composographs," pictures that were mere inventions but sure show stoppers. One page-one composograph portrayed silent screen star Rudolph Valentino meeting Enrico Caruso at the gates of heaven after the actor succumbed to a burst appendix at the age of thirty-one. Appendicitis wasn't glamorous enough, so papers competed with one another in making up reasons for the Latin Lover's death. Several decided he had been murdered by a jealous lover. Each new revelation was shouted in Second Coming type that was two inches high. The display type was the largest then available. It was to have been saved to announce Christ's second coming, but several tabloids figured why not use it for Valentino's departure.

Jazz journalism's preoccupation with sex, crime, sport, and sentiment was criticized by some in the self-respecting journalistic establishment and copied by others. Frederick L. Allen, writing in the *Atlantic Monthly*, was among those who had seen enough. "What makes yellow journalism really dangerous," he argued, "is not so much its appetite for scandal as its continued distortion of the news in the interest of undiluted entertainment." Casper S. Yost, editor of the *St. Louis Globe-Democrat*, decided to do something about it. In April 1923 he presided over the first meeting of the American Society of Newspaper

Editors, an organization designed to quarantine the profession from the growing popularity and carelessness of the tabloids. Yost urged the nation's editors to "establish ethical
standards of professional conduct." ASNE's professional canon called for "truthfulness,
impartiality, fair play, and decency" nonbinding on members. J. Willis Abbot, editor of
the *Christian Science Monitor*, objected. His paper had been launched fifteen years before
in the deliberate hope that journalism "might injure no man, but would bless all mankind."
He wanted the organization to have the right to punish irresponsible editors. The era's
"appetite for sensationalism," Abbot argued, had led to an exploitation "of that which is
offensive in life and repugnant to ordinary decency." Arthur Vandenberg, editor of the
Grand Rapids Herald, agreed. Editors, he believed, had the obligation "to tell the country
that we mean what we say when we talk about ethics." A majority of editors, however,
shared the view of E. J. Stackpole, veteran editor and publisher of the *Harrisburg Telegraph*,
who believed that "there is such a thing as ethics in newspaper work," but that it was "the
ethics established in the business office and was tied to box office receipts." Moses Straus,
editor of the *Cincinnati Star-Times*, saw a growing cynicism in the press. "We know that
whether a newspaper is ethical or unethical, it is still quite successful," he observed. That
was why "the profession of journalism is based on no clear idea of what journalism is."

The Rise of Radio News

During the Great Depression and World War II, Americans increasingly turned to radio.
Twice as many Americans reported that they'd give up a newspaper before they'd part with
their radio. By the beginning of World War II, there were more radios in America than
bathtubs or telephones. The simultaneity of experience that enabled listeners to hear events
as they were happening made radio a trusted source of news and information. The medium's
persuasive power was apparent when Herb Morrison in May 1937 broadcast the explosion
of the German dirigible *Hindenburg* as it attempted to dock in Lakehurst, New Jersey.
Broadcast journalism was largely invented by Edward R. Murrow, posted by CBS News
in Europe, as Adolf Hitler began his conquest of the continent. Murrow broadcast from
London during the Battle of Britain in the summer of 1940 when the German Luftwaffe
nightly bombed the British capital. "This is London," he famously began his broadcasts,
"being bombed again." On September 18, 1940, after a particularly intense German bombing raid, he solemnly said, "There are no words to describe the thing that is happening.
There's the courage of the people, the flash and roar of the guns rolling down the streets,
the stench of the air raid shelters." Murrow was an inspiration to a generation of journalists, including Eric Sevareid, who joined the CBS News team reporting the fall of France.
As German storm troopers high-stepped triumphantly down the Champs-Élysées, Sevareid
famously reported, "Paris lay inert, her breathing scarcely audible, her limbs relaxed and
her blood flowing remorselessly through her manifold veins. Paris was dying like a beautiful woman in coma, not knowing or asking why."

In the United States, radio commentators interpreted war news to an anxious public. Hans V. Kaltenborn of the National Broadcasting Company had the widest following, and reported the war from Britain, Italy, France, and Germany. Kaltenborn organized the Association of Radio News Analysts to help broadcast journalism serve as an instrument of informed consent at a time of national peril. Kaltenborn likened a reporter's job to "the duty of a public servant" in giving listeners the information they needed to know. Gabriel Heater, Elmer Davis, and Lowell Thomas developed a national following for their radio commentaries. So did Raymond Gram Swing, whose carefully crafted two-thousand-word, thirteen-minute summary of the news for the Mutual Broadcasting System over a 120-station network won him a nightly audience of 37 million on both sides of the Atlantic. "To get to the meaning of foreign news these days," he reported at the beginning of World War II, "items have to be added up, not pulled apart." Hitler's fundamental miscalculation, he predicted, was that "the ordinary Englishman and the ordinary Frenchman would fight to check a single man in his ambition to dominate the world. And so would an American."

After the war, Swing urged peaceful coexistence between the United States and the Soviet Union and along with other journalists was forced to testify before Joseph McCarthy's Permanent Senate Subcommittee on Investigations on charges that Swing was a "Communist sympathizer." McCarthy used his televised hearings, watched by 20 million Americans, to claim widespread Communist infiltration in government agencies and the U.S. Army. The Hutchins Commission Report "A Free and Responsible Press" noted that the social responsibility of the press required that journalists not only report facts but the truth behind the facts that give them meaning. This is what Elmer Davis, writing in *Atlantic Monthly*, urged reporters to do in checking the paranoiac spread of "McCarthyism." Journalists had been "objective," Davis wrote, in reporting McCarthy's charges, but not in checking out their truthfulness. David argued that there was a difference between "news and the whole truth. Objectivity often leans over backward so far that it makes the news business merely a transmission belt for pretentious phonies." The editorial board of the *Christian Science Monitor* decided not to print McCarthy's continuing flood of accusations until they could be checked out. On March 9, 1954, Edward R. Murrow devoted his *See It Now* prime-time news show on CBS television to McCarthy, showing McCarthy bullying witnesses and pointing out his false allegations. "The actions of the junior senator from Wisconsin have caused alarm and dismay amongst our allies abroad," Murrow reported at the conclusion of the program, "and given considerable comfort to our enemies. And whose fault is that? Not really his. He didn't create this situation of fear, he merely exploited it and rather successfully. Cassius was right. The fault, dear Brutus, is not in our stars but ourselves." McCarthy never recovered from Murrow's program and on December 2, 1954, was censured by the Senate.

Journalism in the Television Era

The second half of the twentieth century saw television emerge as the go-to medium for Americans eager to get the news. CBS and NBC began covering national nominating conventions in 1952. John Chancellor became NBC's senior correspondent. In September 1957 he was the first network reporter to arrive in Little Rock, Arkansas, to cover the forced desegregation of Central High School. Chancellor and NBC's camera captured a mob scene outside the school, when angry white protesters closed in on fifteen-year-old African-American student Elizabeth Eckford, shouting death threats at her and Chancellor. "Television was holding up a mirror of these people for the outside world to look at," Chancellor recalled, "and the image in the mirror was not pretty. Little Rock was the first national crisis seen on television by the whole country." President Dwight Eisenhower, watching from the White House, went on national television, announcing that federal troops were being sent to Little Rock "to prevent anarchy and mob rule" and to enforce the Supreme Court stand that the nation's schools be desegregated. The episode, Chancellor believed, "showed how powerful television might be. Television coverage is important particularly when what it is covering is important. Then, it can make history move much faster."

Walter Cronkite understood the importance of network news coverage in ending the Vietnam War. Polls found that Cronkite as anchor of the CBS Evening News was "the most trusted man in America." After the Tet Offensive in January 1968 inflicted heavy casualties on American forces and their South Vietnamese allies, Cronkite flew to Saigon for his own fact-finding report. His February 27, 1968, prime-time special detailed growing American casualties in the conflict and urged a negotiated settlement of the stalemate. "We've been too often disappointed by the optimism of American leaders both in Vietnam and Washington to have faith any longer in their silver linings," Cronkite said in his closing commentary. Cronkite, who had previously supported the war effort and its escalation, now called for a phased reduction of American forces in the region. "For every means we have to escalate," Cronkite told the American people, "the enemy can match us, and that applies to invasion of the North, the use of nuclear weapons, or the mere commitment of 100 or 200 or 300,000 more American troops to the battle. And with each escalation the world comes closer to the brink of cosmic disaster." President Lyndon Johnson, watching the telecast from the White House, reportedly turned to his aide George Christian and said, "If I've lost Cronkite, I've lost middle America." Weeks later, Johnson announced he would not seek another term as president. The war dragged on with diminishing support from the American people until Congress refused to further fund the fighting during the administration of President Gerald Ford.

Cronkite also became the nation's leading correspondent on the space race, which pitted the United States against the Soviet Union in an effort to land a man on the moon and safely return him to earth. Cronkite had reported the Soviet launch of *Sputnik* on October 4, 1957, the first time an artificial satellite had been shot into space. "If the *Sputnik* isn't a threat to our national security," Cronkite reported, "it is a threat to our sense of security." On May 5, 1961, Cronkite reported America's first manned space flight when

Alan Shepard's Mercury Redstone rocket completed a fifteen-minute suborbital mission. Nine months later, John Glenn became the first American to orbit the earth. Cronkite was unapologetically enthusiastic in his coverage. "We all shared the excitement," he remembered. "Could we do it? That was the big question. Everyone was looking up. We were looking to the stars." An estimated worldwide audience of 300 million was watching the launch of *Apollo 11* on July 16, 1969. Its moon landing four days later left Cronkite speechless. "Whew, boy," he exclaimed, taking off his glasses and smiling broadly, while shaking his head and wiping away the tears.

Some extraordinary reporting in the 1970s helped force the resignation from office of an American president. Five men were arrested on June 17, 1971, for breaking into Democratic National Headquarters at the Watergate Hotel in Washington, D.C. President Richard Nixon's press secretary, Ronald Ziegler, put out the story that this had been "a third rate burglary," but two young reporters for the *Washington Post*, Bob Woodward and Carl Bernstein, continued to investigate the case, finding that the Committee to Re-elect the President had bankrolled the break-in. For months, the *Post* was largely alone in painstakingly putting together the complicity of the Nixon White House in the crime. On the eve of the national election in 1972, Cronkite weighed in with the CBS News special "The Watergate Affair," which charged that "a high level campaign of political sabotage and espionage without parallel in American history" was under way. Nixon won reelection and his top aides threatened news organizations they'd "pay" if they didn't lay off the story. Undaunted, the *Post* and CBS, joined by the *New York Times*, and other leading news networks, aggressively pursued the case. A special prosecutor and grand jury brought indictments of key presidential advisers. The Judiciary Committee of the House of Representatives voted to impeach the president, and Nixon was forced to resign his office on August 9, 1974.

During the final quarter of the twentieth century, three television networks, CBS, NBC, and ABC dominated the American news landscape. By the mid-1980s, two thirds of all Americans were getting all or most of their news from the networks' half-hour nightly news shows that featured Tom Brokaw anchoring at NBC, Peter Jennings at ABC, and Cronkite's successor, Dan Rather, at CBS. On the evening of November 9, 1989, Brokaw reported "the beginning of a new age in Europe." The Berlin Wall had been erected at the height of the Cold War in 1961 to prevent East Berliners from fleeing to the democratic, western sector of the city. Brokaw reported from the Brandenburg Gate amid scenes of jubilation as East Berliners were taking hatchets to the hated wall and pouring into the streets. "Crowds have gathered to celebrate their new freedom," Brokaw reported, holding in his hand before the camera a small piece of the shattered wall. "This is the day the Cold War ended, not with a bang, but a street party."

Brokaw, Jennings, and Rather reported the news not only from their New York studios but from the scenes of some of the most important stories of the period. On February 5, 1994, Jennings was in the central market of Sarajevo when a bomb went off killing sixty-eight. His dramatic and sustained coverage of ethnic cleansing in the region would later prompt the Clinton administration and the United Nations to send a military force to the region. For months afterwards, Jennings continued to make civilian suffering in Bosnia a major story in America. One of Rather's major exclusives was his reporting in August 1990 from Baghdad on the eve of the first Persian Gulf War. Rather managed an exclusive interview with Iraqi president Saddam Hussein just before the outbreak of fighting that saw a multinational force, led by the United States, Britain, and France, expel Iraqi occupation forces from neighboring Kuwait.

Rarely in American history has the nation relied more on its journalists than on September 11, 2001, when four commercial passenger liners were hijacked by nineteen Al Qaeda terrorists and crashed into the twin towers of the World Trade Center in New York, demolishing the buildings, and the Pentagon outside Washington, D.C. A fourth plane crashed near Shanksville, Pennsylvania, when passengers fought to take control of the plane. In all, 3,016 people were killed and America was at war with Islamic terrorists. The over-the-air news networks and cable stations joined by online web users gave nonstop coverage to the tragedy. Dan Rather called it "the Pearl Harbor of terrorism." No story he covered had "affected Americans as personally" or had "so profoundly changed our lives." Brokaw remembers "trying to get our people through something they were utterly unprepared for." Brokaw toured the devastated World Trade Center site, where "thousands died violent deaths" at what was now "a holy place" of national consecration to fight to preserve freedom "from appalling inhumanity." Jennings was on the air for sixteen hours of consecutive coverage in the aftermath of the bombings. As events unfolded he remembered feeling "immersed in confusion and suffocating in chaos." Jennings believed that his forty years of experience as a broadcast journalist prepared him for events on that day. "When everyone is getting worked up, it's my job to really focus, give good information, and sober, quiet perspective."

Journalism in the Twenty-First Century

In the new millennium, barely one third of all Americans watch the network news and their average age is over sixty. The World Wide Web, which had come into existence in March 1989, enjoyed 40 million users by 1995. By 2000, one hundred countries were online. In the aftermath of 9/11 the number of computers going online has tripled every eighteen months. Two hundred fifty thousand web pages are added every week to a universe of 2 billion text pages. Nearly half of all American households were online by 2005, the year that data traffic on the Internet surpassed the telephone as the dominant form of communication. In December 2007, the Internet replaced radio in advertising revenues. Access to information in the twenty-first century is becoming as important as access to fossil fuels had been to twentieth-century commerce. News organizations have had to adapt themselves to this new mobile landscape, where users can access news and information wherever they are with devices so small they can be put in a person's pocket. John Sturm, chief executive officer of the Newspaper Association of America, predicts that there is hope for the American newspaper in this new digital landscape. "Newspapers are no longer a one product medium," he observes. "We're no longer simply ink on paper. Thirty-seven percent of all online users use newspaper websites. Reader surveys show that this is a 20 percent increase from a year ago. The Pew Center for the People and the Press reports that one third of all Americans get their news online. Sturm's conclusion is that readers, whatever their age, will continue to hunt for news they feel they need to know, but that the digital world of text messaging and blogs are where they'll get this branded content.

What will the digital future of news mean to the responsible reporter? Gary Meo, a senior vice president of print and Internet services at Scarborough Research, says that "portability" and "convenience" have become major values for younger news consumers. To Meo's mind, this implies that the "how" and "why" of a story will take on increasing importance. This will put a premium, Meo believes, on people coming into the profession who understand the context of events that give them meaning. "Virtual doorstep delivery," Meo says, will be how news in the future is transmitted, but the content of that transmission will be to communicate news citizens need to know quickly and economically. Jane Hirt, managing editor of the *Chicago Tribune*, says that "reporters will have to learn how to make their stories more concise" for readers who may not feel they have the time or interest to "drill down deeply."

When Benjamin Franklin emerged from the Constitutional Convention, he was asked by a fellow citizen what kind of government the founding fathers had given the nation. The old editor answered, "it's a Republic, if you can keep it!" Responsible reporting in the new millennium still requires readers with a genuine interest in the world around them and reporters who give them a picture of the world upon which they can act. In assessing press performance on the eve of the television era, the Hutchins Commission cited the famous saying of John Adams: "Mankind cannot now be governed without the press, nor at present with it." That assertion has never been more true for responsible reporters than today as our beleaguered republic lives its first uncertain days in a challenging and rapidly expanding digital universe.

Responsible Reporting and the Law

JANAN HANNA

You are a young reporter who has just landed your first job at a news outlet. You are full of drive and ambition, eager to impress your bosses by diligently ferreting out the facts and finding good sources. Then you hit a roadblock. A recalcitrant public official with information you need utters that dreaded little word that sends journalists into a tailspin: "No." It might be "No, you cannot attend our meeting." Or "No, you cannot view those documents." And then there's always "No, you cannot publish what I said."

This may be a knee-jerk reaction by a low-level official who either fears or loathes the media and takes no solace in the fact that what you are seeking might be completely routine and uncontroversial. In other cases, such denials may be a strategic attempt to thwart the publication of sensitive information that could cause embarrassment.

What should a responsible reporter do in such circumstances? Initially, try persuasion. Indicate that you are only doing your job. Remind the official that it is customary and essential for the media to report on, say, zoning changes, recent arrests, proposed municipal budgets, a criminal investigation, or the outcome of a recent court hearing. Being persistent and respectful will often work. The official will know that you are determined to get the information and might back down and recognize that your request is reasonable and in the public's interest.

Often, however, if you are not well known and have not yet developed trusting relationships with sources, persuasion will not work. In those instances, knowing about the law that governs the relationship between the media and the government—the rule that spells out what information the government is or is not required to disclose—will be a great help to you. Each state and the federal government have such a law, known as the **Freedom of Information Act** (FOIA). These acts also include Open Meeting Acts provisions, requiring government agencies to conduct their meetings in public. These laws are based on the belief that the government's business is the people's business. Therefore, the workings of the government, as well as the documents it generates, are by law subject to public scrutiny.

Reporter Confidentiality

There may come a day when you find yourself with a great story that uncovers government corruption or sheds light on a pending investigation. You may have gotten the story by promising your source confidentiality. After the story is published, and sometimes, even before it is published, you may be issued a subpoena—a court order requesting that you disclose the source of your information. Here again, there are laws (and staff lawyers or pro bono lawyers from press associations) to help you out. Many states have **"privilege"** or **"shield"** laws that protect a reporter's notes, confidential sources, tape recordings, video footage, and photographs from government scrutiny. In some cases, particularly if the information you've uncovered has bearing on a criminal investigation or matters of national security, you may be forced to comply with the request. In most cases, however, **shield laws** place a very high burden on the party seeking the information. They typically must show that they have a compelling need for the information and that you're the only person who has it.

Defamation

Another part of the law that responsible reporters must understand are the laws of defamation and privacy. Reporters can be sued civilly for publishing false information that damages a person's reputation. If the person is a public figure—a celebrity or a government official well known in the community—the person would have to prove that you knowingly published false information with actual malice. A private plaintiff need only show that you were careless in publishing damaging information. In addition, the person must show that disclosure of the information caused him or her harm.

All these laws involve a delicate balancing act between the First Amendment and some other interest—typically national security and/or privacy. They are inspired by the principle that, in a participatory democracy, the public must be provided with information about how its government conducts its business.

The War on Terror

These are tense times for reporters. Government action and court rulings over the last several years have been particularly hostile toward the media. Reporters have been jailed for refusing to turn over the names of their sources, suspected government "leakers" have been subjected to polygraph tests, and the government has sought to bar publications from reporting stories in the aftermath of the September 11, 2001, terrorist attacks on the United States. Taking your job seriously and recognizing the awesome responsibility you have as a government watchdog means pushing back, using the tools of open government available to journalists.

Open Meetings Act

The federal government, every state, and the District of Columbia have an open meetings law that requires public agencies to give notice of meetings and conduct them in public. They are also required to keep notes and minutes of the proceedings. The scope of each state law varies. Known as "sunshine" laws, the open meetings laws contain a number of exceptions that allow public bodies to conduct certain business in private. These include discussions of student disciplinary matters, pending litigation, collective bargaining, acquisition of real estate, and personnel matters. See the First Amendment Center (http://www.firstamendmentcenter.org/press/information) and the Reporters Committee for Freedom of the Press (http://www.rcfp.org) for general and state-by-state comparisons. One of the most widely invoked exceptions is "pending litigation." Since almost any issue could, conceivably, lead to litigation or require the services of a lawyer, public bodies use that exception most frequently. Reporters should question public officials who routinely close meetings on pending litigation grounds, and request that minutes from these closed meetings be kept and released once the matter is no longer confidential.

Freedom of Information Act

Every state has a Freedom of Information Act modeled on the Federal act, which was first adopted in 1966 and was most recently amended in 2007 (5 U.S.C. s. 552). The law requires government agencies to disclose certain records, upon written request, within a certain amount of time, and, in some cases, in an electronic form. The law gives reporters (and all members of the public) the right to file a lawsuit if their requests are not met. Reporters, including freelance reporters, are exempt from paying any fees associated with making records available. Agencies covered include those in the executive branch and cabinet offices, such as the defense, state, treasury, interior, and justice departments, and independent regulatory agencies, such as the Federal Trade Commission, Federal Communications Commission, and Consumer Product Safety Commission. There are exemptions to disclosing information under the Freedom of Information Act. They are subject to interpretation by the courts. They include: national security, internal agency personnel rules, trade secrets and confidential commercial information, personal privacy, law enforcement investigations, and federally regulated banks.

The Reporters Committee for Freedom of the Press, based in Arlington, Virginia, has been offering free legal assistance to journalists since 1970. The committee publishes summaries and detailed text of the federal law and each state law. In addition, the committee has a hotline offering free legal advice to reporters. The committee's website gives practical advice on freedom of information issues and guides reporters on how to create effective freedom of information requests. The site also contains an open government guide, a First Amendment handbook, and a means for reporters to access electronic records.

Shield Laws

Currently, there is no federal shield law that protects a reporter from divulging the identity of its confidential sources, although courts have provided protection to reporters under certain circumstances. A proposed federal shield law is pending in Congress (as of 2008). Like its counterparts in thirty-three states and the District of Columbia, the proposed federal law bars the government from forcing a reporter to disclose information unless the reporter has witnessed criminal conduct or has information bearing on national security or a possible terror attack. There must be a showing that the reporter is the only source of the information sought and that there is a compelling public interest in disclosing the information that outweighs the public interest in gathering and disseminating news or information (H.R. 2102: Free Flow of Information Act). State laws vary, but are similar in scope. They protect a reporter from divulging the identity of confidential sources in most civil proceedings absent a showing by the person seeking the information that they have exhausted all other avenues to obtain the information. Reporters typically are not privileged from disclosing information that has a bearing on a criminal investigation. Most of the laws and proposed laws define a reporter as someone who earns substantial income by disseminating information on matters of public interest. Presumably, some bloggers would fall under this category.

For a state-by-state comparison of the shield laws, see the Reporters Committee for the Freedom of the Press website.

Responsible Reporting and the First Amendment

Responsible reporters need to realize that the First Amendment is not without its limits. Reporting information that harms a person's reputation could cost you and your organization hefty damages. The law of defamation is complex. Courts typically decide on a case-by-case basis whether a reporter and news organization should be held liable for defamation. And state laws vary widely. However, cases typically turn on whether the subject of the article or newscast is a public figure or a private figure. For a public figure to prevail in a cause of action, he or she must show that the information was false and that the reporter knew the information was false before publication. A party suing must also show that the information in fact caused harm. It is a very high burden of proof, one that most public officials cannot maintain. On the other hand, a private person need only show that a reporter or publication was negligent in reporting a defamatory falsehood. (See http://www.firstamendmentcenter.org/press/topic.aspx? topic= libel_defamation.)

Privacy rights found in the Constitution can also impede the information-gathering process. Individuals are afforded privacy under the Constitution, and state laws allow for private civil actions where a person is harassed, recorded, or photographed in places where he or she would have a reasonable expectation of privacy (including public places, in some cases). As with the law of defamation, any publication of information gained in violation of a person's privacy can be defended on grounds that the information was newsworthy and accurate.

3

The Digital World and Responsible Reporting

FREDERICK R. BLEVENS

Responsible reporters in the twenty-first century find themselves competing with citizen journalists in a digital world somewhat resembling the press of colonial and early republican America, when journalism was personal and partisan and where the buzz in the local tavern was about the latest pamphlet or paper to hit the streets. Editors often aimed to insult political opponents. Rumor and innuendo were often passions in the pages of the party press at election time. Today, citizen journalists and bloggers have taken the place of their argumentative forefathers. They are often more interested in making their case than reporting the news. Early printers needed rich patrons to reach the literate. The technological revolution of the late twentieth century makes it easy for anyone at a keystroke to claim he or she is reporting news worth knowing.

The Journalist and Digital Gatekeeping

Rarely has information been more available for citizens and less credible. Citizen journalists today often place the "editing" process after publication, as they rush to report the rumor before someone beats them to it. Few rely on professional obligations to weigh the evidence and build their stories fact upon fact while vetting their story for taste, newsworthiness, and journalistic ethics. Corrections do occur in the public sphere after publication, when more and more readers chime in, but this self-correction is not particularly timely or consistent. This makes the job of today's responsible reporter all the more monumental. He or she is the gatekeeper for a generation of readers who rely less and less on the mainstream media for news of the day.

In the digital world it is becoming increasingly difficult for citizens and the courts to decide who a "journalist" is. It's no longer simply somebody with a press card, who works for a news organization producing print or broadcast content for a mass market. Instead, people with a modem and a point of view are claiming the same privilege of free speech as a free press. Their claim is finding legal traction. Judge David Sentelle, ruling in the case of a Bush administration official who allegedly outed a CIA agent, asked if the privileges of a reporter to protect the confidentiality of sources "also protect the proprietor of a Web log, the stereotypical 'blogger' sitting in his pajamas at his personal computer posting on the World Wide Web…to inform whoever happens to browse his way?" Many in the public share Sentelle's sentiment.

Today's bloggers are independent and autonomous, and operate without editing, without oversight, without any formal adherence to ethical standards. Like their early American counterparts, they function efficiently and effectively with minimum equipment and without allegiance to powerful news proprietors. Many are fiercely partisan, sometimes vicious in their invective, and, much like the partisan pamphleteers of colonial times, they post notices in public places, occasionally operate under false names, endure scorn and ridicule, and owe nothing to any corporation. Yale law professor Jack Balkin believes that bloggers and journalists in the mainstream soon will blend into a new kind of workforce. In about a decade, Balkin says, "there may be no clear distinction between reporters on the one hand and bloggers on the other."

Blogging and Responsible Reporting

Responsible reporters need to know that news delivery on the web is redrawing the boundaries of who journalists are and the role journalists play in educating the public. As with any revolutionary movement, assumptions are being challenged and limits are being tested in courtrooms, newsrooms, and living rooms. Most in the blogosphere want to replace traditional media; most in the mainstream want traditional media to evolve or migrate methodically to the web. That is at the emotional core of the tension between the two. Bloggers say they now control the news agenda; mainstream journalists say bloggers would have nothing to write without the news produced daily in traditional media. Bloggers say they deserve the same First Amendment protections granted traditional media; mainstream journalists say bloggers cannot join that club until they accept the same canons, conventions, and ethical practices that guide traditional media. Bloggers and mainstream journalists clash over who should create such standards or monitor them and how journalists can be both socially responsible and free and unfettered.

Where does all this leave beginning journalists who want to be responsible reporters? They will find themselves competing with a new brand of "reporter," the "civic journalist" who is essentially untrained in newsgathering but claims the same rights and privileges of journalists in reaching readers. **The aim of the civic journalist is less to inform than persuade**. Like early American pamphleteers, many in the blogosphere see proclamation as an engine for moving public opinion. New media analyst Christopher Hanson says blogs break down into two types: "I Blogs," "a wilderness of self-absorption," and "Lynch Blogs," those driven by ideology. Each type is seen by some citizens as offering news worth knowing.

There is no rulebook or obligation of citizen bloggers to obey the canons of socially responsible reporting. Many of these bloggers are finding their own way, very much like early American journalists did as they fueled the fires of colonial dissent and political partisanship in the early republican period. The result then and now has been a free-for-all in which **citizens find it increasingly difficult to separate the credible from the incredible, the sourced from the unsourced**. The danger is an outsourcing of the facts around which civil discourse takes place. But facts matter. And the responsible reporter's job and training have long been geared toward going after them and providing citizens with a daily account of the news, which can become the basis of public action. The purpose and practice of the citizen blogger is often to persuade readers of a particular point of view. The Internet provides motivated bloggers with a superior space for debate, recruitment, and the authoring of urban legends. They find the World Wide Web to be an excellent instrument for facilitating political and social networking. The Internet, in their hands, is creatively equipped to inspire wild and creative expression. What is needed for the next generation of socially responsible reporters is the mastery of this webbed world through tools and platforms that seek first to serve citizens with information they need to know.

For those keeping score, the journalistic triumphs in the blogosphere are not, in the scope of journalism history, particularly significant, but they can help us understand the potential of the medium. A blogger exposed Bill Clinton's affair with Monica Lewinsky. One forced Trent Lott to resign as Senate majority leader because of comments interpreted as praise for Senator Strom Thurmond's racist positions. Still another reported that Dan Rather's exposé on President Bush's military service record was based on faked documents, forcing the veteran newsman to step down from CBS. CNN chief Eason Jordan was forced to resign after a blogger posted comments in which Eason said the U.S. military was targeting journalists in the Iraq War. Bloggers had their fingerprints all over the primaries and presidential campaign of 2008.

The philosophical tensions and distrust between journalists on the web and those in America's mainstream media have made it extremely difficult for traditional journalists to cover the blogging phenomenon. Many observers believe that the mainstream media approach the blogging community with great trepidation. Some even assert that mainstream journalists show deference to their blogging colleagues because their belief in free expression outweighs whatever contempt they may harbor for the bad behavior of the blogging community. Jon Carroll of the *San Francisco Chronicle*, an early blogger, says the future depends on the two camps getting on the same page. "The stand-alone journalists are here, and they are digging out facts and leading crusades," Carroll says. "They are also printing gossip and distorting facts—but, hey, so are we. It is about time that all media folks began working together for the common good, defending reporters and bloggers in trouble and, by the way, outing our own when they mess up."

Carroll's plea for togetherness makes sense until we consider the very disparate practices and conventions of bloggers and responsible reporting practiced by mainstream journalists. Responsible reporting is purpose-driven. It sees journalism as a public service because of its obligation to give citizens news that makes self-actualization in a democratic society possible. **The press is free so that it might serve.** This freedom makes citizens stakeholders in the journalistic enterprise. Ultimately, journalists work for them as much as for the companies that employ them. The obligations of public service extend to publishers. A publisher needs to avoid the arrogance brought on by the belief that press freedom belongs only to those who own one.

Serving the Public Interest

Toward the end of the analog era in the 1990s, when television and print were showing the first signs of the growing competition from the online world, the public was clear in its insistence that reporters behave responsibly. A survey by Louis Harris and Associates showed that one third of Americans depended solely on local television for news, more than twice the number who favored newspapers and twice the number who depended on thirty-minute daily network newscasts. Seventy-five percent of those polled said they supported the media's watchdog role, which obligates responsible reporters to be on the lookout for government and corporate corruption. Two thirds of those polled said a major job of a free press was to protect the public from abuses. Sixty-three percent agreed that the press plays an important role in democracy. Yet, Harris and others have found that the public distrusts the press. Sixty-five percent of Americans told Harris they wanted the press to "simply report the facts" and stay out of the business of solving problems or correcting "what they believe are inaccuracies and distortions in the statements of public figures." Eighty-four percent wanted a "fairness doctrine" that would prevent broadcasters from using their stations to promote one-sided viewpoints about controversial issues of public importance. Seventy percent favored court-imposed fines for inaccurate reporting.

In the digital era, not only Echo Boomers but their parents are turning to the web for breaking news and news in depth. Nearly 30 percent of news consumers now access news aggregation sites like Google, Yahoo, MSN, or AOL as their first or second source, while just 11 percent are going first to their own daily newspapers' websites. For young people, the Internet is by far the most dominant news provider. At the turn of the century, news consumers were using the Internet only to supplement their reading; today, it dominates, especially among the under-thirty-six age group. Research is also showing that younger consumers are developing a news reading habit at a much younger age and, therefore, offer a remarkable opportunity for local newspapers that aggressively develop, produce, and distribute news on their local sites.

The challenge for responsible reporters in the twenty-first century will be to demonstrate journalism's ability to inform readers and viewers in a way that helps to create an informed electorate capable of making rational decisions in the exercise of their civic obligations. The intrusiveness of digital technologies greatly complicates their mission. Many websites in December 2006, for instance, posted the grainy video of Saddam Hussein's hanging, captured on a cell phone and broadcast to the world. Millions saw it on YouTube. A Google search brought it to laptop screens in seconds around the wired world. Broadcast news networks in the Arab world showed the incident. Eventually, American news networks showed them showing it. Airing the video triggered a new round of violence in Iraq from groups opposing the public humiliation of their former leader. This was a case in which the intrusiveness of mini-cams not only reported events but shaped them. In a global society, responsible reporters and editors face daily challenges to professional conduct created by advances in digital technologies. Increasingly, they face the reality of story conferences, when the question is asked, "Why aren't we showing what the competition is showing?" and not, "Is it worth showing?"

The current controversy over the role of the press in waging the "War on Terror" has strong parallels to the Cold War debate over how a free press could be made a responsible one. A commission at that time was funded by *Time* magazine magnate Henry Luce to investigate the matter. The **Hutchins Commission**, composed of sixteen of the best thinkers of the period, urged the press to live up to its responsibilities in "the maintenance and development of a free society." Freedom of the press, the commission concluded, can only survive as a "moral right...conditioned on its acceptance of this accountability. Its legal right will stand unaltered as its moral duty is performed." In the years since, the report has become a rallying cry for those demanding a socially responsible press that serves its citizens well. Theodore Peterson has observed that the press has the moral duty to provide information necessary for citizens to carry out their civic responsibilities in an increasingly complex and ambiguous world. Media owners "need not publish every idea, however preposterous," he has argued, "but they should see that all ideas deserving a public hearing shall have a public hearing." Denis McQuail recently has taken Peterson's argument to mean that "communication is too important to be left to professionals." McQuail insists that, ultimately, it is the responsibility of an informed public to hold publishers accountable in meeting their social service obligations.

The Obligations of Social Responsibility

Public and civic press movements in the late twentieth and early twenty-first centuries have emphasized the social responsibility of the press. Hutchins-based social responsibility can be found in university curricula as well as newspaper master plans, midcareer programs, and ethics manuals. Newspapers have devoted more space to opposing editorial opinions, created ombudspersons and reader representatives to field and write about complaints, and opened their editorial boards to outsiders. Newspapers have devised new and controversial coverage philosophies that adopt many of the communitarian goals that position journalists as partners with the government and citizens to solve social problems.

Many of the opponents and practitioners of what came to be known as the "civic journalism" movement of the 1980s and '90s have wanted to push the news industry into activism. Their focus has been to empower citizens with the tools to participate in a journalism of the people. "According to the gospel of public journalism, **professional passivity is passé; activism is hot**," says press critic Alicia Shepard. "Detachment is out; participation is in. Experts are no longer the quote machines of choice; readers' voices must be heard." Within the digital landscape, citizen journalists eschew detachment and use technologies such as the Internet to state their case and claim the same status as professional reporters. With a computer and Internet connection, any citizen, in theory, can wield the same power as the wealthy local publisher who owns a printing press. This effort at democratization presents a remarkable challenge to those who view journalism's social responsibility and communitarian obligations as an antidote to the recklessness of an unfettered press. The "new frontier" of citizen journalism, sometimes called the "pajama revolution," has by the first decade of the twenty-first century morphed into a form of "journalism" that is part chaos and part participation that looks more like a chat—and, at times, a screaming match—over the backyard fence.

The challenge for responsible journalists in the digital age will be to give citizens verifiable news worth knowing at a time in which many using this technology appear to have an allergy to faithfully finding and following the facts. This work is time consuming and not always glamorous. It contends daily with the corporate demands of journalism's bottom line. Knight-Ridder, the newspaper chain that started the user-friendly civic journalism movement, is a case study in the threats and realities of the newsgathering business. In 2006, it sold most of its assets to an even larger conglomerate, the McClatchy Newspapers. The sell-off was characteristic of the growing concentration of the news business in the Internet era, where money, and lots of it, is necessary in an increasingly competitive marketplace. Responsible reporters find that the citizens who demand public service from the news media are also the stockholders who demand that these organizations turn a tidy profit. For young men and women now coming into the profession, this does not mean there no longer will be a need for traditional, mainstream journalists. Instead, Bureau of Labor Statistics data seem to suggest that the rise of the web will mean more jobs in journalism—if you know where to look for them. As news operations sell more and more of their content to digital distribution platforms that are more efficient, expedient, and useful to news consumers, new work opportunities for responsible reporters who can tell stories online under deadline will be created.

The ultimate challenge of digital journalism is to better understand how the public actually consumes—and now participates in—reporting and reading the news of the day. Online interactivity has intensified a public willingness to participate in the ever-expanding communication playground. This threatens the idea of accountability that has long been at the heart of responsible reporting, and is making the future of responsible reporting as frightening as it is promising. How the socially responsible mainstream "old media" blends with the random and chaotic libertarian "new media" will redefine journalism, the rights and responsibilities of reporters and editors, the ethical obligations of publishers and news distributors, and how the government and politicians view the press. Libertarian philosophy, with the freedom to choose responsibility over irresponsibility, is the guiding principle of the Internet. The question is whether the principles and policies of social responsibility, handed down to civic-minded journalists, can harness a viral media that today provides a little bread with lots of stones.

Collaborative Newsgathering

AMY SCHMITZ WEISS

The newsroom you enter today is being radically transformed. News operations are integrating media platforms, journalists, and technologies as part of the news production process. For years, broadcast journalists worked in teams. Now, more than ever before, print journalists are getting in on the act.

As a former online journalist and now as a scholar in this field, I have witnessed a transformation over the past ten years in newsrooms I have visited in the United States and internationally. It has become a place where the journalist needs to work with multiple individuals in the process of getting the story done. Why? The specialization in telling a story for one medium is no longer the status quo in the newsroom. The story is published on the website, in the print newspaper, via podcast, and on the broadcast news. Thus, the production of a news story requires skills and expertise from several individuals at the same time in the newsroom. Working as a collaborative group is more important now more than ever.

According to a recent study of journalists by a graduate student at Northwestern University, online managers and producers surveyed said that teamwork and collaboration ability was a daily requirement of their jobs. Understanding how to work collaboratively in the newsroom will help you to become a better journalist and a responsible reporter. First, it requires a different mentality of how to work. Second, specific steps can be taken during the newsgathering and reporting process to start working collaboratively.

First, spend time with your colleagues in other departments. Spend a few hours a day or over a series of weeks to watch how they do their work. (For example, watch how an online producer compiles news packages for the website or how a designer makes a Flash template for an online multimedia package.) Getting to know what your colleagues do can give you an understanding of how you can shape your story for this multimedia news environment and when you need to ask your colleagues to help develop an item for your story. Your colleagues will respect you for taking the time to understand how they work and relate to their daily routines and schedules. Then, when you have a news story that you would like to collaborate on (whether it includes writing, designing, or producing), the news process will flow smoothly.

Take a look at examples of news stories that are co-authored or multi-authored in various media (online, broadcast, print). See how each story is organized and produced. Contact the journalists involved to ask them how they worked on the project, how many journalists were involved, how long the process took, and what forms of collective decisions took place. Some journalists may not be willing to share details of their triumphs and challenges with you, but many will gladly discuss them with you. Understanding these examples will train your mind to think of your story from multiple layers and perspectives, which is necessary when working collaboratively.

Be open to suggestions and flexible in your approach. A collaborative newsroom environment does have its ups and downs. You will find that some people are happy to work together while others find it threatening. As a responsible reporter, be flexible. Understand that the structure and format of your story can change. Don't be stuck to one form of working. Respect and understand the various perspectives of your colleagues and the news audience; it will greatly help you in working in a collaborative news environment.

As you begin to change your mindset of how you do your work in the newsroom, you will then be ready to implement collaboration at the newsgathering and reporting stage.

Start thinking collaboratively at the newsgathering step—when you have the story idea. When you have an idea, talk with others in the newsroom to get their suggestions. Consider establishing professional relationships with as many people in the newsroom as you can—not only within your news subject area (for example, local, national, or sports) but also in other departments (for example, business and features). Also, talk with staff in different departments such as the designers, producers, and programmers. They can provide you with ideas you may not have considered before. For example, a colleague from the business desk may give you a different angle to your story or suggest a source that you may not have known about. A designer may suggest an illustration to accompany your story, while a multimedia producer may suggest posting a two-minute clip of your audio interview with the story on the website. These contributions may help your story to be richer in context and depth.

Be transparent with your story as it develops. Post drafts of your story to a blog, wiki, or intranet in your news organization to get insight from your colleagues and the news audience. You can create a wiki or another shared digital workspace that you and your colleagues can access at any time, anywhere. This will depend on the type of story you do. You may not be able to share details of your story if it is a controversial or sensitive topic, but if you have an investigative piece that extends across several days or weeks, the contributions from others may help you to dig up some new details, data, or sources to include in your story. Recently, some news organizations in the United States have been doing investigative pieces using a method called crowdsourcing, in which the public is asked to share sources, information, or other forms of data with the news organization for a news story, which the journalists may or may not use.

In conclusion, collaboration is attainable in the newsroom; it happens in many instances and we may not realize it. We can recognize collaboration at one of the most basic levels of doing journalism—in our mentality of how we do our work and at the newsgathering and reporting process. These tips can help make you an adaptable journalist; they can help you professionally, but, more importantly, they can help you in producing the best and most accurate story for today's multilayered news environment.

Data Base Reporting

ART GOLAB

In her travels around town, *Chicago Sun-Times* consumer affairs reporter Stephanie Zimmerman noticed that some neighborhoods had an unusually high concentration of disabled permit parking signs. The signs reserve parking spots in front of the residences of disabled people for their exclusive use. All that is needed to use the spot is a disabled vehicle license plate or hanging placard issued by the state. Seeing that some blocks contained three or more of these disabled parking spots, Zimmerman suspected that there might be some abuse of the program. But with 95,000 disabled plates and placards issued by the state to Chicago residents—and 11,400 designated disabled parking spaces in the city—how could she tell which parking spots were legitimate?

As one of the paper's database reporters I was brought in to help. Thanks to **computer-assisted reporting**, we were able in a week to do what would have taken a team of reporters months to do before the introduction of computers to America's newsrooms. Using a desktop computer, we were able to match the addresses of holders of disabled license plates and placards to the addresses of the disabled parking spots. We found that nearly 10 percent, or 1,097 of the disabled parking spots, were at addresses where no nearby resident held a disabled plate or placard. Further investigation by reporter Eric Herman uncovered the fact that at least 260 of the parking spot holders were dead. And so a front-page story headlined "Dead People Parking" was born. It was a story that could not have been written without the computers and relatively simple computer programs that have come into common use in newsrooms in the last fifteen years.

Sure, governments, banks, and other large institutions have been using computers to do significant tasks since the 1950s, but the personal computer revolution put that power on the desktop of every reporter starting in the 1990s. More recently, the spreadsheet and database software necessary for analyzing large amounts of data has become simple enough that no programming skills are required. A boot camp run by the National Institute for Computer-Assisted Reporting can teach reporters the basics over the course of a long weekend.

Many versions of the Microsoft Office software already running on many reporters' computers contain both the spreadsheet program Excel and the database program Access, both powerful tools used by the *Sun-Times* team in their analysis of parking data. Reporters are finding how helpful Excel can be in sorting and doing math. It can, for example, rank a list of all city employees by salary and calculate who got the biggest raise. It can do the same for test scores for every school in a city or state. The database program Access allows the easy comparison of two sets of data, such as parking spots and license data.

These tools allow a creative reporter to put together two sets of data to come up with something new and newsworthy. In 1989, *Atlanta Journal-Constitution* reporter Bill Dedman, a pioneer in the field, combined home loan rejection data with census data to uncover a pattern of racial discrimination. His series, "The Color of Money," won a Pulitzer Prize.

Mapping software can now take computer analysis to the next level, enabling both the reporter and the reader or viewer to visualize information. The *Sun-Times* used Arcview mapping software to examine the work of city crews that boot cars with accumulated parking violations. We were able to turn the locations of forty thousand booted cars into dots on a city map. This mapping software also allowed us to count the number of dots within any geographic boundary. What was shown in this case was that minority neighborhoods were getting kicked hardest by the boot.

You might ask where all this data that modern journalists analyze come from. The simple answer is that government agencies make information available if you know where and how to look for it. The federal **Freedom of Information Act** and similar laws in most states give reporters the same access to electronic records as to paper records. Though privacy and other restrictions apply, in general all records paid for by taxpayers and maintained by government agencies should be accessible to the public and the media at little or no cost, whether on paper or in electronic form. It should be just as easy to get a CD containing the standardized test scores of all the schools in a school district as it is to get a paper copy of the district budget. In many cases, in fact, it is easier for an agency to provide electronic records, especially for large sets of data, because a CD can be burned or an e-mail attachment sent with only a few keystrokes, while paper records must be located and copied. And sometimes it is not even necessary to ask for the data because they are already posted online and available for download. The U.S. Census Bureau, for instance, is an excellent example of an agency that employs this practice.

Responsible reporters soon realize that just getting data isn't enough. Anyone with a computer science degree can do that. It takes a skilled journalist, however, to confirm that numbers on a screen actually reflect problems in the real world. That's where **gatekeeping** and news judgment come in. It takes reporters to put a human face on social problems. And it takes trained writers, photojournalists, and graphic artists to translate those numbers into something that anyone glancing at a newspaper or watching a news report can easily understand.

In "Dead People Parking," *Sun-Times* reporters put a human face on the story by interviewing neighbors who expressed frustration at disabled spaces that went unused for years. Interviews of residents connected to the spaces revealed that many of them were frustrated as well, because the city was slow in removing the signs after disabled relatives had died. And the *Sun-Times* even found some people using their dead relatives' spaces for themselves. The story was done in early 2007, and the web version included a list by street address of every parking spot that had no one licensed to use it as well as a color-coded map showing the highest concentrations of disabled parking spaces. In a sign, however, of how quickly things are changing in journalism, a year later the online component of that story would be completely different. Instead of having to scroll down a thirty-seven-page list of street addresses, a reader would be able to type his or her own address on a web page and get a customized map of all the disabled parking spaces within a few blocks.

Currently, achieving this type of interactivity requires the talent of hard-core programmers who work in the information technology departments of media organizations. However, software is being developed that will eventually make it much easier for responsible reporters in the future to add interactive web content to the stories they tell.

Where Is the News and How Is It Gathered?

4

Sourcing and Interviewing

CATHERINE CASSARA-JEMAI

In the course of a day's work, general assignment reporters may talk to people as diverse as elected officials, kindergarteners, cancer patients, and prison inmates—people who are used to dealing with journalists and people who are meeting a reporter for the first time. In addition to the people on their beats, reporters' regular sources include documents—everything from police incident records, to court records of the most recent divorce filings, to company financial reports. While some stories are predictable, entail routine reporting, and involve sources who are familiar with journalists, breaking stories may require that reporters take initiative to find the information they need and will involve contact with people the reporter has never met. This chapter provides a map of how to find story sources and use the information they produce.

The Use of Multiple Sourcing

An adept reporter spends the day talking to and collecting information from people whose names never show up in his stories—the clerk of the convenience store where the reporter buys his morning cup of coffee, a police officer the reporter runs into on the beat, the fire department dispatcher, or the city manager's secretary. Reporters who succeed at their work are those who understand the importance of developing genuine rapport with all of the people they encounter in the course of their days—whether they are at work or off-duty. No dispatcher has to call a reporter in the middle of the night to give him or her a heads up that there has just been a fatal accident in the reporter's coverage area, but if that reporter has earned the dispatchers' respect the reporter may get the call and be gathering the story on the scene rather than hours later from the police blotter. It is the receptionist and administrative assistants who answer the reporter's deadline calls seeking the mayor or the public works director. Where there is rapport, the person at the other end of the line may point out that while the mayor is not in now, he will be out of a meeting in half an hour. Where there is no rapport, the reporter will simply be told the mayor is not in.

The surest way to develop rapport with sources is to approach all of them with personal interest and professional respect. Reporters gather a lot of information as they make their rounds. They reap the rewards of discretion as they follow the leads they are given. A beat cop or a shift sergeant or a city hall employee who is identified to a boss as the source of a lead will never share another one, and neither will any of his or her friends or acquaintances.

In the course of a day a reporter may interact with many different types of people, but the people interviewed can generally be sorted into four categories: professionals who are used to dealing with journalists, private people who encounter journalists regularly through their civic or other activities, professionals who rarely encounter journalists, and private people who may be meeting a reporter for the first time. To be effective and responsible, a reporter needs to keep those distinctions in mind. The reasoning is simple.

Elected officials, city managers, the director of the chamber of commerce, the chief of police, and other people who work with journalists regularly usually understand how the reporters work and how they are going to use the information they gather. Because success in their own work often requires reaching the public through journalists' coverage, it is in their interests to be accessible. They may be more or less cooperative depending on their interaction with an individual reporter, but they are familiar with the reporter's need for information "on deadline." On the other hand, these people have their own agendas that can be advanced or perhaps even held up by press coverage, a reality that savvy reporters get used to taking into account.

Similarly, there are private individuals who encounter journalists in the course of their public activities; for instance, the president of the school's parent-teacher organization, the president of the local chapter of the League of Women Voters, or the president of the local historical society. They may not interact with journalists every day, and they may not always understand exactly how the reporter's routine is structured, but they have encountered reporters before and are willing to cooperate and help with a reporter's information needs because they, too, need to reach the community through the press. For these and for all other sources, the start for every responsible reporter is to identify yourself and the news organization you are a part of.

Many sources may not be used to dealing with journalists. These include dentists or doctors, lawyers who do not try cases in court, insurance agents, bankers, and even teachers. While they may not be averse to talking to journalists, they are unlikely to understand a journalist's routines or to understand that journalists often need the information they are seeking "yesterday." Given these circumstances, a reporter often has to be polite and yet persistent and be willing to educate the source on how media routines work, when information is needed, and the form in which it is most useful. With these sources it is often necessary for the reporter to explain what information is sought and what will be done with it, while demonstrating that **the reporter doesn't have a hidden agenda**. These are often the type of sources who want to be allowed to read what the reporter writes before it goes in the paper. No reporter should agree to this condition. News organizations generally forbid the practice.

Ground Rules in Sourcing

Reporters often encounter private people who through chance—whether good or bad— have been thrown into the public spotlight. These sources might include winners of prizes at a county fair, relatives of victims of man-made or natural violence, or the victims them- selves. But whether the source is the father of a child who has drowned or the mother of a child who was accosted on the school bus, a reporter needs to take great care with the interview and the handling of the story itself. The reporter must write the story carefully, respectfully, and with discretion, understanding that people who aren't familiar with jour- nalistic practice may not know when and how to request that information be kept off the record.

Reporters should always be prepared to explain to anyone they talk to the ground rules of requesting that either some of the information they have provided not be used in a story or that if the information they have provided is used their identity may be withheld. If someone provides information "on background," that generally means that the reporter can neither write about the information nor quote the source. To use the information the reporter would need to find another way to get the information. Information provided **"off the record"** can be reported on but not credited to the individual who provided the information—what is generally referred to as an "anonymous source."

As a rule, reporters should not readily agree to receive information they will not be able to credit to their sources and they should explain to their source that the story will not run unless their editor agrees to use the information this way. There are stories for which any reasonable reader or editor would understand why a source has asked not to be identified—particularly someone engaged in an illegal or embarrassing activity. However, the reporter needs to discuss the situation with the editor before heading out on the story. The responsible reporter needs to carefully distinguish exactly when the story is so impor- tant or valuable that that outweighs agreeing to anonymity for the source. And as a rule, the reporter's immediate editor will know the identity of the source even if the name of the source is not identified in a story.

A reporter developing a story on sports gambling on a college campus, for instance, may very well encounter sources who have a great deal to lose if their names appear in the story as either clients or providers of the service. And, while it may be possible to get some factual information about sports betting and other gambling on campus from official sources, it is likely that a reporter and editor will decide that there is a real value to pursuing an interview with either the student running the gambling ring or his or her clients, even offering anonymity up front in order to obtain the interview. A similar circumstance might arise if a reporter writing a story about a successful service providing financial credit counseling to students wanted to interview some of the students whose debt is so bad they need the help.

Anonymous Sources and Tips

Year in and year out, serious journalists and critics of journalist conduct—often the same people—discuss the problems inherent in the use of anonymous sources. If readers are not given the identities of a reporter's sources, critics argue, they are not being given the information they need to evaluate the credibility of the information. On the other hand, proponents of anonymous sourcing argue, without the opportunity to offer anonymity to key sources many important stories would remain unwritten. The reporter receiving information off the record should be careful to discuss the situation with an editor, weighing the source's motives and the relative value gained by using the information.

Reporters often get tips that develop into stories that will be produced that day—what are referred to as breaking news stories—or tips that suggest a topic that will need investigation and study before it turns into something. In fact, reporters are often sent out on a story because their editor or someone else in the newsroom got a tip. Wherever a story idea comes from, the first question the reporter needs to consider is what might be motivating the source of the tip to make sure that a reporter's news judgments are made independently. Reporters work creatively to generate a list of people and documents that might confirm the tip, shed light on the topic, and confirm the accuracy and the direction of the story. It is important that the reporter learn to balance the adrenaline rush triggered by an exciting tip with equal doses of discretion and skepticism.

It can be uncomfortable to return to the newsroom to tell the boss or the assignment editor that there is nothing to a hot tip, but it is extremely important that the reporter learn how and when to stop chasing an erroneous lead. While a reporter may have an idea about the veracity of a story, an editor will generally want concrete evidence confirming or denying a lead. Over time, a reporter's track record may lead editors to trust his or her judgment about the validity of a tip. Once a reporter has confirmed the validity of the story idea, the reporter will need to generate a list of additional human and documentary sources that fill out the story. Good reporters will also be looking for context that will help them produce stories that give their readers the information they need to make their own judgments about the topic. A responsible reporter chasing a breaking story needs to find alternate sources that can shed light on the topic because obvious sources are often unavailable on deadline. And deadlines in the digital universe are 24/7.

While they were investigating the government cover-up that followed the break-in at the Democratic National Committee's headquarters in the Watergate in 1972, Bob Woodward, Carl Bernstein, and their editors at the *Washington Post* came up with a rule of thumb that governed whether they would publish sensitive information they uncovered. If three independent sources confirmed it, they could use it, but if there were fewer than three confirmations for a fact, they would have to wait to break the story another day. Reading news in most newspapers and online sources suggests that it would be hard to find many reporters who hold themselves to such a standard today, but it is likely that their work would be better if they did. Judges of news competitions and people charged with critiquing newspaper quality frequently look to see how many sources reporters cite in their news stories. They do this whether they are evaluating hard news or feature stories. They understand that sourcing reflects the quality of the writing and reporting.

Seeking Multiple Sources

Finding multiple sources for a story is important, whether it is coverage of the local city council, a story about the Girl Scouts, or reporting on pending federal legislation. While it may never be possible to arrive at a completely objective story, **reporters who bring more voices into their stories have a better chance achieving balance, fairness, and impartiality, the hallmarks of responsible reporting.** A reporter who gathers a lot of information from multiple sources can produce a story that is more likely to reflect the complexity of a story than a reporter who is new to the job and may worry that he or she is somehow betraying a source by seeking out other sides of a story, but in the long run everyone is better served by the result if that is what the reporter does.

It is natural to feel gratitude to a good source, and the realities of day-to-day beat coverage require that reporters develop rapport with their sources; however, rapport and gratitude must always be balanced by fairness, and fairness mandates giving equal play to the various sides of any story. That is a citizen's legitimate expectation of any story. Beat reporters with the best track records are those who have good relationships with their sources but who are also respected because of their fairness.

Journalism students are often told that the first place to look for story sources is prior coverage the news organization has already given the story. While that is certainly a starting point, it should never be considered enough. In addition, reporters old and young get used to consulting the "experts," the government officials and organization representatives who are reliable sources. This often leads reporters to overlook people who are just as valuable—the nonexperts—such as neighborhood residents, rank and file workers, and consumers, who may have just as much to say and can speak from lived experience. It is important that novice reporters develop the confidence and people skills to enter communities and talk to residents. As news organizations try to make their coverage more attractive and meaningful to readers, editors will push reporters to write stories balancing "expert" opinions with those of community residents.

Each reporter coming to a story, or returning to one, needs to ask, "Who else...?" and "Where else...?" Who else might have ideas or feelings about this subject? Where else might I find information that will contribute to my understanding of the story and improve my reporting of it? Interviewing is a critical skill in responsible reporting, and the best way to interview someone is in person. Reporters have also long relied on the telephone as a means of contacting sources. The Internet now competes with the phone for many contacts, but both the phone and Internet pose challenges for the best reporters and hamper beginners' newsgathering efforts.

A reporter who conducts interviews in person is at an advantage for a number of reasons. When face to face with a source, the reporter has access to information about personal interests and habits as well as nonverbal cues that would be otherwise lost. Experienced reporters become good at building rapport with sources they have never seen. Beginning reporters are more likely to build rapport with their sources in person. A reporter who can see his interviewee will be able to recognize and overcome distrust much more quickly. Beyond that, interviews about sensitive topics get further in person because it is much easier to end an interview on the phone than in person.

In-person interviews are always more productive because they give reporters access to physical and personal details about a subject that might well be missed over the phone or Internet connections. Such details often put both the reporter and the subject at ease. These contacts give the reporter bits of physical description of the person or setting that add color to the story and heighten its veracity with readers. An experienced reporter always gets a phone number when completing an interview to check facts or obtain a little bit more information when the story is written.

Sourcing and Professional Courtesy

If it is necessary for geographic or other reasons for an experienced reporter to conduct interviews over the phone or Internet, the reporter must be careful to be respectful and polite in initiating contact with a source. Journalism professors, who are otherwise used to dealing with students, are still frequently annoyed and angered by the presumptions of beginning journalists who initiate Internet contact seeking material for stories. "For my journalism class I have to write a story about you for the alumni newsletter. The story is due on Friday, so if you don't have time to meet for an interview maybe you could answer the five questions below. I need the answers Thursday." While this particular message is apocryphal, it is unfortunately very reminiscent of too many e-mails sent to potential story sources across the country every semester.

It is not only beginners who overlook the niceties in pursuit of a story. An experienced reporter at a medium-sized paper complained that he never got any information when he filled in for the police reporter. It was not necessary to hear both ends of the conversation to understand the problem. The reporter who normally covered the police beat conversed first with each dispatcher before asking for an update on what had happened or might be happening in that town, and he never forgot to say "please" and "thank you." The man who filled in was brusque, terse, and demanding on the phone. Most likely the dispatchers were irritated by his manner and, as a result, would do nothing more than answer exactly and only the questions he asked.

A reporter covering the public safety beat, or the city hall beat, for that matter, quickly learns that **the best tips often come from someone who is close enough to a story to know about it but is not directly involved**. For instance, a planning officer for one town may tip a reporter off that the federal government is conducting an investigation in an adjacent town. A police dispatcher from one town may give a reporter a heads up about a breaking story in another community.

Picking up the vocabulary of a story topic is vital, even if the reporter is conducting an interview within minutes of being assigned a story he or she knows nothing about. Though a reporter is not a lawyer or an economist, if assigned a story that involves law or economics, he or she will need to get up to speed on those topics fast. The source will be happier if the reporter admits to covering something for the first time. If a reporter does not understand what the interviewee is saying and writes it down anyway, hoping to get an explanation later, the reporter will probably not be able to use those notes to produce a comprehensible story. However, admitting ignorance only works once—in the newsroom or on the street. An editor or a source who has to plug a gap in the reporter's knowledge will generally only want to do it once.

Working a beat, reporters often find that a productive approach to a story is "I am new to this beat/town/story; can you fill me in and give me the story?" As long as it works it is the most fruitful approach to getting both the facts and the background of a complicated story—when asked of people on all the sides of a story. Strategic ignorance can also be helpful. This approach does not declare ignorance but instead suggests the possibility that the reporter might really know what the source is talking about. Generally once the source gets started the reporter can figure out enough to elicit the details and find out what needs to be known.

Responding with something vague like "Oh really? Is that so?" followed by consultation with a trusted source elsewhere, can be the best approach to sources who are deliberately trying to test a reporter who is new to the job. Unfortunately, sources who frequently but reluctantly encounter beginning reporters will set out to "test" them by offering outlandish tales or phony tips. Reporters should not let this sort of episode get them flustered, and if they are flustered they have to learn not to show it.

Sourcing through Paper Trails

When you are dealing with paper records or websites, you need to ask, "Who prepared this? Is there an agenda that shapes the information? Is there a way to confirm the information? Is there a person who will be able to elaborate on the story behind the document?" The fact that a website comes from an advocacy group as opposed to the government does not mean the reporter should not use the information, but if the information is used it is all the more important not only that the reporter credit the site for the information, but also that the story explain the particular interest of the group or source.

Working with documents is another situation when sources can come in handy. For instance, a reporter might ask a city clerk to explain how to read a government document. It is vitally important that a reporter understands how far to read when encountering documentary sources. Frequently, the meat will deliberately be buried in the heart of a document. The director of public relations for General Motors gleefully told the story of how the story broke that the automaker giant was suing *Dateline NBC* for its handling of an exposé on the alleged danger posed by gas tanks on one of the company's trucks. The suit against the show, which the company won, was filed in Indianapolis because that was where the show's producers staged the mock crash, dramatizing the gas tank pyrotechnics with the use of a little explosive charge. While GM made no public announcement of the filing, company officials knew that the story was in the public record and would break whenever a reporter reading the case filing bothered to read as far as the third page. Not only does the adept reporter need to learn how to read a document, the responsible reporter also needs to understand the jargon it's written in and to translate that jargon into language readers will understand.

Reporters need to build an extensive understanding of where and how interviews can be supplemented with information from documents. One of the first steps a reporter on a new job needs to take is to understand public record laws in that state. **Public records** can range from divorce records to applications for liquor licenses, zoning permits, financial filings required of publicly traded companies, and environmental impact statements. Many reporters stop their hunt for documents with online or official sources, overlooking the value of the public library. Librarians know their way around the books in their collection that may offer a reporter background on an unfamiliar story, but they also offer much more, including state and federal websites, town and city historical references, and online databases of all sorts. Documents, like experts, often require that the reporter become familiar with language peculiar to the people and the process that created them. Reporters have to know not only how to read and translate this language, but also how to find the sources, quotes, and color necessary to enliven a story drawn mainly from documents.

The more interviews a reporter conducts and the more that is learned from related documents, the easier a story will be to write. **Beginning reporters often stop with one or two sources, thinking they have the story.** Because of this, they may not have enough information to have the luxury of choosing the quotes and background material that tells the story most effectively. With information from multiple sources the reporter can find the underlying logic one needs to write the story well, using what's telling and setting aside the quotes and details that are less cogent. Without adequate sourcing and interviewing, a reporter is left trying to cobble together a story from incomplete information. That's a position no responsible reporter need be in.

Efrem Graham, a colleague teaching at Bowling Green State University, is a news anchor at the ABC TV affiliate in Toledo, but he used to work as a print journalist. Assigned to the business beat freelance for the Associated Press, it was his job to cover newsmakers in the media and TV industry. The more powerful the people you cover, the harder it can be to get access to them, but Efrem was very creative. Since he knew that he might occasionally pass the key figures on his beat on the sidewalk or share space with them in an elevator, he wanted to be able to take advantage of those opportunities. For this reason he covered the wall near his desk with photos of the people on his beat—and their spouses—so that he would recognize them if he encountered them in passing. The point is that you should always be prepared to meet your source in unexpected places. He did. You will.

Sourcing Three Stories

Let me illustrate the importance of sourcing in three ways—through a story where I had a mountain of information to work from, a story where I knew next to nothing about a source before I met him, and, finally, a story that presented several challenges for me and the reporters I worked with.

As a reporter on a small daily on the coast of Maine, I was usually running from meeting to interview and rarely had the problem of having too much information from which to choose. The exception was a story about a Holocaust survivor who had written a book about her experience. The author was coming to speak at a library in Saco, Maine, and I not only got advance notice about the event, but also received a copy of her book. It was a welcome change to be able to read the book and interview the author before I had to write the story, but I was still working on a deadline so I had to read the book overnight and work to carve a story out of a mountain of material.

I was facing several challenges. First, I had to find a way to take advantage of all that material without making the story so dense that readers would not be able to make their way through it. Secondly, the very topic itself posed problems. It was important that I allow the inherently heart-wrenching human interest aspects of the story to come through without resorting to sentimentality or cliché—which would diminish the power of my writing to convey the pain of her experience. The key in this story, and ones like it, is to **select the facts that give the story its emotional salience**. These moments capture the lived experience. Be on the lookout for them. Elevate them to prominence when you write the story. The result in this case was a story my editor felt was one of the best I had ever written.

Several years later I was a general assignment reporter working for a larger daily in Maine. One afternoon I suddenly found myself covering a story about nuclear disarmament. I was dispatched to a suburban home to do an interview with an advocate of nuclear disarmament. When I got there I was introduced to a man dressed in Swazi tribal clothing—a bright cotton cloth was draped across one shoulder and an animal fur was draped over his other shoulder.

Ben Dlamini had received a doctorate in education from the University of Massachusetts-Amherst and was going to spend the summer urging Americans to demand nuclear disarmament. Dlamini noted that the fallout from a nuclear war between the United States and the Soviets would be as devastating for us as it would be to small remote African countries like his own. If you have no time to prepare for an interview—and in this case, I didn't—start by asking the obvious. Don't be shy. It'll start the conversation. I asked what brought Dlamini to Maine. I still remember his answer twenty-three years later. Ben had a passion for the planet's survival. That's why he had come to Maine, and that's what needed to be communicated in the story. What helped here was starting the story with the most significant thing he had said. You, too, should learn to think it through. Ask yourself what it is you want the reader to remember. If you do that before you start writing, chances are the reader will get where you're going.

During the summer of 1996 I reported for Pennsylvania's *Bucks County Courier Times*. One memorable story involved reporting on that state's steel industry; Pennsylvania routinely showed up in lists of the states with the most asbestos lawsuits, and a large steel plant in the newspaper's coverage area had been the focus of asbestos litigation in the 1970s and '80s. Now the story was resurfacing because of an effort by twenty companies that made or used asbestos to collapse all asbestos lawsuits into one mega-suit and to limit the amount of damages payable to victims or their survivors to $1.3 billion. A federal appeals court had thrown out the settlement, but the companies appealed that decision and considered taking the case as far as the Supreme Court.

Asbestos was used not only in insulation for buildings but also at steel plants, shipyards, and other companies where workers needed protective gear in order to work in conditions with extreme heat. Sixteen companies that had been sued by workers had gone bankrupt, and another slew of bankruptcies were on the horizon. The looming bankruptcies had triggered a new round of lawsuits as the workers, their attorneys, and trade unions realized the bankruptcies meant that settlement funds were drying up. In turn, the surge in the number of suits had driven the companies to propose the consolidation of all asbestos suits into one and to push for the cap on their liability.

With the advantage of time and distance, it is easier to summarize the story succinctly, but at the time we were faced with some significant challenges. First we needed to understand complicated legal actions and their potential implications for readers of the paper. This meant we had to try to understand what had happened when the first asbestos suits were filed decades earlier. After we had read legal documents, medical research, and claims in court by lawyers for both sides, we needed to find a focus for a series of stories that would run in the paper.

That summer there was a palpable sense that the window for legal recourse for injured workers and their families was closing and there was real frustration since the people in question might not get sick for years. Chest X-rays could identify whether asbestos fibers were present in the lungs of people who had been exposed and were not sick yet, but the challenge was to find those people and get them to go through the screening. The community faced an unknown number of workers and an unknown number of the family members who had been exposed to the men's work clothing.

As a rule, the best way to make very complicated stories like this compelling to readers is to find people whose stories illustrate the larger issues. But this is not always easy. The people who had gotten sick quickly had died years earlier, and while the company had not gone bankrupt, the plant in question had closed. The union's concern was not with people who were sick but rather with those who might get sick in the future.

We needed to find a way to convey these facts to readers who were new to the area or too young to remember the earlier story. It was a real challenge to find the people we wanted to build the story around—workers who could tell us what it was like to work in the plant, the families left behind from the earlier round of illnesses, and the people who once worked in the plant and were now sick or still waiting to find out if they would get sick.

We pulled the story together by creating a timeline and an overview of the legal actions and their implications, and by conducting human interest interviews that made the story understandable and compelling. In the final analysis, **serving citizens is the best possible reward for responsible reporters**. Being careful and comprehensive about sourcing and interviewing makes such service possible.

Interviewing

STEVE SMITH

Responsible reporting often requires getting a quote from a participant in or observer of a news event that gives your story an authenticity and validation that no third-party account can. Whether reporting in print, broadcast, or online, few things give a story the winning edge as much as finding just the right quote. In radio broadcast news and increasingly in online reporting, reporters have the ability to get a sound bite of the actual newsmaker. This is referred to as an "actuality," which is a recorded segment of an interview with or statement by the newsmaker or observer. For years, print reporters were told by editors to get better quotes from the sources they interviewed. In digital America, online stories often allow listeners to hear the actual quote coming from the originator's mouth. This is a powerful tool that not only makes the story more interesting, but also removes doubt in the listener's mind as to the authenticity of the quote.

In today's digital world, a simple compact flash or mini disc recorder can provide a broadcast-quality interview from which to edit actualities. This new technology gives reporters (even those with little or no technical audio experience) the ability to record volumes of content at a news event. Since broadcast news stories have the limitation of very short time restraints, the challenge is to get and choose statements from the newsmaker that can summarize the event accurately and concisely.

The reporter's responsibility is to place the statement in proper context, if it is not evident from the actuality itself. If a statement can be interpreted several ways without hearing the surrounding interview, it is your obligation in your copy to make the particular meaning perfectly clear to the listener. Irresponsible reporters sometimes advance a possible alternative meaning never intended by the newsmaker in order to create controversy and conflict in their story. They know that a story with controversy, conflict, or something sensational will often be placed higher in the newscast order.

For example, let us say fictional Jane Jones, a candidate for city council, was speaking at a local political event. You recorded Jones saying, "If you looked at what drives my opponent to make many of his business decisions, you would say John Doe is a crooked businessman, but he always seems to stay just within the letter of the law." If you then used just the portion of Jones's sound bite saying, "John Doe is a crooked businessman," it would be sensational but would change the meaning of Jones's statement entirely. The listener could incorrectly infer that Jones was calling Doe a lawbreaker, which she clearly was not. This is a misquote, even though it comes directly from the newsmaker's own mouth. Writing a story in this manner is not only unethical but can actually be considered libelous if the reporter clearly and with malicious intent misrepresented the intended meaning of Jones's statement. Reporters will often flirt with this tactic in order to make a story sensational while keeping it just barely legal. Obviously, these are not the actions of a responsible reporter.

Good reporters gather as much information about an event in advance of covering it. Government meetings, news conferences, and scheduled events provide the opportunity to study up on what is going to happen, who is involved, and previous positions taken by the principals. Accidents and crimes do not usually offer the same opportunity to gather background information in advance. However, being aware of weather conditions, police and emergency response procedures, current events that might have played into the news event, and common knowledge about an area can often help in asking more relevant questions at the scene.

Be well versed in what to look for at each type of event. Learn which types of bystanders make good witnesses and which do not. Bystanders with no firsthand observations should be used only to point you to those who actually observed the event. Whenever possible, get quotes directly from the actual newsmakers, as they most validate the story and their words have the greatest impact on listeners.

When conducting interviews, always keep your specific audience in mind and determine which information would be most relevant to their lives. Several years ago as news director for a local radio station in the Blue Ridge Mountains of western North Carolina, I sometimes covered stories of local people who were killed in traffic accidents. The main focus of these stories was usually the identity of the victims, because they were part of the community and had business or personal relationships with many of the listeners. On one occasion there was an incident in which several people were killed in a one-car accident on a local road just off the Blue Ridge Parkway. While investigating, I discovered that all of the victims were tourists from another state, which immediately changed the focus of my story, as none of my listeners would know these folks, or where they worked or where they lived. However, a big concern of local residents is the dangerous road conditions in our area created by the huge volume of tourists sightseeing on unfamiliar local roads.

When interviewing the officer who responded to the accident, I asked how often tourists are involved in traffic accidents and what the most common cause of these crashes was. He stated that usually it is their unfamiliarity with our mountain roads and their lack of attention to driving while sightseeing, and I instantly knew I had my quote, my actuality, and my story. When the story aired, my lead was "leaf-looking while driving proves deadly once again for High Country tourists." My entire story was built around that one definitive quote from the responding officer.

When interviewing to find that definitive quote, public affairs reporters should not use questions to lead the interviewee to a predetermined conclusion but rather to the discovery of facts the reporter then places in proper context. While previous knowledge will help in knowing where to look and perhaps what to look for at a news event, young reporters particularly need to make certain they do not go in with presuppositions that will inhibit their ability to find the facts.

Responsible reporters do not repeat a question in order to get the answer they want, but rather ask a second time in rephrased form only for clarification. No journalistic good comes from creating a story based on presuppositions. **Reporting is not about finding facts to fit presuppositions**, but instead honestly going where interviews and your investigation take you. Always be careful to give the context necessary to give that reporting meaning.

An old saying is, "You took the words right out of my mouth." Remember that responsible reporting takes those words out of the newsmaker's mouth and uses them powerfully, truthfully, and clearly, in the way the speaker truly intended.

5

Going Online

BRUCE C. SWAFFIELD

Journalists today are using the Internet to research information, write better stories, and verify facts. From gathering news to checking proper Associated Press style to collecting background details, writers and editors rely on the World Wide Web because it is fast, efficient, and comprehensive. But journalists are not the only people using the Internet to make their work and lives easier.

According to the Pew Internet and American Life Project Surveys (March 2000 to April 2006), the number of U.S. adults online has risen from 15 percent in 2000 to 75 percent in 2006. The survey conducted between February and April 2006 revealed that **on a typical day 66 percent of all Americans use the Internet, 53 percent send or read e-mail, 38 percent use a search engine to find information, and 31 percent seek news**.

The *World Factbook*, published online by the U.S. Central Intelligence Agency, says that that in 2005 there were more than 1 billion Internet users around the world—a sizable amount considering there are only 6 billion people on the planet. The countries with the most users included the members of the European Union (239 million users), the United States (205 million), and China (123 million).

There is no doubt that the World Wide Web will continue to grow in both popularity and size. Just how big is the Internet right now? No one truly knows for sure. However, in February 2007, a search on Google using only the letters "www" produced results for more than 7.5 billion websites in four seconds, while a search using "http" netted more than 2 billion websites in three seconds! Keep in mind that there are billions of other websites that do not begin with either "www" or "http." The truly staggering fact is that thousands more sites are added each hour of every day. The successful journalists of tomorrow will have to know how to find the information they need, and they will have to do it quickly. There will be no time to do random surfing on a search engine. The best writers and editors will have to know exactly where to find what they need; in short, they will have to be expert navigators in the growing universe of cyberspace.

Searching for Online Information

In the past, journalists had to count on information in newspaper files (often called the morgue) in order to do research. Now, however, almost everything is available online, from newspaper archives to personality profiles to government documents. For example, political reporters are accessing various websites to learn more about how city, state, and federal governments operate. Many public records are available online, including meeting agendas, city ordinances, property deeds, death certificates, and police records. Court reporters access dockets and proceedings online on a regular basis. Crime reporters now check the police blotter by going to a website rather than police headquarters.

Those in the newsroom also rely heavily on the Internet. Copyeditors use the Internet to verify details, check information, and correct misspellings. Sports writers never have to leave their desks to obtain statistics and player data from professional team websites. Feature writers can go to the web to generate new ideas for stories or to research a subject. General assignment writers use the Internet to keep abreast of what is going on in their area and to learn what other media organizations are covering. Even photographers, photojournalists, and videographers go to the Internet to see how a story is being handled by the competition.

Never before has so much material been available in seconds. No longer is there any need to spend precious time making phone calls to confirm details or names. Most libraries have numerous databases online, available and accessible to everyone. Just about everything a journalist needs, in terms of details, is available on the Internet. The real trick, though, is in knowing when, where, why, and how to access helpful websites. For today's reporter, basic common sense and practical experience are the two keys to going online. Journalists have a responsibility to make sure the information they use and pass along to viewers and readers is 100 percent accurate. Any doubt or uncertainty about certain elements, even persons or events, means the resources cannot be used. Every piece of news must be verified.

Going online to gather facts, figures, and details for a story is not as easy as it seems. There are literally billions of websites on the Internet that offer all kinds of information, from opinions to personal experiences to honest facts. Half of the success in using the Internet is in knowing where to find certain bits and pieces of information. The other half of the equation is identifying what is reliable and accurate. Once you know where to locate the material you need and how to evaluate it, your stories will become more accurate, more interesting, and more detailed. Remember, reporting is all about giving readers and viewers the right information so they can understand and evaluate the event or subject for themselves. Great reporters gather *all* of the important details to make the public more informed and educated. Mediocre reporters only pass along basic information; they do not go beyond the five Ws and one H. Nor do they dig deep into a story to present the unusual elements that make a story interesting and helpful. Because of the power of the Internet, it is possible for every writer to become a great reporter. The secret is in knowing where to find what you need. Locating information, quickly and efficiently, is critical to your success. How you go online, many times, can either make or break your career.

Navigating the Internet

Most journalists use the Internet daily. They use it to get the news, to analyze certain situations and issues, to understand what others are saying, and to see what might unfold during the next twenty-four hours. There are a thousand and one other uses, but the most important element is that the Internet can bring the world into your laptop in seconds. Journalists tend to know their way around cyberspace, perhaps a little better than the average user. But the best writers have learned how to use the Internet rather than to allow the Internet to use them. In other words, they have set up an organized approach to using the Internet. To save time and work, many persons have created shortcuts and links to the most useful websites. Bookmarks also help writers to navigate the Internet quickly. For example, many journalists have developed a certain group or cluster of sites that they know are reliable and accurate. With just a click of a mouse, they have a clear, up-to-the-minute panorama of the world on one small screen. In an instant, it is possible to see how a national or international story is covered all over the world by going to Google News. A few seconds later, we can watch live coverage of a soccer match overseas. Whatever our interest—news, sports, travel, cooking, weather, fitness, health, or even research—we can remain current quickly and easily if we know where to find what we want.

For the most part, journalists are skillful organizers. They have learned, through years of training and experience, how to arrange a story by presenting the most important facts and details first. The same kind of structure needs to go into using the Internet as a resource. A majority of reporters have a daily routine when they go online. First, they visit several places on the Internet in order to learn the latest news and information. They have developed the habit of reviewing several news websites each day, including weekends and holidays. A good, top-ten list might include the websites for the following media organizations:

1. The *New York Times*
2. The *Washington Post*
3. The *Christian Science Monitor*

4. The BBC
5. *China Today*
6. The *Jerusalem Post*
7. The *International Herald Tribune*
8. *USA Today*
9. Associated Press
10. Local dailies and area television stations

In fifteen minutes or less, you can get an overview of what is going on all over the world. This element is, by far, the most important advantage of the Internet. The time spent doing your homework each day will save you countless hours in the future as well as help you write more detailed stories. Keeping up on current events and historical developments is crucial for any reporter. Think about some of the background information writers need to have in their heads. You can't know everything, of course; there is just too much going on in the world. But going to the Internet each time you need to write a story can be extremely time consuming. A little knowledge of history, by keeping abreast of current events, will take you a long way. Writing a feature story on a family who came to the United States from the western coast of Africa is much easier if you know something about the recent civil wars in Liberia and Sierra Leone. Even doing a sports story on a new baseball player from Latin America becomes less daunting if you are somewhat familiar with the culture and lifestyle of the athlete's home country of Venezuela. The point is not to wait until you need certain types of information and then run to the Internet. Try to expand your knowledge each day as you go through the same group of websites.

Each writer's list of popular news sites will be different. What does not vary, however, is how reporters approach the task. A few guidelines can help you work quickly and efficiently. First of all, as you visit each site, see what stories are on the front page; also note how each article appears and how much space is devoted to it. Internet news sites are much like newspapers in layout and design: the most important stories appear at the top, and those with less significance are toward the bottom. Ask yourself how each article is presented (for example, with or without photos) and if there are related links that might be helpful. Take a few moments to think critically about the treatment of each event. Does the story offer all of the necessary information from an objective point of view, or does there seem to be some sort of bias or prejudice on the part of the writer? Remember to take notes as you go through each website just as you would during an interview. Scan the editorials on each site as well. What is the lead editorial, and are there any op-ed columns? Write down your brief thoughts on how these important issues could have an impact on the public. Depending on your individual tastes and preferences, it is a good idea to review other sections (business, lifestyle, sports, food, travel, and so on). Whatever you do, remain focused. Do not jump around, if at all possible. Stick to one publication at a time. Do not allow the Internet to lure you into surfing across the web. Random searches usually lead nowhere and they waste time. Going from site to site may be interesting and fun, but it will produce little knowledge and yield few useable results.

Develop a sound method and logic for your daily work and research on the Internet. Once you have a system that works best for you, get into the habit of using it each day. Discipline yourself so you do not become lost in cyberspace. Too many people, reporters included, find themselves running out of time because they became caught up in exploring the Internet. Save the surfing for weekends and holidays—times when you are not facing a deadline. Remember that great reporters always take notes. Avoid thinking you will remember where you saw a certain article and even that you will recall all of the contents. Write it down, but do not get in the habit of printing out each story or piece. Do your analysis and note-taking as you are reading and reviewing each site. Otherwise, you will have to reread each individual article all over again. Think, for a moment, about the effect of covering a city council meeting and recording the event rather than taking any notes. Back at the office the reporter has to listen to the meeting all over again. It is always easier to take notes as you go, using a recording or print-outs only as needed.

Building a Database

The amount of information available on the Internet is staggering. From encyclopedias and phone books to business directories and government guides, it is possible to access practically anything by going online. Unfortunately, many people do not go online until they need certain materials. Reporters cannot afford to wait. They must be thoroughly familiar with the Internet and know where to search. As a young journalist, you should begin early in your training to build your own database of resources. Even before you begin working in the field, you can jump-start your career by collecting important sites that are useful for a working journalist. The most helpful websites you locate and find can be kept in a folder or file for future reference. It is a good idea to maintain a separate folder for each subject, but make sure you are specific about the contents of each one. Do not use general labels such as "Resources." Help yourself by being as detailed as possible; that is, use titles such as "Journalism Resources." In this folder or section, you could file many different types of websites and addresses, such as the following: the Society of Professional Journalists, Poynter Institute, Associated Press Stylebook, Codes of Ethics, Freedom of Information Agency, the Newseum, and the Freedom Forum are common, helpful choices. Include the web address and a brief description for each entry in the file so you can locate the best source fast and efficiently when you need it.

Another section could be "Reference Materials," where you could place all kinds of information from dictionaries to encyclopedias to almanacs. A great place to begin your work is to go to eduScapes (http://eduscapes.com/tap/topic9.htm), an educational site that was started in August 1998 by Annette Lamb and Larry Johnson. Some of the links available are language translation sites, a science and history timeline, a Blue Pages directory for government offices, and a medical encyclopedia.

There are dozens of sites on the Internet that currently offer the types of information you may want to include in your personal databases. One of the best for journalists is by

Christopher Callahan, author of *A Journalist's Guide to the Internet*. (See http://reporter. umd.edu/.) He has put together useful sites in sixteen different content areas, which include the following:

}   Maps, sources, and directories
}   Courts and the law
}   Federal government
}   State government
}   Local government
}   Online newspapers
}   News groups

Each section contains excellent sources that anyone can use in developing a comprehensive list of personal resources. For example, below is detailed inventory of what Callahan includes in his section on maps, sources, and directories:

Phone Directories

Telephone Directories. Switchboard and Yahoo! People Search are among the computerized telephone directories that allow name searching with limited address information.

Criss-Cross Directories. InfoSpace has valuable criss-cross directories that enable users to find names and phone numbers with addresses only. Reporters also can easily find neighbors' names and phone numbers.

Phone Number Reverse Directory. InfoSpace, InfoUSA, and AnyWho provide a reverse function that enables users to find addresses and resident names with just the phone number.

Maps

Mapblast, Yahoo! Maps, *and* MapQuest *give users the ability to quickly call up detailed maps of any area of the country, down to the specific location on a block.*

World Atlas *from MapQuest.*

Expert Sources

ProfNet *and the* National Press Club *have databases that reporters can search by area of expertise to find potential sources.* Reporters' queries also can be posted via ProfNet and MediaMap's SourceNet.

The Poynter Institute *creates a new site several times each month for major current stories.*

Kitty Bennett, *news researcher at the St. Petersburg Times,* has created a one-stop site for finding expert sources.

Other Desktop News Sources

Encyclopedias. Find the full-text versions of the *Columbia Encyclopedia* and *InfoPlease*, which has almanacs and encyclopedia.

Congressional Research Service. CRS, a research arm of Congress, provides legislators and Congressional aides excellent nonpartisan briefing papers on many complex issues. CRS environmental-related reports are available through the National Library for the Environment.

Issues Background. Public Agenda Online provides detailed background on a wide variety of public policy issues.

Fast Demographic and Economic Facts. The Census Bureau's Statistical Abstract of the United States contains a wide range of statistics describing various social and economic aspects of the country.

CIA World Factbook. Political, economic, demographic, and geographic information on the world's nations.

Story Ideas. Tip sheets on more than eighteen thousand investigative stories, provided by Investigative Reporters and Editors Inc.

Math Help. Robert Niles's site for the math-challenged journalist.

Conversions. ConvertIt provides calculators to convert various measurements, time zones, and so on. Another good conversion tool is Online Conversion.

Inflation Adjuster. Columbia Journalism Review's inflation calculator allows users to quickly convert dollars from a past year into recent years' value, adjusted for inflation.

The Elements of Style. William Strunk Jr.'s classic work on the rules of writing and grammar.

Bartlett's Familiar Quotations. Insert part of a famous quote and find the correct citation, or search by source. Also available is Simpson's Contemporary Quotations.

Roget's Thesaurus.

American Heritage Dictionary.

Literature References. Bartleby provides full-text of many literary reference books.

Web Ownership. Uncovering the registered owner of a commercial website (ending in *.com, .net, .org, .biz, .info,* or *.name*) is a two-step process. First, go to Internic WhoIs, which will tell you the registrar of the site. Then go to that specific registrar (look for the who-is button on that site) to learn to whom the website is registered and how to get contact information. For international web addresses, go to Domain Search.

Personal Resource Pages

As a result of the exhaustive work by Callahan and dozens of others in the field, reporters can easily find the materials they want and need. There is no excuse to waste valuable time surfing the Internet or going through massive search engines. Much of the work has already been done. Build on what is already on the Internet. Take a quick review of the following sites and decide which links are most valuable for your own personal resources pages:

} Journalists' Tools (http://www.refdesk.com/jourtool.html) by Bob Drudge offers eighty-eight sections, from the *Associated Press Stylebook* to *Who Owns What?*

} The Journalist's Toolbox (http://www.americanpressinstitute.org/pages/toolbox/) by the American Press Institute includes a blog search, weather charts, annual event calendars, and interesting databases.

} Journalism Resources (http://bailiwick.lib.uiowa.edu/journalism/) by Karla Tonella deals with such subjects as cyber-journalism, media law resources, listservs, online newsletters, and citation style guides.

} The Poynter Institute Online (www.poynter.org) has information on current news, careers, design/graphics, diversity, ethics, leadership, photojournalism, writing/editing, and television/radio. This site is a must for any writer or editor. It contains "everything you need to be a better journalist."

} The Society of Professional Journalists website (www.spj.org) covers freedom of information, the code of ethics, a diversity toolbox, anti-profiling guidelines, information about conferences, and tools for leaders.

} The National Press Club in Washington, D.C. (http://www.press.org/library06/resources.cfm), has a Reporters' Resource page with state of the union addresses, an Internet public library, a link to information and services on more than 184 countries, U.S. facts and locations, demographics, experts arranged by topic, business directories, and government resources.

There are hundreds of other websites, of course, but this list is an excellent place to start. As you find more resources, you can add them to your files. Whatever you do, make your categories as specific as possible. Use headings similar to those used by others—titles that are familiar to you. If there is some doubt as to where to place certain information that you find on the Internet, cross-reference the website by placing the resource in two or more files or folders. In this way, you will always be able to locate what you need, even years from now when your mental filing system may be slightly different.

Each time you add new sites to your files, make sure you back up your work. What you are doing now is the beginning of a lifelong project. Never risk losing years of work and research because you did not take the time to save the information both on a hard drive and on a CD. Almost everyone these days has one or more stories about losing files due to a system failure or a hard drive that crashed. Until computers become 100 percent reliable, back up everything you do. Not only will you save yourself time, but you will save yourself from trying to re-create all that you lost.

Responsible Reporting and the Internet

Deciding exactly when to go online for information presents a challenge for reporters. The best and most reliable facts are always gained from talking with people, whether by phone, in person, or by e-mail. The Internet should never be used as an alternative for good, solid reporting. The only time most reputable publications and broadcast companies even allow the use of "canned" quotes from sources is when the information comes from a corporate press release that is published online. Even then, it is always good practice to confirm the information with the firm's media relations office or a company executive.

Journalists must exercise extreme discretion and care when using the Internet. Those who are in the business of reporting the news have to make a sharp distinction between gathering the news and merely copying what other media organizations have already reported. There have been many reporters in recent years who compromised both their reputation and that of their employer because of laziness; they have used the Internet to harvest general information about an incident, and then written the story as if they had collected all the details themselves. Essentially, they gave the false impression that they actually covered an event when, in fact, they were miles away. Not only is such "reporting" an act of deception, but it is also one of betrayal. The writer has both lied and deceived the public. **Report only what *you* see and know.**

If you are working on a feature story about a local public figure, for example, use the Internet to help you with background information and details. Learn as much about the person as you can before you conduct the interview. In short, do your homework. A word of caution, though: do not automatically believe or accept everything you read on the Internet. Anyone at any time can go online and publish almost anything, even about wonderful people. Be judicious in your research; question each source you encounter. You will find numerous sites, perhaps even hundreds, that will give you all kinds of related information when you search for someone's name on Google, Dogpile, or Yahoo. Check out the sites that seem the most promising; that is, those that contain a familiar organization or publication. But do not stop there. Check out where the person works; go to the company website. Most businesses and recognized groups nowadays have links to administrative and staff personnel, which may include brief biographical material on various employees. You might even find a person's entire resume posted on a company website. Perhaps a prominent CEO is coming to your city for a speaking engagement or to take part in a local meeting, and you have been assigned to cover the convention. Your editor also has asked you to write a story before the event. You have a phone number for the keynote speaker so you can conduct a phone interview. But how will you know what questions to ask, especially if you are not familiar with the person's area of expertise or the subject of the meeting?

By combining your skills as a reporter and using the Internet as a resource, you can find out everything you need to write a clear, cogent story for the reader. The first step is to learn as much as you can about the conference by looking at the schedule. Most groups have a dedicated website so participants can obtain more details and specifics on the convention. Find out the web address and review some of topics and sessions. Also, see if there are representatives from the area who will be attending. Make note of local individuals you can contact. The second step is to understand the theme and purpose of the meeting. If the subject is unfamiliar, consult your personal database of resources and research the subject. It is not essential that you become an expert in five or ten minutes, but make sure you know enough to ask intelligent and insightful questions. People are always happy to talk about their line of work. Know enough to get them talking and take down everything they say. The third, and final, step is to find out as much as possible about the particular speaker. What are the person's major accomplishments, successes, and achievements? If you cannot find information on the web about someone, ask the company's media relations office or even the person. There is never any harm or penalty in asking. On the other hand, there are many risks in not having all of the information you need. Again, use the Internet as a resource; it is only one of many tools you have at your disposal. Going online can be immensely helpful in providing the information you need—quickly and accurately—in all three cases, but you must know when and how to get details from other sources.

Starting Your Search

Here is a hypothetical case of how a reporter might start an online search. Assume that I am coming to your city for a conference on international education. You have probably never heard of me, except for some promotional materials you received from the organization that is sponsoring the meeting. You learn that I teach journalism at Regent University, I have been a professor for twenty years, and that I began my career as a journalist in south Florida. Before you call me, you want to learn more about my background. Where is the best place to start?

First, search my name (Bruce C. Swaffield and Bruce Swaffield) on any of the search engines. Instantly, you will discover the many articles that I have written—for *Quill,* Poynter online, CBN.com, and various professional journals—as well as conferences I have directed. The best source of information, however, will be my faculty website at Regent University. There you will find more biographical information, a picture, even a complete resume (also called a curriculum vitae) covering the past three decades of my life. In your research, you learn that I have worked at Regent for the past four years and I have held full-time positions at two other colleges, in Ohio and Virginia. You also see that I began my career as a reporter for a daily newspaper in 1974. Along the way, between going to school at Kent State University for a degree in journalism and going back to school at the University of Miami, I held various other jobs: stocking shelves in grocery stores, cleaning airplanes, working in a foundry, and publishing my own monthly magazine. I now have a master of arts and a doctorate in composition and literature, and I teach journalism.

At this point, you might be wondering why I am a keynote speaker at this upcoming conference. What do I know about teaching and learning in other countries? Good question. Digging deeper, you uncover more details on my website: I have traveled to about fifteen countries, from China to Italy to North Cyprus, and I have done a great deal of work in multiculturalism. In addition, you realize that I am the founder and director of the Worldwide Forum on Education and Culture, which meets annually in Rome, Italy. Now you can go to the Worldwide Forum website to uncover more details about my interests and work. Finally, you can use the Internet to contact colleagues of mine who can give you a more personal perspective.

With all of this information, you are ready to call me for some quotes for your advance story on the conference. You can ask smart and direct questions because you are prepared. Your brief time spent in research on the Internet will pay off in a strong, poignant story guaranteed to impress your editor and your readers. The fifteen to twenty minutes that you invested up front will pay huge dividends in your future success as a reporter. Editors and readers remember good writers.

As you can see, knowing how and when to use the Internet is critical for reporters. By all means use the Internet, but make sure you do not abuse it. Never lose sight of the fact that the Internet is merely one piece of equipment in your tool box to enable you to do your job better.

Accessing Information

Accessing the Internet is possible almost anywhere these days. Airports, malls, coffee shops, downtown buildings, hospitals, and even entire cities are becoming wireless. Never has it been easier and more convenient to go online. The ease of having this resource so readily available may have a dramatic impact—good and bad—on how journalists cover and report the news in the future. The positive benefits are that detailed information is available quickly anywhere in the world. The negative side is that writers and editors might forsake the time-honored skills of traditional newsgathering for the sake and convenience of fast and easy reporting.

In this age of growing participatory journalism, there is always the temptation to cover a story merely by accessing information online. With the billions of sites today, a reporter does not even have to leave the home or office to read the so-called facts on a certain event or incident. News and information can be found on thousands of blogs, media websites, and listservs. The real question is: How reliable is such information, especially that reported by citizen journalists? Reporting the news involves more than mere fact-finding or collecting information via the Internet. Readers and viewers can perform this task for themselves. They are relying on you as a trained reporter to get the true story; they trust that you have verified all of the details and that you have spoken personally with sources named in the story. In good, honest journalism there is absolutely no place for using information from other media outlets or for using opinions expressed in blogs or websites. Accuracy and objectivity are the heart of true journalism. The best reporters report best when they obtain facts and details from knowledgeable sources—those who are involved in or affected by an incident. There is no room for subjective analysis or interpretation on the part of any reporter.

Every now and then, some reporters believe they are good enough to fool the public. They think no one will notice the difference between borrowing facts from an online source and actually covering the story themselves. The risks and dangers of trying to write a story while sitting in a coffee shop, a mall, or the newsroom are several: first, anyone who is familiar with the location or facts will see right through the details and descriptions; second, most editors and readers are savvy enough to know when something sounds superficial; and, third, any reporter who plagiarizes a story is violating the public's trust. All journalists have a social responsibility to inform and serve the audience. The community is counting on you to do your job honestly and with integrity. You are their eyes and ears at city council meetings, school board sessions, in the courtroom, on the street, and at any public event. You have an obligation to keep people informed without bias or subjectivity. In deciding to become a reporter, you accept not only the tasks but the commitments and duties as well. There is no room for compromise. "The duty of the journalist is to further those ends by seeking truth and providing a fair and comprehensive account of events and issues," states the preamble in the Code of Ethics by the Society of Professional Journalists. "Conscientious journalists from all media and specialties strive to serve the public with thoroughness and honesty. **Professional integrity is the cornerstone of a journalist's credibility."**

Whether you go online before you plan your story or during the writing process, the important element to remember is that nothing can take the place of attending an event, being at the scene, or talking personally with someone. Never take the easy way out by using the Internet as your one and only source. **The Internet is a *re*source, not a source.** Use the Internet as a tool—something that will enable you to do a better job, and not something that will do your job for you. Just as a carpenter uses a hammer as a tool to build a house, reporters go online to help build a story. And just as a hammer cannot build a house all by itself, the Internet alone cannot build a story. The reporter is the architect and builder of the story. Journalists should use tools like the Internet to help them put all of the pieces together.

Today's writers have to use all of the resources, tools, and gadgets that will allow them to report the news as quickly and accurately as possible. Increasingly, the Internet is helping reporters and editors publish stories with a minimum of time and a maximum of details. There are some drawbacks, however. Not everything on the Internet is correct, and not every site can be trusted. Like anyone else, journalists have to learn how to discern which sites are credible. It is not always easy to determine what information in cyberspace is true and factual.

Remember that anyone can have a website. Many of the most popular sites today have been created by a person or company, and the website was put online by paying a certain fee to a web hosting company. Basically, anyone with a new domain name and a credit card can establish a site on the Internet. All sites have domain indicators that signify a certain category. Top-level domain (TLD) names are indicated by the following abbreviations: *biz* (business), *com* (commercial), *info* (information), *name* (any person), *net* (network), or *org* (organization). All of these TLDs are open to anyone. Countries around the world have TLDs as well: *us* (United States), *uk* (United Kingdom), *it* (Italy), and so on. There also are restricted TLDs, such as *aero* (airline industry), *edu* (educational institutions), *gov* (governmental entities), *mil* (U.S. military), *museum* (legitimate nonprofit museums), and *pro* (licensed professionals). In order to obtain a restricted TLD, the group or organization must register with a recognized agency and possess the appropriate documents or credentials.

Backgrounding a Story

Knowing the TLD helps the public determine which sites are most reliable, which are acceptable (as long as they are verified), and which are questionable at best. Let's say you are working on a story about a local rapper who has finally made it big. Before conducting the interview, you go online to learn more about rap music. You type in "History of Rap" on Google and receive 5.7 million results! Here is the first page of results:

} in depth site on the history of rap
www.rapworld.com/history/—1k—Cached—Similar pages
BBC—Radio 2—A Brief History of Rap
Mark Lamarr presents a two part history of Rap Music.
www.bbc.co.uk/radio2/r2music/documentaries/rap.shtml—43k—Cached—Similar pages

} The History Of Hip Hop
The **History** Of Hip Hop. written by Davey D.
www.daveyd.com/**rap**title.html—1k—Cached—Similar pages

} Kurtis Blow Presents: The History Of Rap, Vol. 1—liners
The **History Of Rap**. How can we truthfully tell this story? There are so many different... To understand the **history of rap**, you need to know two things:...www. rhino.com/Features/liners/72851lin.html—20k—Cached—Similar pages

} The History of Rap.
It was not known as "**rap**" at that point in **history**, his releases were called "country narrative records" or "talking songs," but the basic "**rap**" idea of...
www.adequacy.org/stories/2002.7.1.101815.3932.html—85k—Cached—Similar pages

} 93.04.04: The Evolution of Rap Music in the United States
In fact, one can trace the **history of rap** back to the West African professional singers/storytellers known as Griots. However, it is not my intention to...
www.yale.edu/ynhti/curriculum/units/1993/4/93.04.04.x.html—50k—Cached —Similar pages

}   Categories
Read profiles of your favorite **rap** and hip-hop artists.… Need help deciding what hip-hop albums or **rap** songs to buy? Read these CD Reviews and song…
rap.about.com/od/hiphop**history**/—17k—Cached—Similar pages

}   Hip hop music—Wikipedia, the free encyclopedia
Hip hop music, also known as **rap** music, is a style of music which came into…It was the first album in the **history** of Australian hip hop to do so,…
en.wikipedia.org/wiki/Hip_hop_music—122k—Cached—Similar pages

}   AllHipHop.com : Daily Hip-Hop News
Hip-Hop pioneer Kurtis Blow is working on a documentary, "The **History of Rap**," focusing on the origins of Hip-Hop, aimed at educating eager fans about the…
www.allhiphop.com/hiphopnews/?ID=4029—42k—Cached—Similar pages

Which of these nine sites are worth accessing? The first one on the list comes up blank. The second one appears extremely promising because it is a documentary; therefore, it should be reliable and accurate. The person who wrote the piece is a BBC writer, so the facts and figures can probably be trusted. The third entry, "The History of Hip Hop," might be interesting, but it is by someone named Davey D. He may know his stuff on hip hop and rap, but the site does not tell me anything about his background or credentials. You move on. Next is the "History of Rap." The site is outdated and there is no known author. Clicking on "The Evolution of Rap Music in the United States," an article published by the Yale-New Haven Teachers Institute, appears. The site has a TLD of *edu,* and the article is written by a teacher. There also is a complete set of references and class lesson plans. This site is a keeper! You bookmark it and continue the search. Jumping over the next site, "Categories," because it seems way too general, you arrive at "Hip hop music" on the Wikipedia site. Wikipedia began in 2001 and bills itself as "the largest reference Web site on the Internet." The web page on rap offers some good information, but I need to be careful. I learn that Wikipedia offers information from many persons. At the "About" page I encounter the following: "The content of Wikipedia is free, and is written collaboratively by people from all around the world. This Web site is a wiki, which means that anyone with access to an Internet-connected computer can edit, correct, or improve information throughout the encyclopedia, simply by clicking the edit this page link (with a few minor exceptions, such as protected articles and the main page)." All that this particular article on rap can offer is a basic outline. As a responsible journalist, I should not quote from the page even if I use proper attribution. I need to make sure everything I include in my story is accurate. On the other hand, I might verify some of the information with the rapper when I interview him. But I am going to let him give me the quote and details, not the Wikipedia website.

The more you use the Internet and review sites that are reliable, the quicker you will learn to recognize a credible source from a questionable one. Always take time to verify the information, including the writer and the website. Do not use anything simply because you see it on the Internet! Use caution and discretion. Your readers and viewers are counting on you.

At present, there is no definitive place on the Internet where you can verify all facts, figures, data, and general information. There are, however, a few sites that allow you to check the accuracy of reports and rumors concerning politics, government, and policy issues:

} The *Washington Post* operates the Fact Checker for weighing reliable information on current campaign rhetoric and allegations. Readers are encouraged to suggest items for investigation and to send in facts or documents that can verify reported information. This site uses the innovative "Pinocchio Test" to indicate the authenticity of a claim made by a candidate or interest group. One Pinocchio is okay, but four indicates the information is a real whopper. Only the most accurate statements earn the coveted "Geppetto Checkmark." (See http://blog.washingtonpost.com/fact-checker/.)

} The Annenberg Public Policy Center (APPC) of the University of Pennsylvania maintains FactCheck for all kinds of news reports. The most popular topics on the website deal with the courts, the presidential race, and congressional elections. There are sections where readers can ask questions and also learn more about the truthfulness of mass e-mails. (See http://www.factcheck.org/.) In addition, the APPC operates a related site containing step-by-step instructions (with actual classroom lesson plans) on how to verify information on the Internet. By clicking on "Straight from the Source," for example, you will be directed to a list of the most reliable websites on more than two dozen subjects ranging from abortion to consumer safety to gun control to taxes and women's issues. (See http://www.factchecked.org/.)

} The *St. Petersburg Times* and *Congressional Quarterly* manage PolitiFact, which helps readers get to the bottom of stories and allegations about political candidates. There is even a Truth-O-Meter showing the accuracy of what is said by and about those running for office. (See http://www.politifact.com/truth-o-meter/.)

As a journalist, you have a responsibility to make sure the details you pass along to your readers, viewers, and listeners is correct. Whenever you are in doubt about anything, take the time to verify what you have found on the Internet with experts in the field. You can also check with trained professionals in local libraries. Many of these individuals have highly specialized degrees in library science; they know how to locate all sorts of information and they can find it fast.

Using Search Engines

How you gather information online depends on your style of writing and thinking. Many people rely on **search engines** to collect new information, while others depend only on published references. The Internet is growing at an incredible rate and it is becoming more difficult each day to use search engines such as Google and Yahoo. It is even more cumbersome to use aggregators and metasearch engines such as Dogpile (www.dogpile.com) and Mamma (www.mamma.com). One search alone could produce millions of results. A recent search on "state taxes" netted more than 57 million results! The results for taxes within a certain state are better but far more than anyone can search. The subject "Ohio state taxes" yielded 1.78 million results—still too many to review in a reasonable amount of time. However, if we search "The Ohio Department of Taxation" (at http://tax.ohio.gov/), the request for information becomes more manageable. At this one website, we are able to find many different types of information. A quick glance allows us to find out, for example, that the state motor fuel tax rate has been 28 cents per gallon since July 1, 2005, and the state sales tax rate is 5.5 percent. Knowing precisely where to begin a search will affect how fast we locate information.

Tomorrow's reporters will need to devise new and innovative ways to find particular resources in an instant. Software engineers all over the world are working on programs that will make plowing through the Internet much easier. Vista by Microsoft is a step in the right direction because it narrows the search parameters. But there is still a long way to go. In the meantime, there are ways to separate information we can use from information we cannot use. During any search, be as specific as possible by utilizing precise key words. As you have discovered already, broad and general searches yield few useable results for your time and effort. You can limit searches in several ways. Searching a general phrase like "water parks" produces 20 million results. Narrowing the search to "Virginia Beach water parks" reduces the results to 1.8 million. But using quote marks around the search phrase cuts the number down to four results!

You also can use an abbreviated phrase when looking for information online. Trying to find information on movies filmed in your area, for example, can be as easy as searching for "movies filmed (add your city)." You need not add "in" because most search programs do not recognize such words as "in," "the," "of," and so on. Also, searching for "St. Louis movies" will turn up all of the films currently playing at cinemas and theaters in the city. Look at what happens when we go to one of the search engines and type in "movies filmed St. Louis." The very first site that appears gives the names of eighteen movies either set or filmed in St. Louis, from *Meet Me in St. Louis* to *The Spirit of St. Louis* to *What's Love Got to Do with It?* (about the early years of Tina Turner). This same website also lists some of the famous actors from St. Louis: Betty Grable, Agnes Moorehead, Vincent Price, Kevin Kline, John Goodman, and so on.

All of this information is great, but can we really trust the site? As reporters, we need to know who compiled the information and if this is one of a million or more personal websites out there that are full of interesting details but little truth. In this case, the information came from a website produced by the 99th AALL Annual Meeting and Conference, held last year in St. Louis. We should be able to trust the American Association of Law Libraries (AALL), which was founded in 1906 and has more than five thousand members. Using reliable and dependable sources always makes our job easier.

A final point to remember when going online is that Internet searches sometimes can be case sensitive; that is, you may have to use capital letters as needed. There is a vast difference in searching for "house" or "House." The first might give you information on actual structures, while the second will give you websites for *House*, the television series, or even the House of Representatives. Fewer and fewer search engines are case sensitive, making the search even more difficult. Where a case-sensitive search at one time for "House" might have produced less than a few thousand results, an all-inclusive search now for "House" and "house" yields millions of sites. In addition, placing quotes around the subject no longer guarantees a limited or restricted search. With or without quotes, a Google search for "house" can turn up millions of possible sites. Adding a descriptor or two, such as "House television show" or "House representatives" frequently helps cut down on the large number of results.

As you build your knowledge of how to conduct online searches, you might want to spend some time talking with a local librarian. These people are experts at finding resources because they know where to look for information. They have been specially trained and know the recognized terms that produce specific results. Reference librarians especially can teach you valuable tricks of the trade. Learn from them and you will have knowledge that few other journalists possess.

Going online for information will never entirely replace being there in person. The Internet is, at its core, a worldwide community of voices talking with one another. We live in an era of participatory journalism. Each voice wants to be heard, but not every voice is knowledgeable, honest, fair, or impartial. As responsible reporters, serving the public, we have to shift through the comments, the statements, and all of the explanations to discern fact from fiction. We have to tell the entire story, and we have to do it by gathering information ourselves. The Internet can help us do our work, but it will never be able to do our work for us.

Arts and Entertainment Reporting

SCOTT L. POWERS

One morning when I was assistant managing editor for features at the *Chicago Sun-Times,* the entertainment editor met me in the space between our offices to tell me about a phone call he had just gotten from singer Elton John's road manager, who that weekend had performed at a large outdoor venue. Our not-altogether-positive review had run that morning.

The road manager claimed that our reviewer had not seen the show. A description of John's trademark flamboyant costumes was wrong, and the reviewer mentioned a couple songs John had not performed. The final piece of evidence: the reviewer had never picked up her tickets—as usual, a pair among the best seats in the house.

Confronting the reviewer, she quickly produced her reporter's notebook, filled with notes from the concert. She claimed that she had gone on a date while on assignment for the show and instead of claiming her reviewer tickets, she used her date's tickets and the evening's activities included a blanket location on the lawn, wine, and a dinner of fried chicken.

"And see," the reviewer said, showing me her notes and admitting her factual errors because she was distracted, "here are the chicken grease stains to prove it."

The lesson? As fun as working an arts beat can be—going to movies, concerts, and plays for free, hanging around with and talking to stars—**mixing work with socializing is a sure-fire recipe for disaster.** For most newcomers to reporting the arts and entertainment, every prior association with going to movies, concerts, and plays has been a social one. But like the dating Elton John reviewer, the arts reporter's full, active attention needs to be on the performance—reporting and engaging with the events onstage or onscreen in order to give readers a full and accurate report.

At its basic level, arts journalism is practiced no differently from any other kind of journalism, with the same types of reporting and ethics that are required for working a police, city council, or business beat. But unlike a news beat, the arts and entertainment reporter at most media outlets will be called on to report and review, a tricky balancing act. One day the reporter will pan a show and the next day will call up someone associated with the show to report out a news story. The only way to be effective is to do both with the utmost professionalism, ethics, and respect for readers and sources and artists.

For the reporting side of an arts reporter's dual identity, there's an additional twist. As with sports, much of the major news centers around planned events. The conclusion of *American Idol,* the last *Harry Potter* movie, a Radiohead recording released only online as a download—all are major arts events that present an opportunity to plan exceptional reporting tailored specifically for a publication's readers.

One such example was the Academy Awards held in 2007, honoring movies released in 2006. One of the movies honored was *Dreamgirls,* the adaptation of the Broadway musical very loosely inspired by the story of the 1960s soul group the Supremes. One of the movie's stars was Chicago native Jennifer Hudson, in her first screen role, and her first national exposure since a controversial loss on TV's *American Idol.* For the *Chicago Tribune,* where I was entertainment editor, this story had the making of a real Cinderella tale for local readers. And it demonstrates that **with the right planning, hard work, and a little luck, a great story can result.**

The movie had its public premiere in Chicago, New York, and Los Angeles on the same day in November 2006, and Hudson was returning home for the local screening. The *Tribune*'s entertainment reporter, Mark Caro, and I planned for him to cover her at the screening. Then, instead of the usual hotel room interview movie publicists usually push reporters to do, Caro had arranged to take Hudson back to her high school the next morning and interview her in that environment. At the premiere, Caro made sure to introduce himself to Hudson, and her family, and friends who surrounded her.

By that morning, Hudson was already receiving rave notices and predictions of Oscar nominations. She certainly heard that news, and her day with Caro at the school produced an insightful, upbeat, and fun piece that ran before the movie opened in December.

And sure enough, January's Oscar nominations included Hudson for best supporting actress. At that point, Caro made a pitch to a Hudson publicist to follow her during the week leading up to the Academy Awards in late February. An appealing story for the *Tribune,* even more so if she won. As is often the case, there was no response—entertainment publicists say "no" to requests more than they say "yes," especially in these days of controlled access and "tabloid" TV, online, and print publications where stars are often held up to ridicule.

Meanwhile, Hudson had scheduled a gospel concert at her childhood church in Chicago for the Monday before that next Sunday's Oscars. Caro arranged to cover the event and spend time with her. After the three-hour concert, Caro rushed back to the paper, filed his news story, and dashed to Hudson's hotel, where, after 11 P.M., she was relaxing with family and friends. It was there that Caro asked her directly if he could tag along in Los Angeles. Her answer, he recalls, was something like: "Sure, honey, you can come to whatever you want."

It didn't hurt our cause that she was between personal publicists at the time—they often prove their worth to their clients by shooing away journalists. Only her movie studio publicist remained, and Hudson made clear to him she was happy to have Caro there—an important result of Caro's previous contacts, including his timing: he was there before all the rave reviews. Caro went to the star-studded parties, dinners, and interviews during Oscar week. He had access to almost every event but the Oscar rehearsals (she was an Oscar-night performer) and was filling his notebook constantly. As Caro was working the West Coast, I was briefing the *Tribune*'s page-one editors about our plans, and by the Friday before the awards, we had a spot on the paper's front if she won.

Our work was far from done. The Academy Awards and newspaper deadlines are not compatible (except on the West Coast). The awards often run past deadline, so Caro spent all day before the show writing most of his story and sending it in to be edited. Remaining to be written: the lead about her win (hopefully not her loss, at least for our page-one ambitions), and the bottom, a quote Caro had arranged to get on the red carpet, as Hudson entered the Kodak Theatre. Again, planning paid off, and the publicist brought her over to where Caro was—having taken water and cookies to his media mates to make sure they moved so he could get to the front—and he got his kicker: *"I am loving every single second of this day,"* Hudson exclaimed, on the red carpet at last. *"Wooo!"*

We had one more surprise, when Caro got inside the theater to the pressroom. The supporting actor and actress awards are usually early in the show, but this night the supporting actress award had been moved to mid-show, about 9:30 P.M. Chicago time as we looked at a 10:30 P.M. copy deadline and the additional pressure to get Caro's story online even faster. But we were ready. All but four paragraphs of his two-thousand-word story that took a week of reporting and months of research were edited and ready to go when George Clooney said: "And the Oscar goes to...Jennifer Hudson." In twenty minutes for the *Tribune*'s website and in plenty of time for a huge page-one spread, Caro was able to put a top on his story that began:

HOLLYWOOD—The most head-spinning week in Jennifer Hudson's life began with her singing at her childhood church in Chicago and culminated Sunday night with her accepting the movie world's highest honor before a Kodak Theatre packed with Hollywood's biggest stars and an international audience of millions.

"I have to just take this moment in," the tearful 25-year-old South Sider said as she accepted the best supporting actress Academy Award for her spotlight-seizing turn as Effie in the musical "Dreamgirls." "I cannot believe this. Look what God can do. I didn't think I was going to win. If my grandmother was here to see me now—she was my biggest inspiration. She had the passion for it, but she never had the chance."

6

Assembling an Online Story

SHAYLA THIEL-STERN

Online journalism or new media journalism has become a popular career for journalists ever since the World Wide Web became a major news source, starting in the early to mid-1990s after the Mosaic browser was developed and more news readers gained access to the web. In only a few years, web journalism grew to become a dominant player in how millions of Americans get their news. In late 2006, Gannett, one of the nation's media giants, announced it was joining a growing trend to converge its newsroom operations. **Convergence** has become the integration of print, broadcast, and online news operations in reporting stories. It enables journalists working in different media to cooperate in producing stories, often from the same location. In the early days of online journalism, the pioneers who worked in the medium were reporters and editors who left traditional careers in journalism with the hope of creating an entirely new way for readers to receive and understand news. Many of these early online journalists had a deep interest in technology, but others simply wanted to be a part of making journalism history. It is amazing to see how fast and far this new way of telling stories has taken us.

When I worked as the music and nightlife editor for washingtonpost.com in the middle to late 1990s, we were all just beginning to figure out how to best use the web's potential to tell stories and reach audiences. Today, teams of online journalists spend much of their time collaboratively researching, writing, editing, and working on multimedia-oriented projects 24/7. These teams include:

Publisher. The publisher of an online news site is in charge of both editorial and business operations and often sets the mission and direction of a website. If the publisher is in charge of an online news site, he or she will still often report to higher business executives within a media company.

Editor in chief. The chief editor of an online news site is the person in charge of all major editorial decisions. This is the person to whom each of the section editors or producers reports.

Producer. A producer's role varies from one news organization to another. In some cases, the producer may edit, rewrite, or design print stories so that they are more suitable for the web. A producer might also write stories to go along with already broadcast stories. A producer's job often involves adding value to stories. Adding value refers to adding multimedia or interactive elements, supplementing the stories with other links to past stories or photo galleries, or simply making the story more readable for an online audience that might include laying the story out differently. Sometimes, producers write their own stories, columns, or blogs. Producers may be called upon to edit various sections of a website. Some producers update breaking news only by talking to reporters and reading the news wires throughout the day. They then design and update the publication's home page based on that changing news.

Section editor. A section editor oversees a specific section of an online publication, such as "Politics" or "Arts and Entertainment" or "Sports." To do this, a section editor often oversees a staff of producers or designers. Their job involves making stories more relevant for web readers and creating new content for that audience.

Multimedia producer. The multimedia producer often builds story packages, which are in-depth pieces on a given topic that incorporate interactivity, multimedia, and graphic elements along with printed information.

Graphic designer. In an online news operation, graphic designers might design the pages of a given website from layout to smaller graphics or logos, and they might edit photos so that those pictures work in the context of the web. Graphic designers develop tables and other visual elements that better illustrate some stories. In online news, graphic designers increasingly must know how to animate graphics and use Flash to design news packages.

Photo editor. As at a magazine or newspaper, the photo editor decides which photos make it online. The photo editor also shoots and edits digital photos, depending on the size of the news operation. Photo editors also oversee and organize online photo galleries and work with multimedia specialists to add photos to news packages.

Video journalist. Video journalists are responsible for shooting digital video to accompany stories that run on online news sites. They often edit, compress, and upload the video to the websites themselves.

Production editor. The production editor ensures that the editing and publishing system are working so that the site can carry on and the process does not slow down. Production editors are sometimes concerned with issues of usability, or whether readers can navigate the website well. Production editors often work with producers, graphics editors, technical experts, and anyone else responsible for publishing on the site.

Let's look at how teams of digital journalists do their jobs by working together.

1. A breaking news producer, the journalist who monitors the Associated Press and Reuters wires and other news sites on the web, listens to police and fire department scanners while watching the news on a television above his or her desk. The producer learns about a twelve-alarm fire at the city's largest chocolate factory and decides this should be the publication's leading story as soon as the producer can post it to the news organization's website. The producer phones the newspaper counterpart's metro desk to learn which reporter has been assigned to the fire, and, in the meantime, posts an AP wire story to the front page of the website to alert readers of this news event.

2. The reporter from the newspaper sends updates on the fire from his or her BlackBerry, then supplements them with details by calling the breaking news producer from a cell phone; the breaking news producer publishes the reporter's dispatches. The producer adds the details to the AP story that already has been published, constructing an entirely new story (the byline goes to the Associated Press reporter and the reporter from the newspaper). The producer will continue to edit and update the story as it unfolds throughout the day.

3. The editor of the online site decides that the fire story is one of the larger news stories to unfold in recent months and sends two online news reporters to film the firefighting process with digital video cameras. When the reporters return with footage, it is uploaded to the website to accompany the written story.

4. The editor then works with a news producer and a multimedia specialist to discuss how they might continue to develop and add value to the online news story. Adding value refers to the process of adding links, multimedia, and interactivity to make a complete package out of an individual news story. They decide to construct a package using Flash or a multimedia software program that allows them to publish the story in a more graphic way and also incorporate streaming sound and video. When there are problems with the audio not working, the multimedia specialist turns to a technical production expert who realizes that the package is too large for the server where it was uploaded and fixes the problem. They then recruit a graphic designer to create a graphic that gives an aerial view of the block where the factory was located. This graphic allows users to click on specific pieces of it and, when they do, more information about that part of the factory pops up on the screen.

5. The online news reporters and producers get to work gathering elements for their special package on the chocolate factory fire. They first find links to stories that have run regarding the chocolate factory over the past twenty-five years and are part of their database. They also add a new story about the economic impact of losing the chocolate factory. They then visit their newspaper's morgue and discover

black-and-white still photographs of the factory when it was first opened in 1910. They turn these over to the multimedia producer, who scans them and creates a gallery of the photographs.

6. Next, the reporters videotape a press conference from the fire chief describing the cause of the fire, and they gather audio interviews with citizens from the city who have memories of the chocolate factory and comments about its destruction. This recorded material is given to the **multimedia producer**, who incorporates it into the final special package on the fire. In the use of Flash to construct the package, the multimedia producer is able to make the photo gallery play like a slideshow while recorded sound bites from citizens play in the background. Readers also can click on the links to the current story about the fire or about past stories on the chocolate factory, and they can choose to click on links of the fire while it burns the building and the video recording of the fire chief discussing the fire's cause. The multimedia producer also creates an **interactive forum** where readers can post their memories of the chocolate factory and ideas for how to rebuild it.

7. Readers are able to visit the website the entire week to view the story package. In the news organization's paper the next day, readers are referred to the online story package for additional information. If the organization has a television counterpart, the news anchors would refer their viewers to the website's URL at the end of the newscast for more information on the story.

Web Reporting and National Tragedy

Today's online journalist is a multimedia producer who builds story packages that often incorporate interactivity, multimedia, and graphic elements along with printed information. This may include audio and video clips. Although many newspapers provided in-depth articles and long series on the September 11, 2001, tragedies, only two online newspapers in the cities where the primary news occurred—nytimes.com and washingtonpost.com—published the photos and obituaries of every person who was killed. John Poole, a multimedia producer and video journalist, working at washingtonpost.com, shot live video and interviews of the burning Pentagon after it was hit by a passenger plane piloted by terrorists on September 11, 2001. Poole, who is now the multimedia producer at National Public Radio, often shoots digital video that runs in conjunction with the stories he's working on. "Visual journalism is important because it's through images and senses and emotions that people experience so much of life, and it has always been the most direct of communications," he said. "This kind of work gives the sense of being there, which is at journalism's core."

Indeed, the web offers new opportunities for journalists to evoke a sense of life through a combination of print and multimedia, and to illustrate and add context to their stories. The addition of this material makes responsible reporters even more accountable to the citizens they serve. It may include links to important official documents, as well as audio and video interviews, and actual video footage of news events. Such stories often provide links to outside organizations, such as those offering critical care in the aftermath of Hurricane Katrina and the shootings at Virginia Tech. "The best thing about being an online journalist can also be the most challenging," says Ben Abramson, online travel editor for usatoday.com. He sees the task of the online journalist as giving citizens news worth knowing without "overloading" them.

Nonlinear Storytelling

In online news writing, the lead generally should not be more than twenty-five words, and some argue that online news writing allows for a bit more edginess in some of its writing because edginess appeals to the online audience and keeps its attention. Furthermore, research has shown that online audiences tend to understand and retain what they read when they can interact with the text in some way. This encourages writing and presenting material using the method of "**nonlinear storytelling**," or letting the story unfold as users choose by clicking on different hyperlinks or graphic presentations. In other words, writers online not only must know how to write concisely and well in print, but also must keep in mind how the online audience wishes to read and interact with the story they construct.

Many news organizations have installed content management systems that allow reporters to use a simple interface to publish stories and multimedia extras. Predesigned **web page templates** are generally available to make it easy to "cut and paste" text from a story onto a web page. This means that strong technical expertise has become less necessary among online journalists hired at major publications. Some news organizations still require online journalists to know HTML and an HTML editor, such as Dreamweaver, GoLive, or Homesite, that allows them to quickly and easily create web pages on the fly. This is especially important for breaking news producers, who often are required to upload stories very quickly. Knowledge of how to add links and graphics to web pages is often helpful.

More and more, online news organizations wish to hire journalists who are comfortable shooting, and in some cases editing, digital video. In fact, some daily newspapers have hired paid freelancers to seek out news and events to cover, and to shoot video footage and write brief stories that they then may upload from laptops in their cars. At the *Fort Myers News-Press* in Florida, these fledgling reporters are called "**mojos**," or mobile journalists, and they are expected to keep the online news sites loaded with fresh news and content throughout the day. Often, online journalists are trained to use digital video cameras and to work through video editing when they are on the job.

For stories that require official documents (such as court or government documents), reporters can scan the material and upload it to the Internet to be directly linked to their stories. This allows readers to view the documents themselves. **Digital reporters often link their stories to audio and video interviews, where citizens can see for themselves individuals who were interviewed.** This keeps journalists grounded in reporting facts that can be verified by users of their sites, but it also requires that reporters and editors screen these materials to make sure that they are appropriate for their readers. The same is true for online forums, where moderators have to be vigilant in screening comments that may be offensive before these comments are posted. When caretaking is done conscientiously, connectivity helps to widen the perimeter of those participating in public debate, while better educating readers to many sides of an issue. The result of this watchdog and community-building role is growing public confidence in journalism as a place of personal empowerment. Web reporting also provides links to outside organizations that often lead to direct action. This is what happened in the aftermath of Hurricane Katrina in August 2005, when concerned citizens linked to the Red Cross and other organizations offering aid to victims along the Gulf Coast.

Responsible Reporting on the Web

Many online news publications were launched between 1994 and 1996, and ever since they have also run on a 24/7 news cycle. This means that online news editors and reporters have deadlines that evolve by the minute. For online reporters and editors, the news never stops. Online reporters face the same daunting daily dilemma. Speed wars with accuracy. Every time. For the responsible reporter, there must be this realization: your most prized possession is not how fast you report news worthy reading, but how accurately. Accuracy is no less a value for reporting online than it is in hard copy. So carefully screen the links you add to stories. Ask yourself, if the information is reliable. Is it trustworthy? Have you fulfilled your gatekeeping role for citizens relying on your professionalism?

Abramson is convinced that **"the Internet offers storytelling opportunities unprecedented in the history of journalism."** Many of us who have worked in this exciting part of the profession would agree with his observation that the options in digitally produced stories are "practically inexhaustible." The instantaneous worldwide distribution of stories produced online demonstrates how far and fast this form of reporting has evolved since my early days of reporting in the online world. The technology of how you do online reporting is in constant evolution, but the values and fundamental decision making of responsible online reporting remains essentially unchanged. That is why responsible reporters entering the webbed world today face unparalleled challenges and opportunities to serve citizens with news that helps create a more just and civil society.

Investigative Reporting

JAMES L. AUCOIN

All great reporting is investigative. What is meant by "investigative reporting" is journalism that encourages the public and its government to correct social and political problems that otherwise could be ignored. Granted, other institutions such as congressional committees, law enforcement, and governmental commissions investigate and make recommendations for reform. Nevertheless, the history of journalism records numerous episodes in which investigative journalists exposed abuses of power, corruption, criminal acts, institutional failures, and other behavior that affected the quality of life in our communities that someone wanted to keep secret or that would otherwise have remained unknown.

Journalism scholars Theodore Glasser and James Ettema have argued that investigative journalism, at least as it is practiced in newspapers and on television, contributes to a public moral dialogue about what needs to be improved in society. In telling their stories, **investigative journalists hold business executives, public officials, and other institutional leaders to traditional moral and political standards**. In this way, they contribute to holding those in power to social accountability. They identify people who share responsibility for problems, and identify innocent victims harmed by the failures of bureaucracy, the criminality of officials, miscarriages of justice, or the negligence and venality of business leaders.

Reporters have engaged in investigative journalism since the beginning of newspapers in America in the seventeenth century. Investigative reports became a staple in newspapers, though, only in the mid-nineteenth century, when penny press newspaper editors considered it their public duty to expose institutional problems. The most impressive period of investigative journalism occurred in the early twentieth century in magazines, newspapers, and books that published muckraking. Reporters Ida Tarbell, Lincoln Steffens, Ida Mae Wells, Upton Sinclair, and others exposed predatory practices of business monopolies, municipal corruption, racial lynchings, unsafe meatpacking, horrible working conditions, and numerous other social problems. Their reports stirred the public to demand passage of the Pure Drug and Food Act, direct election of U.S. senators, child labor laws, trust-busting legislation, and other reforms.

The most famous example of modern investigative reporting is Watergate, in which in the 1970s *Washington Post* reporters Carl Bernstein and Bob Woodward documented misdeeds in the administration of President Richard Nixon. The misdeeds included illegal campaign spending, the break-in of the Democratic Party Headquarters, and the cover-up of crimes. Investigative reporting kept pressure on Congress to investigate the White House and contributed to President Nixon's resignation.

Watergates, though, are rare. More typical investigative reporting is represented by the work of a reporter such as Eddie Curran of the *Press-Register* in Mobile, Alabama. Curran's investigation revealed a sweetheart contract for construction of two warehouses between the state of Alabama and G. H. Construction, secretly co-owned by Lanny Young, an associate of the state's governor, Don Siegelman. Curran's reporting on that story and others ultimately led to federal corruption-related convictions of Siegelman, Young, former Siegelman cabinet member Nick Bailey, former Siegelman chief of staff Paul Hamrick, and others.

Curran received a tip about the warehouse while he was researching a landfill deal involving Young. His source told him that Young was a secret owner of a newly formed company the state had hired to manage the warehouse constructions. At first, state officials would not confirm that such a project was in the works, though the state planned to issue $16 million in bonds to finance it. Curran worked for three or four weeks tracking down leads and trying to access documents before finding the information that opened the door. "I basically broke it open—to the point that they [the Siegelman administration] canceled the project—by going to the state comptroller's office and looking up payments to G. H. Construction," he recalled.

G. H. Construction was a company with no staff and no work record, yet state officials had hired it to oversee construction of the warehouses. The company stood to make $1.7 million on the deal, an amount that construction experts interviewed by Curran said was excessive for such a project. "I found two large payments [listed in documents at the comptroller's office]," Curran explained, "and more importantly, two payments for two 'boundary surveys.'" G. H. Construction reported that the surveys had been done by a subcontractor. By talking with employees of the survey company, though, Curran discovered that one of the surveys "did not exist." He also found out that the company had not submitted a bill to G. H. Construction for the survey. "In fact, the bill from the [survey] company to G. H. Construction was forged by G. H. Construction, apparently without the [survey] company's knowledge," Curran explained.

Curran also read documents related to the proposed bond sale and eventually squeezed out of the Siegelman administration the state's contract with G. H. Construction. For Curran to see the contract, though, the *Press-Register* had to get its lawyer involved. State officials claimed that the contract was not a public document. The *Press-Register* argued that it was. The newspaper won.

Curran conducted a series of interviews to clarify the information he had discovered in the documents. "Several people lied to me," he recalled, "but I was able to prove that with the records I found." Ultimately, he took what he found to state officials to give them a chance to provide a logical explanation for how the project had been handled. When they could not do so, the newspaper published Curran's story on April 29, 2001. It would be the first of many investigative stories that Curran would write about the Siegelman administration. Siegelman lost his bid for reelection in 2002 and was convicted of corruption charges in 2006.

Curran's investigation of the Siegelman administration's warehouse deal is typical of investigative reports published and broadcast by newspapers and TV news outlets throughout the country. It started with a tip. The tip led to Curran's search of public records. Sources provided additional information and helped Curran understand what he had read in the records. The records helped him evaluate information he got from sources. Finally, he took what he found to the targets of his investigation to allow them to respond. Only then was the story published.

7

Beat Reporting and Community News

DAVID R. DAVIES

Reporters who cover community news in the nation's newspapers and for radio and television face an enormous responsibility to get the story straight. In many American communities, they may be the only authoritative news source for what is happening in the community. Local news is where people live. It's news they care about. New technology can make newsgathering hyper-local and geocoded with a focus on particular neighborhoods and Zip Codes, down to the block and apartment complex. **Crowdsourcing** at the local level now allows citizens to network with newsroom professionals in producing reporting that exceeds the resources of many news organizations. These foot soldiers are being organized all over the nation in the twenty-first century as beat reporters were amassed in the twentieth. Their purpose is the same: to report news worth knowing.

Reporting Local News

"I think intensely local, professionally gathered news is due for a comeback," says *Seattle Times* columnist Danny Westneat. "It's the one thing you can't get anywhere else." Westneat is on to something. Annual polls show that the public appreciates local news more than any other news it gets. And local news is where most journalists begin their careers in the news business.

While starry-eyed students of college journalism programs may see themselves headed to the *New York Times* or CNN just after graduation, they more likely are on their way to covering the cigarette tax controversy in Mississippi for the *Hattiesburg American* or the cleanup after **Hurricane Katrina** for WLOX-TV in nearby Biloxi or in networked journalism, where news organizations work collaboratively with citizen bloggers in investigative reporting and in reporting the news of the day. Once on the job, graduates will find themselves entering newsrooms that are in the process of being rewired to cover local news efficiently. Many newsrooms continue to rely on beat reporters, specialists who cover one subject exclusively—education, police, or city hall—as well as general assignment reporters, who cover different stories on different subjects each day. At smaller newspapers and TV stations, each reporter might be assigned a number of different beats as well as general assignment stories outside of those areas. Beat reporters and community journalists have the advantage of building up considerable expertise in the subject they cover. More and more newsrooms operating in the new online universe require reporters who understand how citizens use the information reporters post. This means newly negotiating the territory between reporters and readers in an environment that is intensely interactive. These reporters increasingly find themselves the hub in an era of citizen journalism, where the professionally trained have never been more needed in exercising the **gatekeeping** obligations of the press.

Curiosity is perhaps the most important trait a responsible reporter can have. To that, add a wide knowledge of local and state issues that can only be gained by extensive reading and preparation. All reporters, but especially those who will make their mark covering local and community news, need a good understanding of how local government, including city and county government and local schools, are financed and how they operate. They also need to know how state and local courts work. There will be no end to keeping up with the news in the state and region you cover. That will give you the context you'll need in order to explain stories to citizens.

Beginning reporters need to be on the alert at all times for news readers will want to know. They need to ask themselves: "What is happening that will be meaningful to my audience? Will this story hurt or help my readers? What would the average person on the street want to know about this subject?" **Some of the best stories are those that affect the lives of citizens directly.** If the local city council is considering banning smoking in city restaurants and bars, then obviously everyone in the city—smokers and nonsmokers alike—will be affected. Other good stories are simply that—compelling stories of people doing interesting things. The account of a skydiving seventy-five-year-old librarian, if well reported and well written, may resonate with an audience more than a seemingly more meaningful story of the smoking ban.

Searching for Story Ideas

The best reporters show strong initiative. They look for news and do not wait for it to come to them. You need to find the news before it finds you. Do this by talking to people on your beat and in your city and scanning the web daily for ideas to inform your reporting. Working the phones is fine, but the best way to find good stories in local communities is by visiting with the people you cover. Twenty minutes spent in the courthouse coffee shop can turn up an unexpected story. So can a casual stroll through the offices you cover. There is no shortage of good stories if you know how to look for them. Ask yourself, "Would this interest my audience?" If the answer is yes, then you've got a story.

The best community and beat reporters don't wait for editors to give them their stories, they know their communities well enough to initiate many stories on their own. In my days on the education beat, a typical week might consist of a local school board meeting, a meeting of the state board of education, a press conference about a new school initiative, a science fair at a high school across town, candidate filings for an upcoming election, as well as one or two investigative pieces that shed light on major issues faced by city schools and students. Your job will be to bring these assignments to life by remembering you are your reader's representative in covering these stories. Always keep that in mind. Try to find out what they would want to know. How will what you are covering affect them? That's your bottom line. That's always what you're aiming at.

Community journalism is often about analyzing problems that require a public airing. These are called "**enterprise stories.**" As an education reporter, I was asked to look beyond the day's news to report the trends that gave the news its shape. These stories would often appear on Sundays and would run thirty-five to forty-five column inches, about 2,000 to 2,500 words. Four or more sources were sought to explain key conditions influencing education in Arkansas, where I worked, and across the region. Documents and reports supplemented the interviews. Thanks to the Internet and public record laws, many of these documents are available at a keystroke. They are often the starting point in reporting news your readers will want to know.

Community-based reporting requires drilling down to get good stories. Don't rely on handouts from official sources for your news. That's not reporting. It's stenography. Know what's been reported on your community in the past. Anticipate what will make news in the future. The way to do this is get out of the office. **Good stories seldom come to you in the newsroom; you must go and find them.** Margaret E. Williams, a veteran of the *Hattiesburg American* who did a stint at *USA Today*, says the best way to find good stories is to pay attention to your surroundings. There can be a story down every corridor if you know how to look for it. Ask questions. Satisfy your curiosity. Keep your reader in mind.

Successful reporters of local news had better mind their manners. That means being on time, and being fair to and treating sources and fellow employees with respect. Nothing can kill a career in community-based reporting quicker than being found out as a phony. Sources are under no obligation to talk to you, and if you betray a confidence or abuse them, they'll begin ignoring you. You'll quickly find that professionalism has practical benefits.

Let me give you a quick rundown of what you can expect in some of the most common beats in local news.

Police reporting: This is where you cover crime in your local community. Reporters either love this beat or they hate it. Those who love it enjoy covering crime, and they like interactions with policemen and women. Your day will start by visiting the police station to pore over police reports. Some of our best reporters have started this way. "It's exciting," says Rob Moritz, a veteran reporter who's worked at newspapers in Arkansas, Tennessee, and Texas. "You get to see a side of the community that you normally don't see. And the stories that come out of it are stories about people and things that are happening to people, so they're very personal stories." Moritz recalls the story of the elderly woman in Little Rock who fought off a would-be rapist by cracking him over the head with her cane. Then there was the policeman who survived being shot in the chest by a suspect he was transporting when body armor saved the officer's life. The dents in the armor were so deep that they'd bruised the officer's chest.

State government/politics: If you work in a state capital, you may get the opportunity to cover that great spectacle of American politics—the state legislature. This beat requires a good knowledge of the political process and state government, and political junkies will love it. While the political process isn't always pretty, responsible reporters realize it's critical to the democratic process. So they look beyond bills to the citizens who will be affected. Covering legislatures requires reporters to spend long hours sifting through documents that threaten to leave you cross-eyed. But the payoff is filing a story that captures the impact the proposed legislation will have on your readers.

Local government: Nowhere is the political process more rough and tumble than at the neighborhood and community levels. Every person in your readership area is affected by these stories. It involves how much they'll pay in taxes and how that money will be spent. It covers fire, police, water, sewer, and trash. It is the municipal clock that marks your life. Sources extend far beyond city hall to businesspeople, civic groups, neighborhood associations, and a wide range of local officials. Anyone who lives and works in the city can ultimately be a source. You may find yourself overseeing interactive forums, where citizens weigh in on what you've written, while giving you ideas of what's worth investigating.

Jami Maday, a reporter at the Queens Chronicle in New York City who covered city and county news for newspapers in Illinois and Indiana, said covering local government made her more in tune with the community she was covering. "It was more than just sitting at a board meeting and writing notes about a new road construction project," she says. The contacts she made while covering government news, she found, helped her in covering other news. You'll find the same thing too.

Education: There's wide public interest in this coverage area and the vast range of feature stories that flow from it. The beat not only covers district schools, but also private ones;

not only kindergarten through high school, but also higher education as well. "The beat has its own built-in audience with the teachers, the school employees, the students, and parents," says education reporter Cynthia Howell Oman of the *Arkansas Democrat-Gazette*. There are few subjects that parents take more seriously than educating their kids. School board meetings may resemble battle zones when curriculum is being contested or taxes proposed or strike dates threatened.

Courts: Virtually any conflict can wind up in court. From crime stories to lawsuits reflecting personal and political differences of the rich and powerful, the courts beat reflects a wide range of human interaction in every community. You'll not only cover hearings, you'll interview judges, lawyers, plaintiffs, and defendants on every imaginable conflict. This will expose you to a wide range of human experience. A court reporter might spend one day covering the legal brawl between two former friends fighting over custody of a Pomeranian, and the next day a court hearing into claims that the state's public schools are unequally funded in violation of state and federal law.

"My best sources were usually the lower-level people," recalls Cary Bradburn, an Arkansas historian who had a long newspaper career at the *Arkansas Gazette* and other newspapers. Many other court reporters say the same. You need people with expertise to guide you to the big stories and the stories behind the big stories. Done well, there are few beats that give your readers more news worth knowing than covering the courts.

Sports: The sports beat has long attracted many of the profession's most knowledgeable specialists and often its best writers. You'll cover local colleges and perhaps professional teams, but also high school athletics, often a local fan favorite, and minor sports from bowling to youth baseball. Good sports writers are quick to build faithful followers who share their enthusiasm. Most sports fans have a favorite national sportswriter or columnist, but many follow local sports writers even more closely. That is the team their son or daughter, or brother or sister, is playing for. That's the school they attended and still have ties to. If you write about sports well, they'll likely develop close ties to you, too.

Business: Business reporting is a vital beat at many local newspapers and television stations. The business section offers readers a picture of the economic temperature of the local community through a wide range of business perspectives, from the local office worker to the town's most prominent businesswoman. It not only depicts the current climate but anticipates future turbulence or comforts readers with sunny predictions. Behind the best reporting on this beat is thorough and relentless research that produces an ability to get behind facts and figures to see the impact of economic trends on the citizens you serve.

Reporting Communities in Context

The key to successfully reporting local news is an intimate knowledge of your community. You can't anticipate its future if you don't know its history. You can't assess current conditions unless you properly appreciate the richness of its diversity, its hopes and prejudices. Every beat in each community has its special requirements. Court reporters need to understand how courts work, the rules of evidence, and jurisdictional differences between state and federal courts. Education reporters ought to understand how national education policy affects local schools, and the mechanics of teacher training and teacher pay. City reporters need to know the difference between an R-1 zone (for single-family dwellings) and R-3 (apartments and multifamily units allowed) to make sense of the planning commission. It wouldn't hurt to know a little about trends in wastewater treatment, since that might come up as the local council considers revamping its sewer plant.

While much of this knowledge comes only on the job, you'll be expected to bring a base of knowledge about government, public affairs, and public finance to the newsroom that you gained in college. Every reporter, no matter the specialty, needs to have a firm grasp of government and how it works. You'll need to know mechanics as well as theory. Taxes are based on the assessed value of a piece of property, and you'll need to understand how and why that assessment is determined in your state. Sadly, not every beginning reporter is as conversant in these and other financial rules as they are of the more complicated nuances of those governing the designated hitter or the penalty for clipping. But you'll need to know these things to make sense of your beat as you cover breaking and routine stories and, just as important, to explain these stories to your readers.

The responsible reporter should never forget the citizens he or she is serving. Remember the fundamentals. "At the most basic level, the most important thing you want to do is to get it right and to be fair," says Jim Stratton of the *Orlando Sentinel*. Set aside your personal opinions in writing news for citizens in your community. Be open and honest with sources. Don't be rude. Talk to as many sources as you can, "the more authoritative the better," Stratton says. Double-check, then triple-check, all your information. All the responsible reporter has to offer a reader is credible information. When your credibility is gone as a reporter, your usefulness has ended. Moritz urges all reporters, and particularly beginning ones, to have a healthy skepticism in covering local news. "Don't believe the first thing that someone says to you," he says. "Look for other things, too. Just because a police officer tells you something is so doesn't mean it's true. There could be another explanation for it." He urges reporters to pay attention to money in the stories they cover, where it is coming from and where it's going.

Cynthia Howell Oman, a veteran reporter, believes that all beginning reporters "need to keep a good calendar." It organizes the reporter's day, month, and year. Bradburn reminds young journalists to always go beyond a single source. "You can't go with one source," he says. "You're going to make mistakes if you do that. **Use multiple sources.**" He finds that's the best way to be "reasonably sure your information is correct." Bradburn urges reporters not to get too close to their sources. It impacts objectivity. Veteran writer

Margaret Williams is amazed how many reporters don't read their own newspapers. It makes them look fairly foolish when they are frequently asked to explain what's in it. Mailyn Ellzey, a broadcast journalist who now teaches the craft, predicts that a reporter's first job covering community news will likely be his or her favorite. Everything is new, fresh. The future has unbounded opportunities for personal growth and professional development.

Reporting and Intellectual Engagement

Responsible reporting of local news requires a natural curiosity and intellectual engagement. If you've got it, you're well on your way to being a good reporter. If you don't have it, you might consider another line of work. A reporter friend tells a story about that. In February 2003, my friend was watching television and learned that the space shuttle *Columbia* had blown up earlier in the day. Immediately his mind was racing. What a tragedy! How did this happen? How will it affect NASA? What's next for the space shuttle program? He wished he was covering this incredible story, but it was his day off, so that was out of the question. He found his son across the house watching television.

"The space shuttle exploded," the father announced with a flourish.

"Oh, yeah," his son replied, barely looking up from his video game. "I saw that earlier."

"Son," my reporter friend said with a smile. "You'll never be a reporter."

Covering Crime and Law Enforcement

CAROLYN S. CARLSON

The media have a responsibility to report on crime in order to help the public avoid victimization and to ensure public oversight of law enforcement. Reporting about crime has never been easy, and writing about crime requires a significant amount of sensitivity, especially when dealing with crime victims.

One of the better known crime victims of the 1980s was Jeanne Clery, who was raped and murdered on the campus of Lehigh University in 1986 by a fellow student she did not know who had gained access to her dormitory through doors that had been left propped open so girls could enter after curfew. Clery's parents, Howard and Connie Clery, later learned that the school had kept quiet about numerous other violent crimes on campus and hadn't done anything about 181 reports of propped-open doors at the dormitory in the four months prior to Clery's death.

Arguing that the dormitory residents would never have propped the doors open had they known of the violent crimes, the Clerys lobbied for a federal law that now requires colleges and universities to give their communities timely warnings of crimes that may recur. The law also requires colleges and universities to reveal to members of the campus community on an annual basis the crimes that have occurred on their campuses.

The Clerys have been a champion of access to records on campus crime ever since the death of their daughter. Their position, and the position taken by their nonprofit organization Security on Campus Inc., is that the more information made public on campus crime, the more people can protect themselves from crime and the better they can judge the actions of law enforcement in performing their duties.

The **Clery Act** now requires that all colleges that accept federal funding, which includes nearly all private as well as public schools, must produce a daily, public police log detailing crimes that are reported to campus law enforcement. Thanks to the work of the Clerys and their supporters, campus media nationwide now have access to information that helps them cover campus crime.

Having access, however, isn't all there is to it. Responsible reporters have to do a lot of work to get all the information they need to adequately cover crime and law enforcement, whether it be for the campus or professional media.

To cover law enforcement, reporters should first try to learn all they can about police procedures by doing their own detective work. Read books and articles about police work. Interview officers. **A thorough understanding of how police do their jobs will help reporters avoid mistakes and write more insightful stories.** Keep tabs on how the department looks from the outside by interviewing public defenders, prosecutors, and officers from other departments. Pick grapes from the grapevine. Know when there are organizational, administrative, or personnel changes in the works.

A beginning reporter must make it part of a daily routine to check the public records that you are entitled to access under your state's open records law. These usually include daily crime reports and an arrest log. These records serve as tips for incidents that might make good stories. Rarely do police reports include enough information for reporters to write a complete story. The reports, however, can direct you to the officers, victims, witnesses, and accused you will want to interview to develop a story.

The basic information you'll need includes:

} Suspect's name, address, age, and occupation
} The charge
} Names of the arresting officers and agencies
} Time, date, and place of the arrest
} Description of the crime
} Names and contact information for the victim and any witnesses

Often the description of the crime is sketchy and you have to track down the arresting officers to find out what happened. If you have an incident with no arrest, you definitely need to talk to the investigating officer to indicate that you're interested in knowing when an arrest has been made. It's not unusual, however, for you to not hear about an incident until it's been resolved with an arrest.

Remember that the public record will tell you only the police side of the story. The victim, the witnesses, and the accused may all have different points of view. You should seek them all out and treat each side with respect.

The victim or victims are especially difficult to deal with because you must be sensitive to the ordeal that they have been through. You must realize that they are still going through an ordeal in having to deal with the police and the media about the incident.

Edna Buchanan, a Pulitzer Prize–winning police reporter with the *Miami Herald,* said the primary reason she held that job for twenty years before she stopped to write crime novels was that she felt an obligation to the crime victims. In her book, *Never Let Them See You Cry,* she wrote, "Sometimes, we are all the victim has got. Sometimes you feel like Wonder Woman, or Superman, going to the rescue. Reporters can find missing kids, lost grandmothers, and misplaced corpses. We fish out people who fall through the cracks. Publicity rescues people tangled in the hopeless mazes of government and bureaucracy. We recover stolen cars and priceless family heirlooms. A story in the newspaper can secure donations of blood, money, and public support—and occasionally that rarest gift of all: justice."

The Society of Professional Journalists' Code of Ethics holds several admonitions that reporters dealing with crime victims need to consider.

} "Be sensitive when seeking or using interviews or photographs of those affected by tragedy or grief."
} "Recognize that gathering and reporting information may cause harm or discomfort. Pursuit of the news is not a license for arrogance."

} "Recognize that private people have a greater right to control information about themselves than do public officials and others who seek power, influence, or attention. Only an over-riding public need can justify intrusion into anyone's privacy."

} "Show good taste. Avoid pandering to lurid curiosity."

} "Be cautious about identifying juvenile suspects or victims of sex crimes." In some states identifying juvenile suspects or victims of sex crimes may be illegal; in some, it may simply be illegal for the police department to tell you the names. If you obtain the names of juvenile suspects or victims of sex crimes from police or other sources, you should consider whether identifying them is necessary to your story. Most media outlets will have policies about these issues that you should know and follow.

The two basic ethical principles at stake are to **seek the truth and report it**, and to minimize the harm caused by reporting the truth. The ethical police beat reporter, according to Buchanan, does all he can to make sure the victim is not revictimized by his stories but instead finds justice.

In addition to the victims, you can talk with witnesses about a crime but remember that the only information that is privileged—that you can use without fear of being sued for libel—is the information in the official police report. Take care when using information not in the official police report, and be particularly careful when your information contradicts the official report.

Remember that the accused are just that—accused—and you must be careful not to convict him or her in your copy. Suspects' stories are likely to be very different from that of the police, and the police reporter is obliged to seek them out, by talking to family members, attorneys, and, if possible, the suspects themselves. The SPJ Code of Ethics has two warnings about dealing with suspects. First, "be judicious about naming criminal suspects before the formal filing of charges." Secondly, it urges reporters to try to "balance a criminal suspect's fair trial rights with the public's right to be informed." Both concerns can be met with sensitivity and thoughtfulness on the part of the responsible police reporter.

Finally, once you've gathered your information from the public records, interviewed your investigating officers, witnesses, victims, attorneys, suspects, and their families, and have taken into account your ethical concerns, it's time to write the story. Most in-depth crime stories lend themselves to a modified **inverted pyramid** style of organization, in which you start with the overall scene and the latest development, advise the reader where things stand now and what will happen next, then go back to the beginning and tell what happened in chronological order, sprinkling the story liberally with quotes from your various sources. If the story stretches out over several days, each subsequent installment will include a condensed version of the chronology, with the latest developments at the top.

The police beat offers the responsible reporter a wide panorama of the human experience that should be described with care, persistence, and energy.

Reporting Race and Ethnicity

TRACE REGAN

Too often journalists fail to be responsible, fair, and comprehensive in covering racial and ethnic minorities.

The reasons for this failure vary. But, fundamentally, journalists may simply need to know more—and *care* more—about the sensibilities, interests, and views of minorities to portray them responsibly and fairly in news stories. That familiarity includes being aware of the diversity of opinion within any particular minority group.

Uninformed reporting about minorities can not only unwittingly offend minorities but also disserve the broader community by creating a flawed portrait of the lives of minority group members. **It's imperative that journalists think about race and ethnicity to minimize missteps when covering minorities.**

Presumably, reporters know they should avoid the blatant use of stereotypes. However, a more difficult issue is the unintended reference to stereotypes. For example, when a sports broadcaster praises an African American quarterback's *intuitive* ability in executing a successful play but credits a white quarterback's *intelligence* in executing a similar play, that contrast subtly reinforces a negative stereotype about African Americans—namely that African Americans are intellectually less capable than whites.

Admittedly, the reporter, in making this comparison, may not have been thinking about race at all, and may indeed be put off by anyone who accuses him or her of being racially insensitive. However, *not* thinking about race may be part of the problem. The more one thinks about race, the less likely one is to offend when reporting on anything that involves race. It should be clear that reporters can offend inadvertently. When journalists reinforce stereotypes, however unintentional these comments might be, not only might they offend, but their accuracy is compromised, and accuracy is of course a cardinal aim of journalism.

Consider this example about a sports writer for the local newspaper in a small Ohio community who wrote a story about the death of a former high school basketball coach. The writer referred to the coach as a fiery *Italian* who was best known for his disciplinarian approach to athletics. It's questionable whether the writer should have referred to the coach's Italian heritage in connection with the coach's fiery persona because doing so reinforces the stereotypical image of the average Italian as an excitable person. Why not drop the "Italian" and simply say the coach was a fiery guy if one wants to describe the coach's personality? Furthermore, isn't this stereotype about Italians a cliché? Not only might this stereotype offend the sensibilities of some readers and mislead others, it's trite writing. Again, had the writer been sensitive to the issue of stereotyping, he might have avoided coupling "fiery" with "Italian."

Besides avoiding stereotypes, journalists need to work at treating minority subjects in the news the way they treat non-minority subjects when the circumstances of the stories are similar. Periodically, one hears complaints about the news media lavishing attention on white victims of crime and paying far less attention to minority crime victims.

For example, a twenty-seven-year-old white woman in a large northeastern city was murdered in her apartment in an attractive neighborhood, home to many young professionals. That story made the front page of the local paper. But when, a couple of months later, a thirty-year-old African American woman was murdered in her apartment in that same neighborhood, the story was not on the front page of that same local paper, and the story received far less coverage. Neither woman was well known. Essentially, it was the same story and same average news day when both stories ran. But coverage of the two murders was decidedly different.

If Jon-Benet Ramsey had been an African American, would the story of her murder have received the same attention the news media gave it? Or consider the case of Tamika Houston, a twenty-four-year-old African American, who mysteriously disappeared from her home in Spartanburg, South Carolina, in June 2005. Reportedly, Houston's family tried but could not get the media to focus on Houston's disappearance; the family certainly did not get anywhere near the kind of saturation coverage that attended the disappearance of Natalee Holloway, who is white, when she went missing in Aruba. Nearly all of the missing person stories that get national and sustained media coverage involve young, white, middle-class women.

Why the difference? It's hard to escape the conclusion that race is a factor, perhaps the primary one, and one that may be largely invisible. The different handling of the missing person stories just cited seemingly reflect a belief, perhaps subconscious, that **majority white audience members are simply more interested in a missing person story when the subject is young, white, and attractive.** Still, are journalists not ethically obligated to treat all members of a community similarly when dealing with the life of a person? Should the decision in missing person stories be determined wholly or even primarily by market considerations?

When Katrina flooded New Orleans, two photos of people leaving a store with food received a lot of attention. The caption accompanying the photo of a young African American man described him as "looting" a grocery store. The caption accompanying the photo of two white residents described them as "finding" bread and soda from a local grocery store. The fact that comparable photos were treated differently by the news media is, at best, suspect behavior. It would be interesting to know whether the journalist who wrote the "finding" caption in the photo of the two white residents would have written the same caption if the photo had been of the young African American man. Similarly, it would be interesting to know if the journalist who wrote the "looting" a grocery store caption in the photo of the African American man would have written the same caption if the photo had been of the two white residents.

Another Katrina photo pictured a naked seventy-four-year-old African American man who was being taken from his home to safety. The man, who was identified by name, had only a towel draped over his privates. If the subject of this photo had been an elderly white man or elderly white woman, would the news media have published it?

Or take the Katrina photo that ran on the cover of a national opinion magazine. The photo showed a fairly close-up shot of a dead African American woman lying face down in a pool of water in the street. She's clothed in a blouse, panties and shorts down near her ankles. Again, if the photo were of a white woman, would this magazine have published it? Whether either of these photos would have been published if the subject had been white is not the essential point, however. The point is simply that, in situations where the privacy or humanity of a minority subject may be compromised, journalists should ask themselves whether they would treat a *non-minority* news subject the way they're about to treat a minority subject. Again, think about race to minimize problems related to race in reporting the news.

In covering the minority community, journalists should also:

*Avoid "parachuting" into the community only when there is a crisis or negative event. The reporter should of course spend time in the community developing varied contacts, making herself known and getting to know places and faces. Churches are a good place to start.

*Avoid seeing the community as a monolith and understand that there may be no one leader who speaks for the entire community. Be alert to the diverse voices that in all likelihood exist in the community and reflect that diversity in news stories.

*Be careful about designating anyone a leader. Many minorities may have a decidedly different take on who is or isn't their leader. Be accurate and play it safe. Use official titles, such as the pastor of the Westside Presbyterian Church or the director of the Bunker Hill Community Center. Even labeling someone a *community activist* may be problematic if the term is simply used to describe someone who is active only in that he is all too willing to accommodate eager reporters looking for a sound bite or direct quote. That's inaccurate and sloppy reporting.

*Don't only look for negative stories. Positive stories about the majority community are frequently reported, and the minority community should be treated similarly. To be indifferent about doing positive stories concerning minorities not only is discriminatory, but conveys to the broader community a less than honest assessment of life in the minority community. Furthermore, reporting positive stories will help encourage some, if not many, in the minority community to talk to you, to trust you when you're doing a story about *difficulties* in the community.

*Avoid using file video of minority criminals when generic video is needed for a story about crime, such as a story about the statistics for various categories of crime in the state during the past year. Images of minority criminals reinforce the view of minorities as criminals, whereas, in majority white communities, images of white criminals do not reinforce the image of whites as criminals.

*Try to cover *process*-related stories and not just *event*-oriented stories (for example, a fire, shooting, or news conference). Stories about developing trends (a parent-driven push for school uniforms to help combat antisocial behavior) or concerns (about bullying in elementary schools), if done well, will pull the reporter into the community and give the reporter greater insight into its residents. That improved sense of the community will enrich the reporter's coverage of the community and benefit the broader public interest.

*Avoid identifying criminal suspects by race unless the description is **exhaustive,** and especially avoid the practice of identifying only minority suspects by race or ethnicity. If the suspect is only identified by race or ethnicity and there are thousands of men or women of that race or ethnicity in the community, how beneficial is the racial or ethnic identification in apprehending the suspect? The harm of stereotyping would seem to outweigh any advantage in identifying a suspect only by race and gender.

*Consider calling a random sampling of fifty or so residents to get a sense of how at least some in the community view a variety of subjects. Or employ the civic journalism idea of periodically sponsoring a small pizza dinner to tap in to community views on the issues. Assembling residents for a conversation can be particularly useful as some people feed off the comments of others and contribute insights that might otherwise never be made known. And of course one of the things reporters might learn in canvassing the community in this fashion is how well the local media are covering the community.

Science and Technology Reporting

SONNY RHODES

Hurricane Katrina. The Indian Ocean tsunami. The feared AIDS and bird flu pandemics. The human genome project. The stem cell controversy. The genetic mapping of mind and memory. Dirty bombs. Dark matter. The expanding universe. Killer quakes. Anthrax attacks. Record-setting wildfires. Habitat loss. Water and air quality. Global warming. It is difficult to overstate the importance of reporting on science and the environment.

Consider this: in February 2007, a United Nations–sponsored group, the Intergovernmental Panel on Climate Change, announced a 90 percent certainty that human activity had contributed to a rise in global temperatures since 1950. The panel, which included scientists and government officials representing 113 countries, concluded that the main cause of the temperature rise was the addition of greenhouse gases to the earth's atmosphere. The temperatures would continue to rise throughout the twenty-first century even if governments acted immediately to require major cuts in greenhouse emissions, the panel stated. The story was reported around the world.

Now consider this: at roughly the same time the panel's report was released, a book titled *Unstoppable Global Warming: Every 1,500 Years* was published. The book's authors maintained that global warming is part of a harmless, natural cycle the earth is going through. Soon after the report and the book were released, the 2006 Academy Award for best documentary in the features category went to *An Inconvenient Truth,* an account of former Vice President Al Gore's efforts to draw attention to global warming.

Clearly, the controversy over global warming is news and will remain so for years to come. It is not alone. Increasingly, stories on science and technology appear on front pages of newspapers and websites and as the leading story on the nightly news. For students who were attracted to journalism because they heard there would be no math, the prospect of reporting on science issues may be unnerving. Indeed, **just thinking about interviewing chemists and biologists might make the bravest reporter hyperventilate.**

I learned, though, to use the same skills in interviewing a scientist that I used with a mayor, a school board member, or a CEO. I asked questions, lots of them, and tried not to worry about sounding foolish. Assume that if you have a question, many of your readers may well have the same question. If I saw I was getting in over my head, that the interviewee was getting too technical, I would say something like this: "Think of me as your neighbor and that we're just talking to each other over the backyard fence. How would you tell your neighbor about this?"

A good reporter is obligated to ask enough questions of authorities to understand an issue sufficiently to explain it to readers. As for the danger of sounding like a fool, I've always found that whomever

I interview is grateful that I am taking the time to get the story right. Few things are worse than mis-quoting someone or misinterpreting that person's ideas. For several years, I've written a nature column for the *Arkansas Democrat-Gazette,* a statewide daily newspaper. I work hard to make sure I get things right. I have assembled my own library, and as an academic I frequently use University of Arkansas resources that I know to be reliable. One of the great things about being associated with a university is the access it gives to faculty members who are experts in many specialties. In preparing to write about plants, fish, mammals, birds, and other aspects of the natural world, I often call on fellow faculty members to share their expertise.

My goal in writing about nature is simple: if I can tell a reader something he or she didn't know about some species of flora or fauna, maybe that reader will better appreciate that species and treat it better. I get my ideas from many sources—newspapers, magazines, radio, television—but also from simply observing my natural surroundings. A good walk, whether it's around my neighborhood or along a wilderness trail, provides enough ideas and experiences for any number of columns. In considering whether to write about a particular subject, I apply the same criteria that reporters and editors use in determining news value: impact, uniqueness, and proximity, among others. I also figure that if something interests me, it will probably interest readers. In writing the column, I try not only to inform but to entertain.

Invariably, with each column I also learn a few things and entertain myself; it's highly enjoyable to create something that may contribute to readers' understanding of their natural surroundings. My column writing also leads to opportunities for me to be a reporter again. A few months ago, a features editor at the *Arkansas Democrat-Gazette* asked me if I would write a profile of the executive director of Arkansas Audubon, which is heavily involved in environmental education. I went to Lexis-Nexis and did key word searches on the names of the director and the organization. More than two hundred articles appeared. By carefully checking the headlines, I found about twenty articles that provided a good sampling of the organization's overall goals and activities. Next, I checked out of a university library about twenty books that covered topics ranging from prehistoric Arkansas, to the history of Earth Day observances, to extinct birds. By the time I sat down to interview the executive director, I knew a great deal about him and his organization. I had also added to my knowledge of the state's history and its wildlife, knowledge that continues to help inform my column writing. The preparation helped me with that story and will help me in the future.

Many science and environment writers and reporters would agree with a recent observation made by Katherine Marks, who reports on environmental issues for the *Arkansas Democrat-Gazette.* Marks points out that in nine years as a journalist, she's covered the environment as well as "local government, transportation, and education. I bring this up because I feel **my job is the same no matter what I'm covering: to shed light on topics a reader might not learn about elsewhere.** I enjoy covering environmental issues because they really touch everyone. What's more important than the air we breathe and the water we drink? What's more, environmental issues, particularly climate change and energy, could be the biggest stories not only of my lifetime, but for generations to come."

That should serve as encouragement to the next generation of responsible reporters who will make stories on science and the environment relevant to millions of readers who will need to know what they know.

8

Covering Speeches and Press Conferences

ANN O'DATA LAWSON

Several years ago at an annual chamber of commerce breakfast, the mayor of a midsized city was delivering his State of the City address. After presenting the year's economic development results, the mayor seemed to take a step back from the podium to signal a shift to his next point when, to the crowd's surprise, he stumbled into the backdrop curtain and fell off the platform. When the story appeared in the afternoon edition of the city's major daily, what do you suppose was the focus? Did the number of newly created jobs capture the headline? Or did his fainting due to a possible cardiac problem feature prominently? Unexpected occurrences often shift news coverage. A city's employment statistics may seem less pressing than a change in leadership. Although the mayor was back to work within the week, concerns about a succession plan and special elections had become prominent community issues.

Covering Public Events

Speeches are not always the stories they start out to be. **A good reporter will look beyond the words of the speech and find a story** in the audience reaction, an opposing viewpoint, or perhaps what remains unsaid by the speaker. The types of presentations that a reporter may cover will vary from meetings to press conferences, but they hold in common one basic element: these speeches are *public* and, therefore, open for fair comment in the press.

Most public speaking textbooks agree that there are only three main purposes to a speech: to inform, to persuade, or to entertain. These three purposes are present in every speech to varying degrees. A speaker needs compelling information in order to persuade an audience, and occasional cleverness in a speech will help hold an audience's attention through the content.

Recognizing the general purpose of a speech is rarely difficult. The press release or pitch letter the journalist receives about this planned event will usually reveal the purpose of the speech. Most political speeches are meant to be persuasive, urging citizens to vote for or against a particular candidate or issue. While press conferences given by a corporation unveiling a new product or responding to a crisis may persuade the public to have a favorable opinion, crime or health-related press conferences are more often informative.

In the public speaking classroom, students learn the essentials of speech construction. Speeches usually begin with an attention-getter, something such as a quotation, startling fact, rhetorical question, or humorous story. The speaker then proceeds into the body of the speech. Good speakers will preview their main points by telling you the three or four primary items that will be covered. After explaining the first point, the speaker will move to the next idea. Each main item should contain supporting material in the form of quotations, statistics, expert testimony, personal examples, or a combination of these.

When all of the main points have been presented, the speaker should briefly review all of them again. This formula is sometimes known as "tell them what you're going to tell them, tell them, and then tell them what you told them." Since the main points are repeated three times, this approach generally helps an audience retain key information. All speeches should conclude in a way that clarifies the point of the speech and the desire for some type of audience action.

As for organizing the material into the main points, a speaker may choose from an assortment of patterns. Some persuasive topics will call for a problem-solution order of the points that defines a problem and then offers ideas for solving it. Other topics might be organized by listing the causes of an issue followed by the positive or negative effects it produces, or a cause-effect pattern. A chronological organization is best for information that needs to flow in a timeline, such as a biographical introduction. A spatial pattern is preferred for explaining locations or movement, such as a building or map. The topical pattern is frequently used when information can be divided into equally important sections. Understanding and recognizing these patterns will help a reporter follow the speaker's ideas.

Whatever the organization, a journalist needs to remember that speeches follow a traditional *pyramid* **structure,** not an inverted one. Presenters usually save the best for last in order to maintain audience interest. Some speakers may pique listeners' attention by starting a story during the introduction and saving the resolution for the conclusion. It is important for a reporter to be present and alert during the entire presentation. If you think you have the main idea of the speech and choose to leave before the speaker is finished, you might be missing the impact.

The difference between a speech and a news story isn't limited to structure. Word choices in speeches need to be more conversational and less formal than they are in a typical story. Content will often be repeated for emphasis because an audience can't rewind what they've heard as they might when they reread lines in a story. Of course, reporters should be prepared for those who have not had training or experience in public speaking and whose speeches may be imperfectly written, inadequately rehearsed, or poorly delivered. A good journalist will look beyond the speech itself to find the news value of the story.

Your coverage of a speech or press conference does not begin when the speaker arrives at the podium. A reporter begins researching the background of the speaker, topic, host organization, and other critical information well in advance of the speech. Reporting a speech is not simply taking dictation; your job is to put the information into context and relay its relevance to your audience.

One way to inform your story is to interview the speaker after the presentation or press conference, when your questions will be more direct. The background research you've already done will add to your depth of questioning and analysis. As an example, think about writing a story about a political rally. Is the candidate's speech given in a vacuum? Surely you would want to ask questions about the candidate's views on issues even if they are not mentioned in this particular speech. You can only ask probing, thoughtful questions if you are well prepared.

Consider interviewing several members of the audience. Reactions to a speech can be demonstrated by applause or boos, but quotations from audience members can reveal the mood of the event with attributed statements. If the candidate speaking refers to his or her opponent, why not contact the opponent for a comment? If newspaper editors only wanted to know the words of a speech, they could print a transcript. Your job is to provide readers with the whole story of the event.

In addition to interviewing, a key tool of a reporter is observation. Find concrete ways to help your audience visualize the scene and hear the words.

When you return to your computer to write and file the story, you'll begin by reviewing your notes. If you have only kept track of key words, you will not be able to ethically quote the speaker. Taking detailed notes is critical to capturing a speech or press conference. The speaker may have quoted others in the speech and provided statistics. Before you include those in your story, verify their authenticity. You may have had the opportunity in your interview to ask questions such as, "What was your source for that number?" or "Who was it who said that line?" If you can't confirm this information through another source, refrain from using it or possibly point out the discrepancy between what someone said and what the facts show.

The discipline of public relations is the source of most press conferences. Accomplished public relations practitioners understand the needs of journalists and strive to provide newsworthy items. However, it is possible for a press conference to be used as a publicity tool. When this occurs, a reporter should critically examine the news value of the event and whether there is, in fact, information the public needs to know. Don't allow the medium of a press conference make you cynical about the message.

Journalists need to be discerning listeners. Every industry from natural gas utilities to health-care administration has its own subculture, terminology, and lingo. The vocabulary of speakers is not always understood by those outside their industry. Ask for definitions. Research the industry. Don't allow unfamiliar words to cloud your understanding of the issues and information your audience needs to know.

Finally, responsible reporters strive to keep their writing original. In a traveling press corps, numerous reporters follow a candidate or politician and may hear the same speech several times a day. A reporter can't lament that there is nothing new to write about. A story must be filed. You are challenged daily to find a unique story on the periphery of the speech because the words themselves cannot be the repetitive focus.

Remember that speeches are not always the stories they start out to be. A well-prepared, disciplined, and attentive reporter will seek the newsworthy story and provide the necessary context. Listen to the speaker, observe your surroundings, discern what is significant. Your writing will benefit and your editor and readers will appreciate it. Now that you are equipped to prepare for, listen to, and write about a speech, apply the concepts to this case study. This event took place at Malone College in Canton, Ohio, on March 23, 2007. You are a reporter dispatched to cover this announcement and you have just received a press release. Take a moment to read the release.

STREIT APPOINTED PRESIDENT-ELECT AT MALONE COLLEGE

[DES: Pls. set all that follows before next heading as a quotation] Canton, OH. March 23, 2007. Malone College announced today at special meetings of the trustees, faculty, and staff that Gary Streit, Ph.D. has accepted the position of president of Malone College. Dr. Streit (pronounced "Strite") will assume the position on July 1, 2007, following the retirement of Ronald G. Johnson, Ph.D. on June 30. Donald Harper, chairman of the Malone College Board of Trustees and of Malone's presidential search committee, made the announcement.

Dr. Streit comes to Malone College from Olivet Nazarene University, where he served in the positions of provost, chief academic officer, and vice president for academic affairs, overseeing major institutional initiatives. A native of Winchester, Virginia, Dr. Streit is married to Marla Streit, Ed.D.; they are the parents of an adult daughter. Dr. Streit earned the A.B. degree in English from Trevecca Nazarene University (TN), the M.S. degree in education-psychology from the University of Knoxville (TN), and the Ph.D. in English education from the University of Illinois.

As Olivet's vice president for academic affairs for the past 15 years, his credentials are impressive. Under his leadership, the percentage of doctorally-prepared faculty increased from 39% to nearly 80%; masters' degree programs increased in number from 2 to 14; a first doctoral program, the doctor of education degree, received approval by the Higher Learning Commission; and total enrollment grew from 1,700 in 1991 to 4,500 in 2006.

In his own words, a college president must "'get it' when it comes to an understanding of how critical it is that an institution's academic muscle must ever be toned and fit and must be ever vigilant in keeping the academic program relevant." According to Dr. Streit, the president "must be able to inspire, motivate, and then lead all of the institution's stakeholders toward a clearer understanding of what it is that we need to continually learn, unlearn, and relearn about ourselves and our institution in order to maintain viability in these ever-challenging times." Dr. Streit continued, "I have known about Malone College throughout my career and am familiar with its solid reputation. Malone College has been laying tremendous foundational work for some time. Especially noteworthy are the past 13 years of sustained growth and development under Dr. Johnson's leadership. I believe that Malone embraces the heart of what Christian higher education is, and also embraces growth, change, and all that makes Christian higher education relevant in 2007—how we address and equip *this* generation as they go on to serve 'Christ's Kingdom First.'"

Described as a high energy, "outside-the-box" thinker, Dr. Streit believes that clarity of mission is critical as any institution of higher education continues to preserve its soul while, at the same time, reinvents itself to address the educational needs of succeeding generations.

Dr. Streit was selected from a field of 30 highly qualified candidates in a national search that began in the fall of 2006, conducted by the firm of People Management, Inc. under the direction of Rob Stevenson and Thomas W. Thomas, Ph.D. On Friday, March 9, the search committee agreed to recommend a candidate to the executive committee of Malone's Board of Trustees at a special session called for Wednesday, March 21st, as well as a specially called Trustees meeting of the full Board earlier today, March 23rd.

According to retiring President Ronald G. Johnson, Ph.D., "I want to express my sincerest thanks to Don Harper and the members of the presidential search committee for their tireless and excellent work. Secondly, I wish to express my strong support for the recommended candidate. Gary and I served on a number of CCCU (Council for Christian Colleges and Universities) and CIC (Council of Independent Colleges) panels during my early years as provost, but I had not worked with him in the intervening years. After renewing my friendship with him and meeting his wife, I believe God has directed Malone to a talented and experienced candidate and spouse, both of whom clearly have exceptional people skills because of their sincere concern for others. They will represent the College extremely well with each of its various publics."

Step One: Assess the Information

Begin by highlighting the information you find newsworthy or interesting. What questions do you have after reading the release? What do you believe your readers would want to know? Where might you begin to research for independent information?

Ask yourself which news values are at work. The story is timely since the announcement is being made "today." Selecting a new college president is significant to a community because colleges are often major employers and have economic impact on a region. Do you perceive any conflict in this announcement? From the press release you gather that the college's focus is on the new president's qualifications for the job and plans for the future. What is your focus?

Ask yourself if there are any references that you should clarify. What potential biases do you bring to this story that you should consider? Are you familiar with this institution, a student, or faculty member? There are many unanswered questions and you haven't even arrived at the press conference.

Step Two: Attend the Event

Imagine that you are at the event and hearing a speech that introduces the new university president to the public. Pay attention to the purpose, structure, and language of the speech. Note specific phrases you may want to quote directly. As you've learned, observation is critical to providing an accurate description of the scene. However, for this case study you are reading a transcript and are unable to observe the context, surroundings, and reactions. Parentheses have been added to indicate when the audience laughed or applauded. In a real situation you would have observed that there were approximately two hundred people present in a performing arts hall to hear the speech and roughly fifteen people at the press conference in a classroom space. Now read the speech.

The Speech

The following was presented by Dr. Gary Streit.

"Thank you. Please be seated. You will be very happy to hear that on this Friday afternoon I have no prepared remarks. (audience laughter)

"Let me introduce Marla to you, Dr. Marla Streit. What can I say? I could say many things, but the best job the search committee did without really knowing it was recruiting Marla to come to Malone College. Actually, this morning while the board of trustees was in the business of electing me, Marla was in the side room grading papers. She is a professor in the school of education at Olivet (Nazarene University). She didn't want to waste any time since she was missing a day of classes. That tells you something about Marla Streit. Marla, do you want to say anything?

(Marla Streit) "We are just glad to be here. We believe we are in God's will. This is my fourth trip here and I was telling the folks at lunch that every time I feel more comfortable here and more at home. We have spent some time talking to some of you, to students, to people in restaurants downtown and being at church on Sunday.

We just want you to know that we feel at home here and are looking forward to the days ahead."

"My journey to Malone College began when I was 15 years of age. It began on a Sunday night in a little mission church in Winchester, Virginia, when I accepted Christ as my personal savior. It was in a very unlikely spot because the church was a mission church. The pastor and those wonderful people, few in number, decided they were going to rent a facility until they were able to build a church building. Well, they rented the chapel of a funeral home. So I committed my life to Christ in the Jones Funeral Home of Winchester, Virginia. (some laughter) That young pastor and his wife began talking to me even then about Christian higher education. They began to mentor me, took me and other teenagers hundreds of miles away to visit a Christian college. There I met Marla. There I made decisions about my career, about my profession.

"We spent most of our working lives in Christian higher education. I am converted! You don't need to convert me about what we can do in these kinds of institutions. And you don't need to convert me about Malone College, because your reputation precedes you. Over the years Malone—the Malone family—is one of those particular institutions I've been interested in because of the great leaders I have known from here. About the time I became a chief academic officer, Dr. Ron Johnson became Malone's president. He mentored me in my early days as a dean. I have watched and admired his work here at Malone. I've known Malone faculty and staff over the years and I know what this institution is about. Over the last several months I've gotten to know you much better. But it is only the search committee members I have really gotten to shake hands with, talked with, and prayed with. We are so looking forward to getting to know the faculty, administration, and students.

"As we start this next chapter of Malone College together, I'm going to be engaging you in conversations in meaningful ways so that we, as a community, can feel good about the future, building on the bedrock that has been so ably placed before us. Look around you, look around this campus. We drink from wells today, do we not, that we did not dig? I'm reminded of that as I sat in the president's dining room this morning and looked at the portraits around the room. It is a daunting responsibility, for this institution now rests with us.

"I want you to know I am really excited about that. I'm thinking of the Philippians scripture today, 'forgetting those things which are behind.' And we dare not! I'm going to wrestle with the apostle Paul a bit here. I do not want to forget those things which are behind in terms of this institution's development. But I want you to know how excited Marla and I are in reaching forward to those things which are before, as we seek the mark, the prize, the high calling of God through Christ Jesus our Lord. These are going to be interesting days of transition for all of us. And I covet your prayers as we pray for you that God will bless these days of transition and bless Malone College in its next chapter of development. Looking forward to getting better acquainted with each and every one of you. Thank you."

Although the speaker said he had "no prepared remarks," the speech follows classic construction. Did you notice that the introduction begins with a humorous line? Although the primary purpose of the speech is to inform, his comment on the Friday afternoon was a lighthearted way to begin an informal address to college employees.

Following an introduction, the body of the speech then progresses chronologically with "my journey began when I was 15 years of age." He continues through his experiences to the present appointment and concludes by expressing enthusiasm in the future. Although this flow of information is easy to follow as a speech, remember that news stories usually evolve differently.

After hearing the speech, you should have additional questions. Stop to make your list and then continue with this case study by reading the question-and-answer session of the press conference.

The Press Conference

Following an introduction, Dr. Streit made the following opening remarks:

> We are privileged and humbled to be here, Marla and I. It has been an interesting journey and I must say it is good to have the search over. (audience laughter) I have been involved in Christian higher education for a long time and early in my career, Malone College was one of those institutions I had heard about. I knew about it by reputation. Malone is a member of the Council of Christian Colleges and Universities, those institutions that are Christian in their outlook and that work to integrate the best of faith with the best of learning. As we sit here today we feel honored to be called to this assignment and anticipate with great excitement the next chapter that we will be a part of at Malone College.

Reporters' Questions

1. What do you see for the future of the college? Where would you like to take it from this point?

   "The first responsible action of a new administrator is to become well informed and well acquainted with the thinking of the people. Immediately in my work, I want to engage this community and have very serious conversations about the present and certainly the future. My impression is that Malone College, because of the solid leadership of Dr. Ron Johnson and his predecessors, is poised for incredibly exciting days of growth and development both quantitatively and qualitatively. For example, I'm reminded of the Great Commission. This college is founded on Biblical concepts and precepts. The Great Commission is to Judea, Samaria, and the outermost parts. So what message? What mission for Malone? What are the implications to this campus, this community, this region, and our world? I believe that any Christian college worth its salt is in the business of creating leadership for the next generation as they become salt and light the world so desperately needs that Malone College can provide."

2. The press release says you are an out-of-the-box thinker. Can you give an example of what this means and how it will apply to Malone?

    "I think they called someone and that person described me that way. (audience laughter) That's okay—I love that. Out-of-the-box thinking is any time you look at problems and situations through different lenses, not just doing the same old, same old or the classic textbook way to address this or that. I'm all about looking at organization structures and asking if form follows function. I'm always interested in finding a better way. Dynamic, out-of-the-box institutions are those that look for ways to expand their mission outside the typical boundaries."

3. I understand you were offered the presidency by a college in Kansas but declined and you stayed at your current school. What made you decide to leave now and come to Malone?

    "I felt like a bride three-quarters of the way down the aisle and very quickly we're going to be married. Before I say 'I do,' I have a few questions. A year ago I was offered the presidency at another fine institution, but at that point I realized the mission of that institution was really not where my heart was. That is not a negative in any way, but to be a leader at any institution, there has to be compatibility and fit. And that's the difference between that situation and this one."

4. Why did Malone choose Dr. Streit? (addressed to Donald Harper)

    "As he just said, it was about finding the person with the right fit. We interviewed several candidates, and Dr. Streit fits with Malone College."

5. Every institution has its own culture and subcultures. How do you plan to integrate into Malone's community, especially with students?

    "Any wise person pays great attention to culture and gets to know the culture. I grew up in the Shenandoah Valley of Virginia. Marla is a North Carolinian. We met in Tennessee. We lived in Illinois. These places are geographically and culturally different, and we've loved all those places. We're interested in culture. A Christian college is a community of people, blended faith traditions and regions brought together in residence halls, chapels, and classrooms. We bring ourselves, with no plan to impose. We want to get to know you."

6. What one or two things do you want to say to students if they have questions about the transition?

    "We're thrilled to be here. Relax and enjoy the journey with us."

Step Three: Ask Questions

Reporters only asked six questions at the press conference. Did they ask one of yours? Was anything missed?

The first question is straightforward in asking about the future of the college. This reporter knows that proximity is an important news value. Readers want to know if the local school will grow, bringing more jobs and more students to boost the economy. What additional information is provided in the answer? Can you think of a follow-up question that could have been asked?

The second question uses language directly from the press release. It is obvious that the reporter found one sentence unusual or interesting enough to need clarification. Had you highlighted this same phrase?

Would it surprise you to learn that the third question was asked by a *student* reporter from the college newspaper? The news that Dr. Streit declined the presidency at another college was not mentioned in the press release or the speech. Where do you suppose the student gathered this information? Preparation and research are apparent. Although other reporters may not have known to ask this question, the information was given in a public forum and is open for all to use. Wise reporters take notes on all the questions, not just the ones they ask.

Following a press conference, reporters may have an opportunity to conduct individual interviews. If that is the case, and you have a "scoop" you don't want shared with other reporters, plan to ask your question after the event. If you aren't sure you'll have a private interview, it may be better to ask a good question and share the resulting information with other reporters than to take the risk.

Step Four: Assemble the Story

Here's how *The Repository*, of Canton, Ohio, reported the story on March 24, 2007. Reprinted with permission.

MALONE'S NEW BOSS MARRIED TO JOB

By Benjamin Duer, staff writer

CANTON Gary W. Streit is a happily married man. So, what would possess him to run off and tie the knot a second time?

He fell in love, of course.

Donald Harper, chairman of the Malone College board of trustees, introduced Streit, 61, as the Christian school's new president on Friday.

"I think you have to fall in love and get married to do this job," Streit said.

Streit will become the school's 13th president when he begins his term July 1. He replaces Ronald G. Johnson, who will retire June 30.

Streit comes from Olivet Nazarene University, where he has held a number of posts, including provost and vice president of academic affairs. Olivet is a private, Christian, liberal arts college in Bourbonnais, Ill.

Streit was selected from a field of 30 candidates in a national search.

MAKING THE COMMITMENT

In Malone, Streit sees the right situation for himself and his wife, Marla. He believes in the college's mission.

That didn't stop him from making Malone's executive committee nervous. Before accepting the job, Streit recalled telling the committee: "I feel like a bride who is three-quarters down the aisle and very quickly we're going to get married."

He had some questions, he explained, "Before I say, I do," he needed some answers.

To Streit, falling in love with a college means that both sides share the same beliefs. He didn't find a connection in Kansas where he declined a job offer. He found it in Malone.

Streit now hopes to use the same "outside-the-box" thinking that helped him win the Malone job.

He'll always ask, "Is there a better way?" he said, to improve educational opportunities at Malone.

For example, Streit said Olivet offered international classes in Hong Kong. He sees similar potential at Malone, which offers few international opportunities—trips abroad and a student teaching program in Guatemala.

Students can expect Streit and his wife at college events. If you run into them on campus, don't be afraid to shake their hands. They want to meet you.

"Relax. Enjoy the journey with us," Streit said.

"I believe God has directed Malone to a talented and experienced candidate and spouse, both of whom clearly have exceptional people skills," Johnson said in a prepared statement.

Streit praised Johnson, saying he would inherit a school with a "wonderful, stable environment."

The writer for *The Repository* uses an unconventional lead, likening a college presidency to a marriage. That theme continues when the declined offer from another college is referenced. This story also mentions international expansion, a topic of interest to the local community. This story shows how a speech is the beginning and not the end of all a reporter will need to know in reporting a speech. If you're asked to cover a speech, remember that **responsible reporters prepare, listen, observe, question, write, edit. Repeat.**

Covering Meetings

LISA PECOT-HEBERT

There are several types of meetings that beginning reporters will be asked to cover. On Monday you could be covering a school board meeting, Tuesday a legislative round table, and Wednesday a town hall forum. While these meetings may differ in content, they can all be covered in a similar manner. The process includes: premeeting preparation (*before*), the meeting itself (*during*), and postmeeting write-up (*after*). The guidelines in each section should be used as a tool to help you write a comprehensive story about any and all types of meetings.

Premeeting Preparation

It is important to conduct research *before* you attend a meeting. Depending on your deadline, this may be difficult to do, but it is imperative that you get a handle on the issues that will be discussed prior to the start of the meeting. Begin by finding out who is calling the meeting to order. In other words, is it a civil rights organization, is it the local water authority, is it the school board? Once you find out who is running the meeting, contact the head of that organization and get a copy of the meeting agenda beforehand. Remember that **sunshine laws** require that you be given access to meetings where the public's business will be discussed. An agenda will identify the key players and will help you decide whom to interview. In addition, because you have names and titles, you can begin interviewing some of these people before the meeting takes place. That way if you run out of time after the meeting or people start leaving after the meeting, you will already have some quotes and background for the story. Don't hesitate to interview sources at this time or ask for names and phone numbers of other key players involved in the meeting.

Besides knowing the time the meeting is going to take place, you should also be aware of the circumstances surrounding the time of the meeting. For example, if a controversial issue is being discussed at a local school board meeting (like whether or not they should cut out free after-school programs) and the meeting is being held two days after the governor voted to decrease funding to all schools by 15 percent, you now have additional information to give to readers that will contextualize your local story.

In your research, you should understand why the meeting is being called. In other words, is it a routine public monthly meeting (in which case you can read the minutes from previous meetings as research), is it being called to give an update on a prior issue that was voted on at the last meeting, or is there some sort of crisis that has arisen that caused the meeting to be held (for example, several racial incidents have been reported in a Chicago suburb, so the local NAACP chapter has called a meeting to discuss a plan of action)?

By getting this information before the meeting takes place, you will have a better understanding of the circumstances surrounding the meeting, whom you will need to interview, and what will be discussed. Now you are ready to attend the meeting itself.

Covering the Meeting

Arrive at the meeting early so that you can make sure the agenda they are passing out (if they have one) matches the one you received earlier in the day or week. The agenda is a document that has the order the meeting will follow but does not always include the names of the speakers. Depending on the type of meeting, most of the scheduled speakers should have name plates in front of their seats. To ensure accuracy, use this to check the spelling of everyone's name. Also, sit in a place in the room that allows you to see everyone so that you can identify who is speaking. This way, you won't confuse who said what.

Take plenty of notes. It is better to have too much than not enough. Bringing a tape recorder can be helpful when trying to fill in quotes, but unless it is a public meeting, you may not be allowed to tape it. So, if they see you recording and ask you to turn it off, detailed notes will have to suffice. A good deal of what goes on at the meeting is not verbal. Be aware of your environment! If there is excitement or anger in the room, let that come through in your story.

Another thing you can do while at the meeting is to think about a follow-up story or feature. If the board does make a motion to suspend all funding for after-school programs, interview parents about how this decision will affect them. This might be a nice story to run the day after the meeting story or as a sidebar to the meeting story.

Postmeeting Follow-Up

Once the meeting is over, you should look over your notes and see where you need to fill in holes. Take this time to do the following:

} Talk to people and ask them to elaborate on points they made earlier.

} Make sure you have all speakers' correct titles and/or affiliations. If not, ask them.

} Get reactions from people regarding what was discussed (or not discussed) during the meeting.

} Depending on the company or organization you are covering, some may have what is commonly referred to as a "virtual pressroom." A virtual pressroom contains expanded write-ups on selected topics covered at the meeting as well as other press materials that you may not have picked up that day. If you have time and are not on a tight deadline, you should take the time to visit the virtual pressroom to see if there is anything you missed at the meeting. If a virtual pressroom is not available, some organizational meet-

SIDEBAR

ings (like the school board) may have a website that could provide valuable information on the history of the organization you are covering.

} Once you get back to your office, think about what other sources are needed for the story to be complete. For example, if the school board decision was made in light of the governor pulling funds from the school system, call the governor's office and try to get a quote from a spokesperson. It is important to remember that you are not restricted to reporting only what happened at the meeting. If additional information is needed to contextualize your story for readers, take the time to gather it. If you are on a tight deadline, a follow-up story the next day on government cutbacks and how they are affecting the school system would be another way to get the complete story out.

These tips should help when you cover your first couple of meetings. Remember that as a reporter you are writing for readers. So when thinking about how you start your story, ask yourself why readers should care about this story and how it impacts them. Here are two examples of meetings I covered that might be similar to meetings that many beginning reporters will be asked to cover.

Meeting Scenario #1

Reporters are sometimes asked to cover stories that require knowledge of a particular subject. I was once assigned to cover a meeting of the American Association of Physicists. A press release sent by the organization's public relations department mentioned a guest speaker who was going to discuss a breakthrough therapeutic device for cancer. There were only two hours before the meeting began, and I did not have a science or medical background. There are a few steps beginning reporters can take to ensure they'll be better prepared to properly cover such a meeting and provide readers with news worth knowing.

You can go to the organization's website and look up information on the speaker. Double check the spelling of his name and his background. Research the organization. Find out information on its history and purpose.

Next, do research on the speaker's specialization. Look into some of the existing cancer treatment techniques to get acquainted with medical terminology. Familiarize yourself with key terms, print out their definitions, and bring them to the meeting. This can serve as a reference sheet when you're at the meeting or preparing to ask questions. Always remember that **it is your job as a reporter to take complicated situations and make them into understandable stories!** Your research will allow you to ask sensible follow-up questions after the meeting is over that may prove important to your readers. Once the interview ends, look for additional handouts on site. You'll never know what you need. Better to have it than not. If you take this step-by-step approach, you'll be able to make your deadline and write a comprehensive story about a difficult subject. This will even be true when you're reporting complicated stories under tight deadline pressures.

Meeting Scenario #2

Some meetings are weekly or monthly, so if you are assigned to a beat, you usually know when they are going to take place and are familiar with the meeting participants. While the previous example highlighted the importance of advance research, this scenario will highlight how postmeeting research can be crucial to your story.

I remember one assignment to cover meetings of a local water authority that were held on the third Thursday of the month. While covering the water authority might not seem like it would be newsworthy, you'd be surprised. There were many stories that flowed from this assignment. Look at it this way: a meeting may not always be newsworthy, but what you learn at the meeting may be!

During one particular water meeting, the agenda included a report from the general manager and his discussion of the approved budget for that particular year. I did not realize it at the time of the meeting, but his report would be an important part of a series of stories that I would later write. The other point the general manager discussed that night was the drought conditions the county faced. After the meeting, I went to the water authority website and looked up old meeting minutes that told me the budget allotments from the previous year. I noticed that there was an increase of about $10,000 from the previous year and wanted to know why. In a phone conversation with the general manager I learned that increasing costs came from attempts to combat the drought and that the county faced mandatory water restrictions if the drought continued. Research showed that the last time the county was under a drought watch the human and economic toll had been high. My editor needed to know that this story was more than an update on the county water system, but was an important news story that had the potential for several follow-up stories.

Sure enough, subsequent stories detailed the dangers of a drought and what would happen if we did not get rain in the next few weeks. The impact on the community included the possibility of mandatory water rations, the environmental impact the drought would have on the county, the devastation of the local farming community, and a potential steep spike in prices of store-bought fruits and vegetables. A final feature story focused on a farming family that was thinking about selling off their eighty-year-old family farm to try and cover the cost of irrigating their crops.

You now see how postmeeting research can lead to other related stories that can be useful to your readers. So, the next time your editor asks you to report on a meeting, go prepared, and be prepared to dig deep for meaning after the meeting. Very often you will find news really worth knowing.

Reporting Religion and Moral Issues

ARI L. GOLDMAN

The mere mention of faith and religion might inspire images of serene churches, sleep-inducing sermons, and boring Sunday school classes. Not much fun or excitement or news there. Nevertheless, the field of religion writing has emerged in the last quarter century as a vibrant and major beat in American news outlets. Many newspapers have "Faith" sections, *Religion and Ethics Newsweekly* is a popular show on PBS, and Internet websites about religion, such as beliefnet.com, have proliferated. And religion is increasingly the subject of documentaries and front-page stories.

The reasons for so much news about religion are many. For one thing, churches have done everything to jazz up their services, using everything from hip-hop music to youthful preachers to grow their audience. On the national level, evangelical Christians, a group widely supportive of President George W. Bush, have emerged as a major force in American politics. Christian evangelicals are riding the crest of a wave of political influence that goes back to the election of Ronald Reagan as president in 1980. The role of religion and moral issues in politics and society has been on the rise ever since. Campaign 2008 was filled with stories about Rev. Jeremiah Wright, the controversial pastor who led the church long attended by Democratic presidential nominee Barack Obama.

In the late 1980s, the world saw the collapse of the Soviet Union, whose Communist ideology suppressed and in many cases outlawed religion. With the collapse of the Soviet bloc, religion emerged as a new force in lands once dominated by atheism. In the 1990s, regional conflicts around the world, from Bosnia to Northern Ireland to Israel, were played out against the backdrop of religious faith. Everywhere, it seemed, people were fighting and dying in the name of religion.

On the domestic level, the pedophilia scandal of the Roman Catholic Church led to the arrest of predatory priests and the resignation of their bishops. The pedophilia scandal shed new light on the responsibilities of all religious institutions to protect children in their care.

The destructive power of religion on the world scene was unleashed in a whole new way on September 11, 2001, with the terror attack on the World Trade Center in New York and the Pentagon in Washington. And the violence in the name of God hasn't stopped, as we've seen on the streets of Bali, London, Baghdad, and Jerusalem.

Religion news isn't just about the local church supper anymore. It is a major issue in our society, and a good reporter has to be smart about it. **Many major contemporary issues have profoundly religious and moral dimensions.** You'll find people motivated by their religious beliefs on both sides of issues like gay marriage, abortion, homelessness, and the death penalty. And America is changing right in front of our eyes. Where a Christian church and a Jewish synagogue once stood are now Muslim mosques, Buddhist temples, and Hindu ashrams.

What is the best way to approach a religion story?

As with coverage of all stories, religion reporting requires an open mind. Achieving an open mind when it comes to religion is often more of a challenge than being open-minded about a story about the fire department or city hall. Much of our religious knowledge is conveyed to us as absolutes. Our faith is right, and the others are wrong, we are told. It is often difficult for the believer in one faith to see the validity, let alone the beauty, of another faith.

One of the greatest challenges facing journalists today is covering Islam. On the world stage, Islam is often portrayed as a violent and fundamentalist faith. It is important, however, to realize that every faith has its own extremist wings. A responsible reporter will search out a variety of voices about Islam. This includes the many moderate voices that are often overlooked. In 1997, the Pulitzer Prize for feature writing went to Andrea Elliott of the **New York Times** for her series "An Imam in America." Elliott totally immersed herself in the Muslim community in New York and showed the complexity of life for American Muslims. She demonstrated that lives lived day to day by most Muslims—people who care about making a living, finding a spouse, getting an education, connecting to a community— were a far cry from the stereotypes of Muslim fundamentalists abroad.

What I ask of my students is to try to view each religion from the perspective of the believer. That often means leaving your own faith at the door of the church or the mosque or the temple. Talk to the adherents of the faith. Try to walk in their shoes (or bare feet). Try to experience their music and their mysteries.

This is not easily done, but the benefits can make for very rich journalism. Religion writing gives you the opportunity to go beyond people's actions and write about their feelings and emotions. Writing about faith gives you the opportunity to write about things that sometimes make journalists uncomfortable. Perhaps this is why religion makes some editors uneasy. Editors want to know the bottom line: Who won? Who lost? What was the score? How much will it cost? What's going to happen next? These questions are particularly difficult to answer when it comes to religion. A good religion writer can tell you what someone believes and how that belief moves them to action. A good religion writer can tell you what was said when the proponents of different religions came together. He or she can describe the religion's context, its history, and its theology. But he or she cannot tell you who was right and who was wrong or who won and who lost. The big religious questions do not have easy answers.

As in any reporting task, it is essential not to make assumptions when writing about religion. The temptation is particularly great when it comes to religion, but resist. A wafer in a Catholic service means something different than a wafer in a Protestant service. And wine in a Christian service is different than wine in a Jewish service. One sacred space might require you to take off your hat, another might require that you put one on. One might want you to go barefoot, another might require you to turn your cell phone off, another might tell you to leave your notebook and pencil at the door.

Ask the people around you—the believers, the regulars—for guidance. Religion and deeply held moral beliefs can be complex and confusing, but understanding them is a vital tool in understanding today's world.

How Is the News Written?

9

Writing the Lead

BRUCE J. EVENSEN

The most important part of any story is how you start it. Punch lines are wasted on people who aren't listening. Three in four people who start your story won't finish it. The majority of them will bail before they finish the first paragraph. That's why **the first paragraph is the most important in journalism.** It gives readers and listeners the news they need to know and gives it to them in a way they'll easily understand. Most Americans have seen thousands of stories before they get to yours. They know what to expect. You frustrate their legitimate expectations at your peril. Citizens want to know the news and how it affects them. So stories are constructed to lead with the most recent, relevant details of the story. Relevance is measured by the greatest effect on the greatest number. Delivering on that obligation is what guides the start of a responsible reporter's story.

The Five W's

There are six common elements that should appear in the first two sentences of every hard story a journalist writes. These elements are the "who," "what," "when," "where," "why," and "how" of the story. If readers and listeners haven't found all of these in the first forty to fifty words of your story, they will begin to wonder why. And while they are puzzling over what the story doesn't have, they'll be unable to fully understand what you have reported. So make it a point to write who, what, when, where, why, and how on a scratch pad for each story as you are organizing your information. This will help you think about the story and what your reader or listener need it to say. Beginning journalists should practice placing at least three or four of these elements in the first sentence of their stories. The remaining two or three elements can be incorporated into the second sentence. These should be simple declarative sentences of twenty to twenty-five words at most. Simple declarative sentences begin with nouns that act on verbs and are often followed by direct objectives or prepositional phrases.

Beginning journalists often have a hard time under tight deadline because they don't know what to say and how to say it when starting their stories. It helps having a list of six common elements that fit every hard news lead they'll ever write. Avoid syntax that muffles meaning. These can often be found in compound sentences that typically join two separate ideas with an "and" or "but" or "if." If that's your temptation don't do it. You will be guilty of putting two pounds of baloney in a one-pound bag. The bag bursts because it can't contain the volume. Similarly, your sentence struggles because two ideas that should be separated are stuck together. Remember to write with the reader in mind. Don't make his or her job more difficult than it already is. The job of the responsible reporter in covering breaking news is often to tell what happened, to whom it happened, why it happened, when and where it happened, and how it happened. Telling your reader and listener these things is a major assignment in fulfilling the social responsibility of the press.

Every lead must pass the "so-what" test. Readers must be made immediately aware that staying with your story is worth their time and attention. They're under no obligation to keep reading. The obligation and opportunity are yours. Make sure the most recent, relevant detail of the story leads the story. Bait your hook with leads that contain news worth knowing. Don't wind up for the pitch. Pitch. Get to it. Deliver. Citizens have limited time and won't let you waste it.

Each sentence should have a single idea behind it, and each sentence of every paragraph should relate to every other sentence in that paragraph. Write in a conversational style. Say "says" and not "according to." Don't use pronouns such as "he," "she," "it," "they," or "them" in news copy, unless these words are part of a direct quotation. The reporter should get into the habit of repeating the proper noun. That will make the reference clear. Be careful about adjectives and adverbs. These are words that express personal opinions. Stories are filled with personal opinions of those you cite. Readers should know their views but not yours. Individuals reading or watching news stories should never know how a reporter feels about the story. That's not news. It's views. Remember that **lack of objectivity is the number-one thing that citizens say irritates them about news reporters.** Attribute information. Say who says so. This will ensure that your readers know whose opinions they're reading.

Searching for Significance

Know what's really relevant to the reader or listener. On February 7, 2000, the Chicago office for Associated Press reported that "two small planes collided over a hospital parking lot Tuesday, killing three people and sending one plane into the roof of a hospital." The second sentence stated: "Windows blew out of the top floor of Midwestern Regional Medical Center as one plane crashed onto the roof and crumpled." Then readers were told that "the two people on the plane, a Zlin, were killed." It wasn't until the story's fourth sentence that the AP reported that "the Zlin was co-owned by Bob Collins, a popular morning radio personality for WGN-AM." AP's fifth sentence said: "He was feared dead, the station said." Collins had in fact perished in the crash. His early-morning radio show was one of the most popular in the Midwest and could be heard across thirty-eight states. Certainly, the possibility of his death needed to be incorporated into a lead that might have said: "WGN radio personality Bob Collins is one of three persons feared killed following the collision of two planes over a Chicago-area hospital." Individuals who might have only passing interest in the story of three people who were killed when two planes collided might have a substantial interest in a story in which a well-known radio personality was one of the three who died.

A similar search for significance might have improved a lead that appeared in a Gary, Indiana, daily on November 24, 2006. Readers are told, "as shoppers in Hammond prepared to take advantage of Black Friday sales, clouds of black smoke billowed from the Jupiter Aluminum Plant, engulfing the area skyline." It is not until the third sentence of the story that readers learn that "no one was injured" in the blaze. The eighth sentence quotes Hammond's mayor as saying "there was great concern" that combustible materials at the plant might have set off a dangerous blaze. The thirteenth sentence tells the reader that forty workers were in the plant at the time of the fire. That same sentence reports that 143 employees work in the building. The concern of union officials that these workers "might be out of a job for an extended amount of time, right before Christmas," was reported in the fourteenth sentence. The story is about more than curiosity caused by shoppers who saw smoke in the sky. It's about forty people escaping a fire that burned for several hours and threatened the surrounding neighborhood. The report is also about 143 employees who may be out of a job as a result. These are the most recent, relevant details of a story that should have started: "Forty employees escaped injury and 143 workers may be out of a job following a dangerous fire that gutted the Jupiter Aluminum Plant in Hammond this morning." The who, what, when, and where are in the lead. A second sentence will focus on how the blaze began, why it got started, and why city officials said it was so serious. The second-day story would focus on the fire investigation and what company officials say about those plant workers affected by the fire. Follow-up stories might focus on the plant's safety record and any potential hazards to the neighboring community.

Covering Breaking News

Let's take what you've learned about writing a lead and apply it. This story begins in the early-morning hours. Imagine you are commuting on a bypass south of a city on your way to work. It's late winter and a freezing rain is falling. It's a quarter past six in the morning. There's a major traffic tie-up as you travel westbound on U.S. Highway 20. You pull over to the shoulder of the road and walk in the direction of a bridge where you see a series of emergency lights flashing. You walk toward the lights. In the dimness of early morning, whom would you be looking to talk to? Generally, when emergency vehicles arrive at a breaking news scene you'll find city police or sheriff's deputies. In this case, the person in charge was a Winnebago County sheriff's deputy. Let's say his name is Tony Taylor. Before you ask him a question, be sure you properly spell his name in your notes. Beginning journalists sometimes don't know what to ask when arriving at an accident scene. It's best to be brief and to the point. Ask Taylor what happened. Have him tell his story. In this case, however, the news source didn't say a thing, but instead pointed. You look at where he was pointing and in the poor light see the outlines of a tow truck. You're surprised you hadn't seen it before. You figure there was so little light and you were so determined to find the guy in charge in the midst of a gaggle of people you had missed something pretty obvious. It's a good idea before you charge in to ask your first question to carefully observe an accident scene or a breaking crime scene. You'll be amazed at what you miss if you don't.

As you cut through the crowd of emergency personnel at the top of the Rock River Bridge, you can finally see the wrecker better and notice that a hook from the long arm of its crane is fastened under the rear bumper of what appears to be a late-model sports car. The car is completely lifted off the roadway and is pointed headlights down. You walk around the front of the car to look at the driver's side. There, quite abruptly, you are within a few feet of the upper half of a woman's torso. Her head, shoulders, and arms dangle through a half-opened driver's window and blow about eerily in the wind. The rest of the victim remains inside a car that shows little evidence of damage beyond a dent in the driver's door. It appears to be a young woman, maybe in her early thirties. It's dark and hard to tell. The body appears to be turning an ashen blue.

You ask Taylor what had happened. He tells you, "Police received a call around two this morning from a motorist who reported that a car going westbound on U.S. Highway 20 at a high rate of speed had swerved off the roadway, plunged down an embankment, and landed in the Rock River."

You could ask Taylor a series of follow-up questions, but he is too busy directing recovery operations to give you any more time. On the basis of what little he said, how can you follow up? There appears to be an eyewitness to the accident. By asking police at the scene, you find that the witness is still at the accident site. The witness is Don Hoak. Since the accident occurred at two in the morning, the viewer might be wondering why Hoak was driving at that hour. He tells you that he is a traveling salesman and was driving home, "When I saw out of my rear-view mirror a car approaching at a dangerous speed.

It was swerving all over the roadway. I slowed down and pulled to the side of the road for fear I'd be hit. The car sped past, cut diagonally in front of me, and plunged down an embankment before crashing into the river."

You ask what Hoak did next.

"I called 911," he tells you, "and rushed down to the water's edge." He adds, "The car was completely submerged, but in the darkness I could see its headlights under the water." You ask if Hoak attempted to rescue the motorist. He answers, "I tried, but there was nothing I could do. The water was freezing cold."

Following Up

You're unable to get any more information at the accident scene. You get back into your car and slowly head for the office, thinking through the missing pieces to this puzzle. You won't be filing your story until a late-afternoon news block and realize there are major parts of the story that remain unanswered. The "who" of the story is obviously missing. The identity of the victim will typically come from the county coroner's office after next of kin have been identified. In this case, it's 1:45 in the afternoon when Winnebago County coroner Elvin Tappe confirms that the dead woman is a thirty-one-year-old Rockford woman named Jody Davis. You need an address. It's 1321 Alpine Drive in Rockford, Illinois. What else do you need to know about this woman and her death? Think back to the accident scene. Remember what you saw when you walked around the wrecker and noticed the driver's side of the car. The car didn't seem badly damaged. Tappe tells you Davis didn't die from injuries suffered in the accident but drowned. You wonder why she was unable to escape the wreck, and he tells you the force of the collision trapped the victim's legs under the dashboard.

Think through what the eyewitness to the accident told you. A car approached him at a high speed and was weaving over the roadway. This happened at two in the morning. You ask whether Davis was drunk at the time of the crash. Tappe says toxicology tests will come back later in the day. You ask what is known of the victim. Is she married? Does she have a family? Where does she work? Tappe reports that Davis was married and the mother of three children, Bill, age eight, Hillary, age four, and Chelsea, who is nine months old. An employee identification card in the victim's personal effects confirms that she worked at Sundstrand Corporation, a major aeronautical employer in the Rockford area.

Over the next hour and a half you confirm that Jim and Jody Davis lived at 1321 Alpine Drive. You call the residence, hoping to understand a major part of the story that remains unclear. You know what happened and to whom it happened. You know when and where the accident took place. You even have an explanation of how the victim became trapped inside the vehicle. What remains unclear is why a young mother of three was driving her car so erratically at two in the morning. There is no answer at the victim's home to help you answer this question. A beginning journalist might wonder whether it is a proper job for a responsible reporter to be poking around a victim's home asking intrusive questions that are none of anyone's business but the family's. This is a perfectly reasonable objection. And if the victim had died at home the objection would be decisive. When, however, there is public behavior that endangers others, the public has a right to know about it. This is the public interest standard that should always be weighed against the right to privacy. The right to privacy is the right to be left alone. The reporter must be aware of responsibilities to both the public and the people he or she is reporting on. In this case, a call to the coroner at 3:15 confirms that Davis was legally intoxicated at the time of the crash.

You have forty-five minutes before your story airs, and you have a critical decision to make. Your story has to answer each of the major questions that your audience might reasonably bring to this story. Many of your viewers might wonder how it could happen and who might have been at fault for allowing a mother of three to be driving drunk at two in the morning in hazardous weather conditions. The issue is not only the poor judgment of the victim but perhaps the irresponsibility of others. You call the victim's home again, and again there's no answer. You don't have time to drive to the residence. You hurriedly look through your notes. There's barely half an hour before air time now. You notice that the victim worked at Sundstrand, so you call there. You discover the division in which she worked and are directed toward a friend of hers. Kerry Wood describes herself as Davis's "best friend." She is aware of Davis's death. It had been reported on Rockford radio within the hour. Wood is very upset. You ask when was the last time she saw her friend. She tells you it was "around midnight. We went out for a couple of drinks." You ask whether Davis seemed distressed. Angrily, Wood interrupts, "She was very depressed! She threatened to kill herself. It was that no-good husband of hers. He'd been running around on her. It's that bum's fault! I hope he fries!"

It's now 3:40, twenty minutes until your local news block goes on the air. The show's news director is going to lead with your accident report. You take one last crack at contacting Davis's husband or a member of the family, and again, there is no answer. You're stuck with what you have, which is actually quite a lot. You quickly tick off the who, what, when, where, why, and how of the story. Jody Davis died when her car went into the Rock River. But who's Jody Davis? She's a mother of three. Should you say "Jody Davis" or "mother of three" in the lead? Who's "Jody Davis"? She's a "mother of three." So, "mother of three" communicates more information than "Jody Davis." All right, so should you write, "A Rockford mother of three died when her car plunged into the Rock River"? It's true but misleading. She didn't die from the accident. She drowned as a result of the accident. Unless you say "drowned" in the lead, listeners will think she died from injuries she suffered in the crash. OK, there's fifteen minutes to go before air time. The lead is starting to look good. "A Rockford mother of three drowned when her car plunged into the Rock River." That's fourteen words. You can comfortably go up to twenty, maybe twenty-five words in the first sentence. So you probably can include a bit more. You have the "who" and the "what" and the "where." The "when" is easy enough. You can add it to the end of the lead. That means that now you have: "A Rockford mother of three drowned when her car plunged into the Rock River early this morning."

Thinking the Lead Through

There's now ten minutes to air, and you suddenly see a problem you hadn't considered. What do you do with the victim's friend? First of all, she and others who have followed the news during the day are already aware of Davis's death. That's not news to them. After all, Davis died at two in the morning, nearly fourteen hours ago. The lead is supposed to be the most recent, relevant detail of the story. You can't lead with the fact of Davis's death. That's old already. The radio and your online competitors have already reported it. Your competitors had reported she'd drowned, but you had information that she was legally intoxicated at the time of the crash. You check the online story of the *Rockford Register-Star*. They don't have the result of the toxicology report. So you rework the lead to update the information. You'll need to attribute it. That gives you a different start to the sentence. It reads, "The Winnebago County coroner reports a Rockford mother of three was legally intoxicated…"

"Eight minutes to air," the production assistant is yelling in your ear. "Where's the lead?"

You might reconsider why you're saying "legally intoxicated": just because that's how the coroner phrased it. So substitute something more conversational and try again. "The Winnebago County coroner reports a Rockford mother of three was drunk when she drove her car into the Rock River early this morning." You read it over to yourself. Twenty-four words. Seems to read all right.

"Six minutes," someone is saying impatiently again.

The second sentence should be a lot easier, you think. You need to say who this woman is and give some indication of why she was driving drunk at that hour in that weather.

"Five minutes," someone is saying, looking at a watch as if this were a space launch.

"Thirty-one-year-old Jody Davis," you type, "of 1321 Alpine Drive had…had…" Had what? What are you supposed to say? That her husband is a womanizing lout?

"Four minutes."

You don't know anything about the husband. You never talked to him. You only have Wood's word for it. And if she's wrong and you write it, it's defamation. And if you say she said it, and she's wrong, it's defamation.

"Three minutes."

Either way you're wrong. And the station is sued. And you're fired. But how do you account for the fact that a mother of three is out driving drunk at two in the morning in the freezing rain? How do you write the "why" when you can't be confident you have it right?

"Two minutes."

OK, OK. How about: "A friend says thirty-one-year-old Jody Davis of 1321 Alpine Drive had been having personal problems."

You hit "print." Out comes a sheet of paper with the two sentences. The copy is rushed to an anxious anchor, who ninety seconds later reads it out over the air.

As it turns out, the victim's family won't welcome media reports that Jody Davis had been driving drunk the night her car disappeared into an icy river and she drowned. It is devastating to lose a loved one, and it is humiliating to have it be known that the individual may have contributed to the tragedy by driving while drunk. They aren't much satisfied when you tell them that the responsible reporter tries to balance the privacy rights of a bereaved family and the public's right to know. In a community the size of Rockford—150,000—a drowning death is a big story. When it is combined with drinking and driving, it is bigger still, because the combination is lethal, and ran the risk that Davis might have harmed others, including the traveling motorist she nearly crashed into. While the public is entitled to these facts—these events all unfolded in public and had a tragic consequence—the public does not have the right to pry into the personal affairs of the deceased and her family. They are not entitled to hear the unsubstantiated testimony of the irate friend of the victim. Beginning journalism students need to know that they and their employer are not protected from a libel suit even if they attribute the allegations made by Wood against the husband. "Malice" is demonstrated in a libel award when the reporter shows a "reckless disregard for the truth." Telling a judge and jury that you were under deadline and couldn't get to Jim Davis to confirm Wood's account is an utterly inadequate defense. And an irresponsible one. The public is not entitled to a specific explanation for Davis's late-night conduct but is entitled to a general explanation, attributed to her friend, that Davis was "distressed." You could make the case that reporting the friend's assertion that Davis was "distressed" is all the public needs to know. There is merit in that argument. Many might wonder, however, what this ominous phrase means. "Personal issues" doesn't tell them what she was upset about, but it does indicate a fundamental truth of the story.

A colleague thinks you should have "played up" Wood's quote that Davis "intended to commit suicide." You didn't, and a responsible reporter probably shouldn't have, because there's no direct evidence that Davis tried to kill herself. In fact, there's some direct evidence that she tried to swim away once her car became submerged, but couldn't because her legs were trapped beneath the dashboard of the car. Avoid trying to be overly dramatic. When people are upset, they say all kinds of things, but that's hardly the equivalent of leaving a suicide note. Furthermore, this is a story that needs no amping up. If your viewers can't get interested in a story about a young mother of three who drowns while driving drunk, there's not much more you can do or should do to interest them in it. In fact, many people *were* interested in the story. The victim was well known in her community, and the extraordinary sadness of the event was apparent to many. It needed no sprucing up to make it more "newsworthy." Just report what you know, what you have confirmed to be true. This is what you owe your audience. They are not well served by your inventiveness nor entertained by your imagination.

As for what the sheriff's deputy reported and what the eyewitness reported, had you gone on the air immediately or filed your story online moments after the mishap, you would, of course, lead with their testimony. At the moment, it was all you had. This becomes a "what" story—a woman was killed when her car plunged into a river. However, **the further you move away from the event, the more you are required to update what is known.** In this case, we later learn that the victim drowned, we learn her identity, and we learn she was driving drunk before the crash. As each new relevant detail comes to your attention, you are pushing it toward the head of the lead. Remember, the most recent, relevant detail of the story leads. That's particularly true of stories that need to be updated over several hours. During that time, with each update, your story becomes less a "what" story and more a "why" story. This is true in your reporting of every breaking news story you'll ever report, including the accidents and disasters that are an unfortunate staple of news we all need to know.

Writing Responsible Leads

Beginning reporters might find it a bit dispiriting to be a breaking news reporter. It can make you feel like a vulture. **The worse it is for someone else, the "better" it is for you,** in the sense that the worse the news is, the bigger the story is. That is why responsible reporting requires more than an appetite to be first with the worst. That is a menu for the cynicism that one sees in so many veteran reporters. Instead, beginning journalists would do well to consider their social obligation to give citizens the news they need to know, to give them a picture of the public world, which will become for many the basis of personal decision making and communal action. The press is the only institution in American life that has a Constitutional protection to keep the government off its back. The reason is to allow reporters the freedom to gather the information of the day and to offer it to our fellow citizens as part of our daily obligation and public trust. A lead that is written well is the first important step in doing just that.

Business and Finance Reporting

EDMUND LAWLER

I recall with great clarity the moment my business writing career began. The news editor of the Chicago bureau of the Associated Press needed a reporter to cover a major announcement at the troubled Continental Illinois National Bank, the nation's seventh-largest bank. There was no one to be found on the business desk, so he turned to my side of the newsroom.

A relatively new hire in the summer of 1984, I was accustomed to covering news from the courthouses and the police stations. On the lighter side, I had recently written a well-received story on the retirement of Bozo the Clown, a longtime fixture on super station WGN-TV. I pleaded that I knew nothing about banks—or money, for that matter. My forte was cops and clowns. The news editor was unmoved.

I was soon in a cab en route to Chicago's financial district. I was about to cover what would become the largest bank failure in U.S. history. In the boardroom of the bank that afternoon I heard bank and government officials describe a mind-numbingly complicated—to me, at least—scenario by which the government would assume about 80 percent of the bank's loan portfolio. The portfolio was an ugly mess of loans gone bad due to the bank's overly aggressive lending policies and a huge batch of nonperforming loans it had bought from a failed bank in Oklahoma.

The feds feared that if Continental went down, it could unhinge the entire U.S. banking system. So it essentially nationalized Continental Illinois National Bank to ensure the stability of the nation's banking system. I listened intently and scribbled furiously in my notebook as the government and bank officials described the bailout. Afterward, I buttonholed every official in the room, desperate to get the story right. I had better, because the story was going to appear on the front page of just about every newspaper in the country. The Associated Press was and still is the world's largest news organization.

Our editors made us well aware that even **the smallest mistake in a story resonates many thousands, even millions of times over and all over the world**. My due diligence paid off. I got the story right, and I continued to get it right in the weeks ahead as I became the AP's resident expert on Continental Bank. It was an exhilarating white-knuckle ride, but I realized that business news isn't much different from the kind of general news that I had been used to covering. Granted, there are a lot more dollar signs and there's a business lingo all its own, but if you can ferret out the who, what, where, when, why, and how, you can write about business and finance.

Certainly an MBA would be helpful, but not many journalists can afford that luxury. And not all have the aptitude to study business at an advanced level. Mastering the business beat is no different from becoming an expert on criminal justice or politics or baseball. You find the right sources and listen carefully. Check and double-check every bit of information, because, like I said, it's complicated. But your story can't read like a product manual. It has to engage the readers, many of whom don't know much more about business than you do.

You need to absorb everything about the particular business discipline to which you've been assigned. If your beat is small business, for example, thoroughly read the roster of magazines targeting that segment, such as *Inc.* and *Entrepreneur.* Attend conferences and make the website of the U.S. Small Business Administration a regular stop on your daily rounds. Reading the *Wall Street Journal* every day, online or in print, must become a regular habit as well as reading the leading general business magazines such as *Business Week, Forbes,* and *Fortune.*

One of the joys of business writing is the opportunity to specialize. I became an expert on marketing, in particular business-to-business advertising in which one company touts its product or services to other businesses, not consumers. I have been writing a column for a business publication on that subject since 1990, and I have written three books on the subject. I have given more than a hundred speeches on business-to-business advertising to audiences around the country and even a few overseas. I could never have done any of that without becoming an expert on the subject, and I could not have become an expert without establishing a national network of sources who know vastly more about business-to-business advertising than I ever will.

A business reporter needs to become savvy about finding and reading the public documents that can often lend insight into the operations of a company. Publicly traded companies are required to file quarterly and annual statements of operations and financial status with the Securities Exchange Commission in Washington, D.C. The information is available online through the SEC's database, called EDGAR (www.sec.gov/edgar). The database is a rich depository of documents that include the annual (Form 10-K) and quarterly (Form 10-Q) reports on a company's financial condition.

Another valuable online resource is Hoovers (www.hoovers.com). It has information on more than 43,000 companies and 6,000 industries. Some of the information is available only through subscription. And another online resource is a company's own website. The better corporate websites include a wealth of information about a company's history, mission, executives, strategy, marketing, and its latest initiatives.

Privately held companies are just that: private. But that's not to say that their affairs don't spill onto public dockets in courthouses, state legislatures, or regulatory agencies.

Mark Twain famously said there are three kinds of lies: "lies, damned lies and statistics." There's not much business reporters can do about the first two, but a sense for the statistical can make a reporter's work more insightful and less vulnerable to corporate or government spin. Look at how long it took the Wall Street analysts, government regulators, and journalists to discover that Enron was nothing more than a house of cards. Journalists should have seen that one coming. I wish I had taken a stats class in college; I wish I had taken an accounting class in college; I wish I had taken a marketing class in college; I wish I had taken more math.

Yet I managed to become the business editor of a daily newspaper and the managing editor of a monthly business publication. I'm convinced I would have done better at both jobs had I acquired a stronger foundation of math and business classes. But it's not too late for you. Eat your broccoli: **take that math or economics class you've long been avoiding.** A certain confidence in math will allow a business writer to not only resist being spun by someone with a stronger command of the numbers, but also to translate the information into a comprehensible, approachable thread for an audience that's not necessarily savvy with numbers.

Combine that numeric confidence with curiosity—an essential characteristic in any beat—as well as doggedness, strong interviewing skills, the ability to navigate through databases and websites in search of information, and a flair for storytelling, and you've got the formula for success as a business and finance reporter.

10

Writing a Newspaper Story

MIKE CONKLIN

In January 1993, police in Palatine, Illinois, a Chicago suburb, were called to open the doors of a Brown's Fried Chicken restaurant in the wee hours of the morning and found a grizzly scene: seven employees shot to death. TV, radio, and newspaper reporters descended on the scene to relay details to their audiences, but, unlike many of their peers, who waited for announcements at the site by officials, an astute crew of journalists from the *Chicago Tribune* spread into the neighborhood.

These reporters applied old-fashioned, policelike techniques. They knocked on doors to interview anyone who might have heard anything. They also took down license plate numbers within a three-block radius, traced the numbers through the Illinois secretary of state's office, and called owners to search for any related information. As a result, they gathered additional details used in the newspaper's coverage.

Writing a newspaper story takes legwork and lots of it. Writing the story can be the easy part. The inverted pyramid with a compelling lead, nut graph material, and details in descending order of importance are the order of the day, whether it's reporting for print or online. The process evolves into making judgments on the value of the information. Many stories almost write themselves.

The lead sets the tone, tackling the most important part of the story. For the most part, it is evident what it should be—death, outcome of an event, money, an so on. If it is easy to write a headline for your article, generally your lead works and the rest of your writing is about organizing information, looking for good transitions, and keeping it moving for the reader with lean paragraphs of no more than three or four sentences.

Do not try to finish your news story with a tidy ending, which unlike feature writing may try to tie things off nicely by bringing the reader back to the original focus. The simple fact is this: news stories don't end. A car crash that killed two people? Police may file charges twenty-four hours later. Another severely injured person may die in a few days.

Information Gathering

Gathering the facts is perhaps an even more important key to a successful news story. The more facts in hand, the more information the journalist has to build the story and inform the reader. Typically, this requires more effort when the news has not been personally observed, as when reporting a meeting or another scheduled event.

In many cases, reporters start with basic information that frequently is no more than a few facts from an editor making the assignment, a sketchy news account from a wire service, or basics obtained from a document such as a police report. This should never be considered enough, and, with deadlines approaching, the reporter needs to set many things in motion without pinning hopes on any single source.

Pulitzer Prize–winning *Washington Post* reporter Bob Woodward has observed that "the great dreaded thing every reporter lives with is what you don't know. The source you didn't go to. The phone call you didn't return." What that means for beginning reporters is that they need to be reminded to not simply wait for that one telephone call they may consider vital to the story. Instead, reporters should consider their inquiries like seeds sprinkled in the field by a farmer. Calls should immediately go to any potential source for additional information, no matter how indirect they may seem. Then it becomes a matter of harvesting whatever blossoms as the phone, hopefully, starts ringing.

Responsible newspaper reporters learn to move in the direction of where the interesting information takes them. They will often start writing parts of the story before the lead as details become available. This way, they are not locking their stories into a structure that proves too confining as additional information is uncovered. This has the additional benefit of helping reporters to not waste time working and reworking their leads. An exceptionally good detail from a source could lead to an entirely new story lead. At the same time, a source may be forthcoming and friendly, but that does not necessarily enhance the value of what he provides. Make judgments on how and where to use information solely on its merit.

It is important for the newspaper reporter to know his or her speed at the keyboard. That's why many of them set a personal deadline for when they will need to start writing. Then, even if elements of the story are still missing, they start. Once they have met their deadline, they are not necessarily done. Late calls from sources could mean vital details for a follow-up or, if the story has been posted online, important updates.

TV and radio also have deadlines, but their errors are not as easily retained by the public. Online news services can often make instant corrections. Newspaper reporters face an added burden. Their work, compared to that of others, might just as well be etched in granite when it appears on paper. It is there for everyone to see. Millions of facts can be contained in a single issue of a daily paper and, on balance, only an infinitesimal number will be incorrect on any given day. But guess what readers seem to remember the most?

Don R. Hecker, as director of the New York Times Student Journalism Institute and editor for staff editor training at the *Times,* offers the following tips for writing news stories for publication:

1. Does the first paragraph, or lead, work?
   } Is it clear and easy to understand? If it's a hard-news story, ask yourself if you could write a headline based solely on the lead. If not, why not?
   } Has the writer tried to put everything in the first paragraph (or worse, the first sentence)? Look for facts you can take out of the lead and use further down in the article.

2. Are all the basics there?
   } Who? What? Where? When? How? Are they all there? The simplest things are always the easiest to forget.
   } Is a comparison with something the reader knows, a baseline, required to help understand the magnitude (the ever-popular football field, or averages or records)?
   } Is there enough history or background to make the story clear to the reader who has not been following the story?

3. Are there unanswered questions?
   } Does the story say what's going to happen next? What are the implications?
   } If obvious questions can't be answered, does the story say why?

4. Is it fair and balanced?
   } When an explicit or implicit accusation is raised, does the target have an opportunity to respond?
   } Are racial, sexual, religious, or ethnic references relevant? Is that relevance clearly established in the story? Is it applied equally to all people in the story?
   } Is there "another side" to the story or to the contentions of the main sources? Is that other side, or sides, presented and are they given appropriate weight?
   } Is the subject matter of the story placed in context by including information from an outside or unbiased observer?

5. How well is the piece written?
   } Is information where the reader wants to find it, or are important details left to the end, or too much detail thrown at the reader in the beginning?

} Does the writer fall back on jargon or insider terms or frequent use of acronyms or initials for things or processes?

6. Do the numbers add up?
   } Does the math work?
   } If an overall number is given, do the details of the story support it?

An Iowa Case Study

An excellent example of what Hecker is talking about appeared in an April 2007 edition of the *Dubuque Telegraph Herald,* an award-winning independent newspaper with a weekday circulation of thirty thousand. The paper's location in a lively Mississippi River community (pop. 57,000), which has three colleges, a casino, and numerous tourist attractions, and borders three states, means there is ample material to report. Still, on a damp, overcast April 24 in 2007, the newspaper had a story dropped on its lap that would be a dream for all journalists with a love for news reporting. On that day, federal officers swept into a quiet neighborhood to arrest John P. Tomkins, who was charged with sending bomb threats to investment firms in an attempt to impact stock prices. The story, similar in some ways to that of the famous arrest of Unabomber Ted Kaczynski in 1996, drew national headlines. The threats were made over a twenty-month period of time and arrived in letters signed "The Bishop." Tomkins, a family man, worked as a machinist, served as secretary-treasurer of his local union, and had been a part-time letter carrier for the U.S. Postal Service.

Erik Hogstrom, a nine-year veteran reporter on the *Telegraph Herald,* was dressing for work at approximately 8 A.M. when the telephone rang. "It was assistant city editor Tom Jensen, who asked me to drive to the intersection of Grant Street and Hillcrest Avenue [in a quiet, residential part of Dubuque's west side] to follow up on a report of a significant police activity," he recalled. As the first reporter on the scene of the arrest, Tomkins's home, Hogstrom attempted to interview any available neighbors and kept his eyes open for "color" that he could add to reports of "on-the-scene" happenings. Much of his movement was limited by space that had been roped off by federal authorities.

When Hogstrom returned to the *Telegraph Herald* office, he continued to work the telephones as well as check with his paper's photographers and other colleagues involved with this story. At one point, he managed to contact by phone a resident of a nearby apartment complex who had witnessed a bomb squad search of two storage spaces used by the suspect. Two *Telegraph Herald* photographers were on the initial scene with Hogstrom, photo manager Dave Kettering, and staff photographer Jeremy Portje. Kettering remained on the scene for an hour and a half, then returned to the office. At that point, graphic artist Mike Day joined Portje and Hogstrom in a return trip to the scene. Day collected information on the suspect's neighborhood for a map, while also shooting video with a point-and-shoot digital camera normally used for taking mug shots.

The photography staff, graphic artist, and website manager Steve McAuliff worked together to post updates to thonline.com. Hogstrom and other reporters and editors supplied them with new, brief-sized miniature stories as things developed.

Hogstrom's eventual task was to construct an "overall" story to lead the coverage, along with a timeline of events and a sidebar on clues used by investigators. Jensen, Kittle, McAuliff, Kettering, and Hogstrom met at 3:30 P.M.—a half hour before the managers and copy editors meet for the daily story budget meeting, to recap efforts up to that point.

Local Dubuque officials played little role in the arrest of the suspect or the investigation. Federal authorities on the scene were tight-lipped on developments, so the *Telegraph Herald*'s staff continued to rely heavily on telephone interviews, the actual criminal complaint, and information from wire stories originating in Chicago, where the suspect was taken. An exchange of some information was made with the *Sun-Times* newspaper in Chicago.

The criminal complaint was one of the most valuable pieces of data, however. It supplied the details of the charges and gave names for reporters to pursue. The *Telegraph Herald*'s archives were searched for past stories containing Tomkins's name, and Google searches led to even more leads to follow. The deadline that night was approximately 10 P.M. for the next day's newspaper, but because a new editorial front-end computer system was being broken in, stories needed to arrive sooner to make their way through the chain of editors, copy editors, and paginators. Because there is only one edition, once the front page and jumps were completed, the *Telegraph Herald*'s website manager continued to update the website as information became available.

The following is an excerpt from the lead story in an issue that was filled with coverage of the developments:

By Erik Hogstrom
TH staff writer

Don Stedman stepped out of his front door into the middle of a federal raid Wednesday morning. "I got up at 8, going to get the paper, and there's 20 people in my driveway," Stedman said. "Every federal branch of law enforcement was walking around."

Dozens of federal agents descended on Dubuque Wednesday, searching the 2067 Grant St. home of a former part-time letter carrier charged with sending pipe bombs and threatening mailings to investment companies in Denver and Kansas City, Mo., in an effort to drive up stock prices.

John P. Tomkins, 42, of Dubuque, was arrested on his way to work at the Adams Co. and charged with one count of mailing a threatening communication with intent to extort and one count of possession of an unregistered explosive device. Tomkins allegedly signed his letters "The Bishop," and federal officials said the bombs would have exploded if one wire had been connected.

"The only reason you are still alive is because I did not attach one wire," The Bishop wrote in one letter, according to the criminal complaint. "If you do not believe me, then go ahead and touch that red wire to the top of the battery pack. There is enough gunpowder and steel shot in that tube to kill anyone in a 10-foot radius when it goes off."

Tomkins appeared briefly Wednesday before U.S. Magistrate Judge Sidney I. Schenkier in Chicago. When asked if he understood his right to remain silent and to be represented by an attorney, he said "yes" to both questions.

Schenkier ordered Tomkins held in custody pending a hearing Monday afternoon on whether he should be released on bond. Assistant U.S. Attorney Mark E. Schneider said the government wants Tomkins locked up pending trial because of the risk he would flee and because he represents a danger to the community.

Tomkins' federal defender, Rose Lindsay, declined to comment. A conviction for mailing a threatening communication with intent to extort carries a maximum sentence of 20 years in prison; possession of an unregistered destructive device carries a maximum of 10 years. Both carry a maximum fine of $250,000.

Federal agents, many with "FBI," "ATF" or "U.S. Postal Inspectors Police" emblazoned on their jackets, swarmed in front of the gray ranch-style house.

In addition to the main story quoted here, there were sidebars, photographs, graphics, and a timeline filling the cover when it came off the presses late that first night after a full day of effort by almost the entire newsroom. Hogstrom worked closely with executive editor Brian Cooper and city editor Ken Brown on the story. Hogstrom's versatility, which had won him many local contacts, was a big reason for his being assigned chief reporter on the story. What happened in the newsroom of the *Dubuque Telegraph Herald* on April 24, 2007, is repeated every day in newspaper offices around the country. Reporting is teamwork for teammates who are not faint of heart.

Traits of Responsible Reporters

There are a little over 1,400 daily newspapers in the U.S. employing approximately 54,000 full-time journalists. They range from the *USA Today*, number one in daily circulation in 2006 with 2.3 million readers, plus a staff of over a thousand editorial workers, to the *Paxton (Ill.) Record*, one of the smallest dailies in America with a circulation of 1,350 subscribers and a full-time husband-wife editorial staff of two. There is a common thread that runs through this industry, and it's that reporters and other editorial employees on newspapers enjoy communicating in a stylized format. They have many of these characteristics:

}   They like to tell stories.
}   They are good at expressing themselves.
}   They appreciate descriptive words.
}   They want to be first to tell readers something they don't know.
}   They like to dig below the surface for facts.
}   They are nosey and like to know the business of others.
}   They like to get to the bottom of something they perceive as an injustice.
}   They don't like to write stories from press releases and handouts, preferring to be original.
}   They are skeptical and question why things happen.
}   They like to network and develop sources.
}   They know when they are being manipulated and dislike it very much.
}   They enjoy putting order into a day's events.
}   They love the printed word.

It is likely that as a beginning newspaper reporter you will be asked to write about anniversaries of major news events, such as the John F. Kennedy assassination, disasters such as Hurricane Katrina, and the 9/11 terrorist attacks. The to-do list also may include writing about significant local events of the past, noting sports championships, criminal cold cases, or closings of old schools. Typically, this is done when anniversaries hit a number of years divisible by five. Then there are the annual articles about traditional Americana: back-to-school, spring breaks, buying a home, garage sales, summer vacations, first baby of the new year, store openings, ribbon cuttings, and high school graduations. Oh, and toss in the occasional obituary. As clichéd and cynical as this may seem, theme-oriented newspaper pieces are a fact of life if you stay in the business for long. Many readers expect to see them, surveys show they generally are well read, and few writers escape doing them.

No matter the size of the newspaper, you use the same techniques and strategies in what you write. **Keep a list of story ideas**. If something on it seems good a month after it first occurred to you, then it is probably a good idea. Otherwise, purge it. This is true whether you're a general assignment reporter or a beat reporter.

Those who work on smaller papers can expect to cover anything tossed their way by an editor and, at the same time, still have regular beats such as police, city hall, the county building, the parks district, courts, or school boards. These are essential areas covered by publications that take seriously their responsibility to make their readers informed citizens. As reporters move up the newspaper chain and find themselves part of a larger editorial staff, generally they become specialists with a narrower range of topics.

Every newspaper reporter battles deadlines, whether it's a court reporter rushing to file a jury's verdict or a feature writer doing a piece for a Sunday special section that has to be submitted Thursday. Journalists, not unlike students writing a term paper, almost always take as much time to complete a story as they are allotted. Sometimes this is a good strategy. Say, for instance, you are a general assignment reporter for the *Omaha World-Herald*. You are at your desk when an editor hands you a sketchy wire-service account of a fatal automobile accident that occurred earlier in the day in Scottsbluff, at the other end of the state. An Omaha family was in the accident, and there are two hours before deadline for your story. By the time the article gets read in the next day's newspaper, it must contain the fullest possible explanation of what happened. Readers may have seen an online version, but they expect more from a newspaper. You are in a position to do this in print because of space, which, with an editors' blessing, can grow by deadline time if you have gathered better details than those you were handed.

If you are to report more facts than the public likely will get from TV, radio, and online accounts, you must start working the telephones ASAP. Calls must be made to potential sources—police, family, neighbors, employers—to flesh out the story. At some point within your allotted time, you must decide, depending on your speed at the computer, to begin putting your story together in a way that will allow you to continue adding details as they multiply. This is the life of the reporter writing newspaper stories. This is also part of its excitement. Many newspaper reporters would agree with Kansas newspaper pioneer Oscar S. Stauffer, who said, "Consider the day lost when your newspaper has not done something to benefit the community it serves."

Sometimes serving readers can be difficult and dangerous. Lori Washington, a reporter for the *Washington Post,* describes the predicament well. "When you go to places where you don't know exactly what's going on," she says, "and you don't know all the ins and outs, it's better to trust your instincts and do something than to just sit there and try to figure out what would be the right thing to do in this situation." Part of becoming a responsible reporter for newspapers is developing the instincts that can be applied in unfamiliar circumstances. While most newspaper reporting is done via telephone, writers, if they have the option, should always try to directly observe the events, or aftermath, of a story. They almost always pick up a detail that can make an article more interesting for the reader. New technology, such as wireless laptops, digital cameras, and cellular telephones with **text messaging,** give newspaper reporters almost unlimited range. There is little excuse for writers not to get out of the office to directly report important, breaking stories.

Good and Better Reporting

Take a look at these two leads and notice the difference extra effort can make.

> LEAD A: HUMBOLDT—A 76-year-old driver was killed Tuesday afternoon when he apparently lost control of his car and struck a utility pole in a residential area here. A Humboldt Police Department spokesman identified the motorist as Willard T. Jones, of Lexington, Ky., and said investigators concluded his vehicle was traveling at high rate of speed.

> LEAD B: HUMBOLDT—A 76-year-old driver, his out-of-control automobile headed straight for an elementary school playground filled with students, was killed Tuesday afternoon

when the car he was driving struck a utility pole at what police concluded was a high rate of speed. The motorist was identified as Willard T. Jones, of Lexington, Ky.

Obviously, lead B is preferable because there is this added news value: the automobile crash could have been worse. The only sure way to learn this was to go to the scene. After picking up this important detail, the reporter was in a position for follow-up questions with school personnel and eyewitnesses to write a more compelling piece.

The responsible reporter can really serve the public on nearly every story. It depends on how you look at the story you've been assigned. When Martha Stewart was released from federal prison in 2005, her every move was scrutinized in what had to be the year's biggest media feeding frenzy. They pored over every delicious detail. How would she look? What would she be wearing? What would be her first meal? What about the reunion with her dogs? It went on and on. I was assigned to report a sidebar on the coverage for the *Chicago Tribune*. I saw this as an opportunity to use the national curiosity—created and fed in great part by the media itself—to do something socially important with my reporting by showing the reality that faces most female ex-convicts after their discharge, which, when compared to Stewart's situation, seemed to provide a stark, readable contrast. Her comparatively desperate plight was similar to that of thousands of women, the vast majority of them black, released every month from U.S. prisons and jails. In a follow-up piece seven months later at the end of the year, I learned that the subject of my story, Cynthia (only her first name was used at her request), had still been unable to find employment.

In another article, I was able to track down and interview a woman who had been discharged years earlier from the same Pennsylvania prison in which Stewart was incarcerated. In this piece, I detailed how most parolees face a humiliating reentry process starting with a long Greyhound bus ride to the parole office they've been assigned. Comments from readers indicated that the stories were well received and became the topic of local discussion. I had capitalized on Martha Stewart as the national story du jour, using interest in her as a means to draw readers' attention to a serious societal problem—recidivism. In addition to seeing my assignment carried out on in a satisfactory (and satisfying) manner, the effort was a reminder in several ways of why being a newspaper reporter is important.

Hardly a month goes by when I, like most seasoned newspaper reporters, am not approached by proud parents asking me to speak to their child about a career in journalism. Generally, the conversation starts this way: "My daughter is a really good writer, and I think she would be good at it." Sounds nice, but the air quickly goes out of the balloon when I tell them, **"Writing isn't necessarily the most important part of the job."** They become even more surprised when I tell them that most newspaper writing, especially on large publications, goes through the hands of several editors before it reaches print. In some cases, the finished article has been rewritten several times and bears little resemblance to the original submission. Then, they are told about what goes into accumulating information to be reported. "Your daughter may be able to write, but she must have interesting material to write about for readers. Does she know how to gather it?" This could mean anything from interviewing the parents of a shooting victim to spending a day in a county clerk's office poring through dusty files. Everyone has a story or two they want to do, but what about after they've done them? Can they keep coming up with ideas?

Newspaper writing is a collaborative effort. No staffer's effort goes straight to print without other sets of eyes seeing it and, in some cases, making changes. Beginning reporters must learn to interact with people inside the newspaper and outside it. It may mean asking uncomfortable questions of people you barely know and working beside people you may not particularly like. That's part of the job. Reading reports, making calls, legwork, research, and asking questions are basic to responsible reporting. These principles are applied to the story of an automobile accident, bank robbery, fire, or appointment of a new city manager. Furthermore, these principles are the same as those used in writing articles of national or international interest. In the end, you must think of it this way: writing a newspaper story is like building a house. The more boards, or details, you have for the job, the more options you have for the construction. And more options mean a better final product. When you are done building the house, it gets turned over to the painters, or editors, for finishing touches.

The Future of Newspapers

Mark Twain, a good newspaperman in his day, liked to laugh that "reports of my death are premature." The same can be said for those who question the life expectancy of newspapers, given the challenge of digital technologies that give readers new and faster ways to learn about the day's events. In addition to the nation's fifteen hundred dailies, recent years have seen an influx of newspapers offering community and ethnic news. There has also been strong growth among **niche publications**, and, in recent years, a dozen free daily tabloids in major markets have been successfully launched. Interestingly, the same technology that some feel threatens newspapers—the Internet, **wireless laptops**, cellular telephones, digital cameras—have become tools for reporters, enhancing their performance. These tools help produce better newspapers and level the playing field for smaller publications with fewer resources. Journalists with Internet access to Lexis-Nexis, public records, newspaper archives, or just about any data bank now have immense research and story backgrounding capabilities. Real newspaper veterans, those whose careers date to typewriters, can testify that simple computer functions such as clip-and-paste, e-mail, and spell-check have made them better writers. These new technologies now make accessing material that would have been unthinkable only a decade earlier possible. They are making newspaper reporting better because it can serve more citizens with information worth knowing. This opportunity is available for beginning journalists as they embrace new technologies in newsgathering. That's why the future of newspapers is filled with hope for citizens who read and reporters who write the news.

Reporting National News

DEBRA A. SCHWARTZ

I am a talker by nature. Listening for me does not come naturally. But working national news showed me I was going to have to follow my mother's longstanding advice: listen. **Acquiring listening skills was the single most important gift journalism gave me as a national reporter.** It was tough for an extrovert like me.

When I was a young reporter for community newspapers in the Chicago area, I just looked for stories that lent themselves to "he said, she said" reporting. Spending tax dollars. Changing village administrators. Profiling a new business. Profiling an environmental activist in the community.

For my first national story, I spent three hours on the phone with an activist in California who was ranting against nuclear power. I had phone ear after the first half hour. But I kept debating the issue with the activist, questioning her point of view, while offering my own. What a mistake! I knew little about proposed changes to the Clean Air Act. At the time, I didn't realize national reporters *did* research. I thought news reporting was all about the voice of the people. I thought it was just writing what everyday people said alongside what government and lawmakers said. That takes interviewing, and I *like* talking to people. I wasn't crazy about doing research.

I didn't realize that in national news the reporter is *obligated* to summarize opposing viewpoints and positions on an issue *before* providing quotes connected to those differing perspectives. I thought the quotes were all I needed. I didn't realize that going into an interview, my sources might attempt to manipulate my thinking to their point of view. Become suspicious of numbers given to back up claims. Do your own math. That requires digging in. Looking at documents. Scrutinizing numbers to determine which are the most credible. That required me to choose whose numbers to believe. The ones from the U.S. Geological Survey? The ones from the National Resources Defense Council? The ones from citizens groups?

Protecting my credibility became a monumental task. Every national news reporter should be careful to guard theirs. It requires reading, going to the bookstore and scanning and skimming the shelves for relevant books and articles in magazines and journals. It also means going to the library to find historical perspectives, and searching the Internet for think tanks and special interest groups with competing positions on the issues. It means investigating to find gaps in what is said and developing an appetite for writing news reports that are fair, thorough, and full of detail. National news reporters need to become intimately familiar with the issues they're covering. Serving the public interest requires it.

Resources for reporters who focus on national news include think tanks such as the Brookings Institution, the Cato Institute, and the Heritage Foundation; activist organizations and industry groups; legislators whose special interests overlap what you're investigating; scholars doing research in what you are covering; and relevant government agencies and departments at the local, regional, and national levels. Beginning journalism students can type **"resource directory"** into their favorite search engines to locate these and other relevant resources. In addition, subscribe to listservs specializing in an area of particular interest. These sites might include: the Society of Environmental Journalists, the D.C. Science Writers Association, and the Society of Professional Journalists Ethics Division. These organizations will help you learn what kinds of stories, angles, sources, and questions other national reporters are thinking about.

Responsible reporters covering national issues become good listeners. They give sources their full attention. They think about what they're hearing. By listening with an open mind, the serious reporter of national news can hear and consider a range of competing viewpoints. This formula works when reporting world news as well. In 2002, I was in Prague reporting on international trade and finance. The meeting was hosted by Vaclav Havel, president of the Czech Republic, and involved a wide range of participants that included Frederik Willem de Klerk, the former president of South Africa and Nobel Peace Prize winner; the prime minister of Malaysia; India's minister of defense; Taiwan's senior advisor to the president; a former U.S. secretary of labor; and leaders of select special interest groups, including the World Trade Organization. This meeting was an ultimate test of my ability to listen carefully, research deeply, and interview smartly for a variety of print, radio, and online publications. It was true for me then, and is necessary for any beginning journalist now, to prepare wisely before going into the arena. If you do that and are an educated listener, you will be well on your way to giving an accurate account of national and international news worth knowing.

Reporting International News

LES SILLARS

On the morning of Saturday, June 4, 1989, *Time* correspondent David Aikman climbed the steps of the Great Hall of the People on the west side of Beijing's Tiananmen Square and turned around. He saw thousands of student demonstrators milling around, and rows of army-style tents with pennants of Chinese universities flying from poles in a stiff breeze. On the north end was a thirty-foot-high, plaster-covered Styrofoam "Goddess of Democracy," a statue that strongly resembled the Statue of Liberty. Protestors shouted pro-democracy messages through portable P.A. systems, while government voices blared through overhead speakers: martial law had been imposed, they said, go home, clear the square.

"I had a hunch something might be approaching a climax," Aikman says. He was a correspondent in *Time*'s Washington bureau at the time, but he had followed the news from China closely that spring. A weeks-long student protest had grown into a major demonstration, complete with hunger strikers camped out on the square's Monument to the Heroes of the Revolution. In late May, he convinced his editors to let him return to Beijing, where he had been stationed from 1982 to 1985.

Walking around Tiananmen Square later that afternoon, he saw students haranguing glum-looking soldiers—"You're the People's Army! You should be on our side!"—and others throwing rocks at the Great Hall and shouting for the resignation of Prime Minister Li Peng. Elsewhere, citizens were building makeshift blockades on roads around the city core, stopping traffic cold and even turning back military vehicles. He went back to his hotel and filed a report to New York. "It'll happen tonight," he wrote.

By the time Aikman returned at 3:00 A.M., the Chinese military had begun a ruthless crackdown. Army vehicles had pushed through the barriers in nearby roads, with some soldiers shooting as they went. At 5:30 A.M., as he crouched behind some bricks in an alley near the Beijing Hotel, he watched a huge convoy of trucks and tanks rumble past and into the square. Soldiers knocked over the statue and dispersed what was left of the crowd with batons and bullets. Aikman saw tracer bullets and heard gunfire coming from, by his count, eight different parts of the city.

Mostly one-sided skirmishes continued around Beijing through Sunday afternoon, with soldiers blasting machine guns into panic-stricken crowds and demonstrators retaliating, where they could, with Molotov cocktails. Thousands died. The Communist Chinese government called it a great victory over the "counterrevolutionary insurrection." On Monday, when Aikman returned to tour the area around the square, it was still unclear what would happen, but a grizzled old man approached him. "Thank you," he said. "Thank you for telling the world what the Chinese government is doing to the Chinese people."

Clearly, Aikman says today, coverage from foreign correspondents had a significant effect during those tense weeks. The presence of the foreign press probably restrained Chinese leaders from taking stronger action sooner and "assured students that the rest of the world did know what was going on," Aikman says. The wave of similar protests that erupted across China following Tiananmen Square likely would not have happened had the students believed no one was watching or listening.

Foreign news gave Chinese citizens more accurate versions of events, despite the party's iron control of Chinese media. As Aikman toured Beijing on a bicycle two days after the crackdown, he saw faxes of the front pages of Hong Kong newspapers plastered to poles and buildings. Word had gone out and was getting back in.

In all cultures and in all societies, "there's always a demand for justice, there's always a demand for freedom, and there's always a demand for truth," says Aikman, who since he left *Time* in 1994 has produced a documentary on the Middle East and written extensively about religious persecution in Russia, China, Egypt, and Pakistan. "Societies instinctively know that they cannot operate on a healthy basis if the truth about core events in their development is suppressed."

International news is also crucial for free societies, and these days perhaps especially for America. The public needs accurate, timely news to help it make wise and compassionate decisions in dealing with other governments and people. "Insofar as we live in a world in which everything is interdependent, sooner or later events in distant places will have an impact upon our own reality," Aikman says. Few people knew much about the Taliban, Osama bin Laden, or Islamic radicals before 9/11, as an obvious example, but since then the threat of terrorism has redefined American domestic and foreign policy agendas and dramatically affected American culture.

American audiences and media are notorious in the international community for their general indifference to events beyond American borders. The volume of foreign news in American media, eroding since the 1970s, shrunk yet further in the 1990s after the fall of the Soviet Union in 1989 signaled the end of the Cold War. But the 9/11 attacks and the resultant deployment of U.S. troops abroad changed that, at least partially and for now. A recent survey by the Pew International Journalism Program suggests that the attacks of 9/11 prompted journalists to pick up stories they had previously ignored or downplayed. About eight of ten newspaper editors said their news hole for international news had increased since 2001, while more than nine of ten said reader interest in foreign news increased as well. More than half said they expected their international news hole to eventually shrink, but that seems unlikely as long as the U.S. military is engaged in Iraq and other Middle Eastern countries.

At its core, to be effective international journalism must connect audiences with the people about whom journalists write their stories. Part of that process, Aikman says, is getting beyond stereotypes—Africa is nothing but AIDS, famine, and civil war, for example, or Latin America is defined by poverty, corruption, and cocaine. "Stereotypes can have an element of truth," Aikman says, but Americans need a deeper understanding. As longtime *St. Louis Post-Dispatch* editor and journalism educator William Woo pointed out in a 2001 Nieman Report, "sooner or later what happens to anybody else—down the street or thousands of miles away, in a country whose name we can barely pronounce—affects us. I tell [students that] good journalists are involved in humankind. If they aren't, they will never be able to write about the world in ways that touch readers nor be able to learn anything about themselves."

11

Writing and Reporting Radio News

SANDRA ELLIS[*]

In June 2001, when the Baltimore Orioles held a press conference to announce twenty-year veteran player Cal Ripken's retirement, it was big news. Ripken had spent his entire career playing for the Orioles. He was famous for playing the most consecutive games (2,632 over sixteen seasons) of any player in professional baseball. Reporters and photographers jammed the large room on the sixth floor of the historic B & O Warehouse overlooking the Camden Yards ball field. Ripken sat behind a long table at the front of the room. All the chairs in the room were taken. TV cameras on tripods filled the space behind the chairs with additional reporters and photographers crowding between them.

Squeezed into the crowd, WBAL-AM reporter John Patti stood near the front of the room, recording the press conference on his Sony MZ-B 100 minidisc recorder. Just to be safe, a second minidisc recorder was rolling as backup. The time ticked by as questions came from all over the room. As soon as the press conference drew to a close, Patti hurried to the parking lot. In the WBAL car he flipped through his reporter's notebook, looking for the quotes that he wanted to pull from the recording. He quickly located the actualities (most no longer than ten to fifteen seconds) and moved each to the beginning of the mini-

---

* Bruce Evensen contributed to this chapter.

disc so that the first five tracks consisted of his chosen actualities. Referring to his notes, Patti wrote lead-ins for each actuality and then recorded them.

The five o'clock newscast was approaching fast, and the Ripken story would be the lead. Patti started the engine and moved the vehicle across the parking lot to get a better line-of-site transmission back to WBAL, located five and a half miles away on a hill high above downtown Baltimore. He powered up the Marti Remote Pick-Up unit, connected the MD recorder to the Marti, then used his cell phone to let the WBAL newsroom know a story was coming in. Back at the station, the recorder was set to receive the signal from the Marti. Upon getting the cue, Patti played the actualities followed by his lead-ins. Once they were recorded, he passed on the details needed for use in writing the anchor introductions. With less than ten minutes until news time, the completion of the story was up to the newsroom staff. A short time later, WBAL listeners heard the five o'clock newscast begin with the anchor saying that Baltimore's own Cal Ripken would be retiring at the end of the baseball season. Patti's sound story, completed just minutes earlier, came on with Ripken himself describing his career, "I'm a hometown guy, my dad worked for the Orioles and as far back as I can remember baseball and the Orioles were it for me. In my career I was able to be drafted against big odds with the Orioles, make it with the Orioles and have a long career with the Orioles. If you add up all the odds, it's pretty remarkable."

The Immediacy of Radio

Radio has always sustained itself with its ability to provide news quickly. It was the first mass medium, capable of reaching millions of people simultaneously. There was a time when news was available every day on almost all radio stations in nearly every part of the United States. Today radio news is more likely to be found on specific stations that are focused exclusively on all-news or news/talk programming. The famous broadcast news pioneer **Edward R. Murrow** described radio as "that most satisfying and rewarding instrument." Murrow eventually, and reluctantly, moved from radio into television but considered radio news his first love.

Out of twelve thousand stations, there are slightly more than two thousand radio stations that provide significant news coverage. Nearly fourteen thousand full-time radio reporters and news producers work for these stations. While faced with the pressure of constant deadlines, radio reporters enjoy a good bit of independence. They work outside the office using portable recording devices to get sound that allows listeners to feel they are at the scene of the meeting, accident, or fire. They interview public officials, eyewitnesses, and victims to get firsthand accounts of what happened. The immediacy of radio means that a radio reporter's goal is to keep listeners up to date on what is happening in their town, state, and the world.

The Work of a Radio Reporter

Bruce Evensen, the editor of this book, remembers a story that reflects the way radio reporters work and how they serve their listeners with news worth knowing. On a Friday night he had reported a police account of a car that skidded off a roadway and their fear that a motorist had been trapped inside. Recovery efforts had been called off and would be resumed the following morning. Early on Saturday, just before arriving at the accident scene, Evensen witnessed another accident. A late-model sports car, stopped at an intersection, was rear-ended at low speed by the driver of a pickup.

"It was fender-bender," Evensen recalls. "I didn't think anything of it."

But Evensen noticed that the driver of the sports car wasn't moving.

"I walked over," he says, "and heard him screaming, 'I can't move my arms or legs! Help me! Please help me!'"

Evensen called paramedics and police, who hurried to scene. The driver was carefully placed on a stretcher and then into an ambulance, which rushed to a local hospital. Evensen gave an accident report to police, who began questioning the young driver of the pickup, as Evensen drove off to the previous night's accident.

"It was a mile and a half away," he remembers. "Divers were applying grappling hooks to a submerged car when I arrived."

There were no skid marks in the wet grass. The car had gone into the river, and the driver hadn't applied brakes.

"The driver trapped inside the car was a teenager," says Evensen. "I remember seeing drug paraphernalia."

When Evensen returned to the office he had two stories to write and several calls to make. If you become a radio reporter you will frequently find yourself in the same situation. Radio reporters don't have the luxury of reporting stories only when all the facts are known. Rarely are *all* the facts known. You go with what you have. Evensen at this point had one driver who was dead, another who was injured, possibly paralyzed, and police were questioning a third person. His first call to the hospital revealed the identity of the driver of the sports car and his condition. A nursing supervisor told him the patient had "a possible broken neck" and was going into surgery at that minute. A second call to the state's attorney revealed the identity of the other driver and that he had been charged with reckless driving. Aware that the patient is in critical condition, you ask what the charges will be if the patient dies. The state's attorney tells you that, in that case, the other driver would be charged with "involuntary manslaughter." Your listeners need to know what the charge means. You find out that involuntary manslaughter is a class-A felony that could lead to a twelve- to twenty-five-year jail term if convicted.

Your radio station will not await the results of the surgery before you file an update on this story. Even before you call the coroner to get an identity of the body found in the other car, you will go on air with what you know. Toxicology results are pending. Finally, later that day, the victim is identified as the sixteen-year-old point guard on the local high school basketball team, which had placed second in state competition just three months before. You remember that this boy was a diabetic and ask if the drug paraphernalia might have been for self-administered insulin shots. The coroner confirms that this may be the case. You tell him there were no skid marks at the scene. He observes that the victim may have blacked out before his car plunged into the river.

Another news block comes and goes, and your news director expects you to update what you know about the story. Later it is learned that the teenager drowned. By mid-afternoon, you're writing and voicing a single story that combines both elements of what you've reported throughout the day. The radio reporter totals it up and comes up with the lead. "A high school basketball star drowns, a man is in critical condition, and a youth may face twenty-five years in jail following unrelated auto accidents north of our city." Quotes from team members and the state's attorney follow. As the hours pass, the two stories take their own trajectories. The city mourns the loss of its basketball hero. The injured man survives his surgery and recovers movement in his hands and feet. The driver of the pickup faces a misdemeanor charge. Radio reported captured events as they evolved, becoming the go-to medium for those interested in breaking news within their community. That is the challenge and reward of being a radio news reporter.

Radio journalists cover many different kinds of stories. The type of station that reporters work for determines what they cover and how much detail they include in the story. New York City's only all-news radio station, 1010 WINS-AM, is known for its slogan "You give us twenty-two minutes. We'll give you the world." Listeners tune in for a frenetic presentation style. In between news stories, commercials, weather, stock reports, sports, and traffic reports, anchors frequently tell listeners the time. WINS news director Ben Mevorach says the station's format is designed for listeners to tune in, listen briefly to get what they want, and then tune out. Reporters at WINS and similar news stations need to be concise. Actualities (audio quotes from newsmakers) in stories are short, frequently only ten to twelve seconds in length. **Radio news is history on the run,** and it is challenging. It is reporting history before all the facts are in. It requires constant updating and responsible reporters who are careful to go only as far as the facts take them.

Covering a Crash

Let me give you an example of the demands involved in radio reporting and what you do about them. It's Saturday morning around nine, and a freezing rain is falling in your community. You monitor a police report that tells you that two planes have collided in midair just north of your city. You drive up Highway 2 in the direction of the crash and encounter a massive traffic jam. You get out of your car and walk in the direction of emergency vehicles that are at the crash site. As you walk, you notice aircraft debris and badly charred human remains, including a severed hand in a glove. The police investigator at the scene tells you that an eyewitness reported seeing the collision. The federal aviation administrator says he's probing the possibilities that weather or pilot error may have caused the crash.

The eyewitness reports that five hundred to a thousand feet up he saw a smaller plane ascending and a larger plane descending.

"The pilot of the larger plane veered left at the last possible second," he reports, "but it was too late."

The smaller craft struck the larger one under the right wing, he recalls. The fuel tank on the larger aircraft "burst into flames," he says. "The larger plane became engulfed in flames, spun into a tight spiral, and crashed onto Highway 2."

You ask about the other plane and are told that it "limped off to the east" and may have "attempted an emergency landing in a cornfield." The witness indicates he thought he heard "its motor quitting."

The radio reporter files the story he or she has. And then looks for more. In this case it means reporting the collision, the likely human casualties, the possible reasons for the crash, and the traffic tie-up that it caused.

Your next step is to pin down how many people were aboard those planes and who they were. You contact the air traffic controller at the local airport and are told that "two planes are overdue" and that "two planes disappeared from our radar screen at 8:44 this morning." According to the airport's flight manifest, a fixed-wing Lockheed aircraft left the airport at 7:55 on a routine training mission. The other plane, a two-seat Cessna, took off at 8:40. You are given the names, ages, and addresses of the five people aboard the training flight and the two people inside the Cessna. The name of the trainer is familiar to you. It's the daughter of a World War II flying ace, who had himself perished six months before while on a routine training mission.

Before filing your updated story, you contact the county coroner, who tells you that "two bodies have arrived, and we've been advised that four more are on the way." You go on the air with what you know, but can see that there's a discrepancy between the number of people presumably aboard both planes—seven—and the number of bodies reported by the coroner—six. There could be several reasons for this. Perhaps someone survived the crash. Perhaps the coroner's office had not been advised that a seventh body was found in the wreckage. Or perhaps the bodies were so mutilated that it was difficult initially to get an accurate body count.

As it turned out, the condition of bodies at the crash site did delay the body count and positive identification. That, however, would not stop a radio reporter from initially reporting that seven people were "feared dead" in the collision of two planes and that the daughter of the city's most decorated World War II flying ace is among them. Later in the day, the fact that seven are dead and that the daughter of the flying veteran was among them is confirmed. The point of this story is that as a radio reporter you report what you know, when it is known, and who claims that it is so, knowing that the next news block will always cause you to add to what the listener has already been told.

Radio reporting deadlines can be challenging. You may have to produce a new version of your story every hour for several hours. The immediacy of your deadline may determine what you include in the story. If you're writing for a newscast that airs soon, you may not have time to confirm or follow up on some details. The best policy is that advocated by Gannett chief executive officer Paul Miller more than forty years ago: **"Substance ahead** of form; balance ahead of speed; completeness ahead of color; accuracy ahead of everything."

The Rush of Radio Reporting

Radio reporting is for those who love the excitement of deadline reporting. For radio reporters, there's a deadline every minute. The challenge is always to be fast without sacrificing accuracy. "Before anyone had ever heard of the World Wide Web, radio news reporters had a clear deadline: NOW," says Milwaukee's WTMJ-AM news director Jon Byman. "We're used to filing news while the news is still happening." "Fantastic" is how WINS-AM reporter Steve Kastenbaum describes his job. "No two days are the same. I love waking up in the morning and not knowing where the editor is going to send me when I check in…not know what's going to happen."

Radio reporters record and edit their own interviews, sometimes sitting in their car and using audio editing software on a laptop computer. Many file their stories, including the audio, via the Internet. Observation is perhaps the most important weapon in a radio reporter's arsenal. They also listen attentively. They capture ambient sound from the scene of a story. Reporters record the sound of feet on a gravel path, traffic on a busy highway, or the cash register at the coffee shop. Imagine a story about a military funeral; the sound of a lone bugle playing "Taps" helps connect the listener to a moving story. Sound makes radio news stories more compelling to the listener.

For radio, the sound at the scene is every bit as important as the photograph is for a newspaper story. Its purpose is to make listeners feel as though they were standing right beside the reporter who's telling the story. It puts them in the scene. With all that listeners do with radio in the background—driving the car, washing dishes, or fixing dinner—reporters must work hard to grab their attention. Well-chosen sound frequently is the final piece that makes a story more "ear-catching." Skilled radio reporters never head out on a story without a set of headphones or earbuds to ensure that they hear everything their recorder picks up.

The Internet now allows listeners to hear their favorite radio station from almost anywhere in the world. Many encourage listeners to sign up for emails detailing breaking news and weather alerts. Stations offer their newscasts in real time through streaming audio via the Internet. Another alternative for news is the use of **podcasts**: audio files found on Internet websites. Radio news operations are using podcasts to let their audience download news stories, talk shows, and newscasts to their MP3 players to listen at their own convenience. Historically a medium focused on immediacy, radio is taking advantage of ever-improving technology to provide the news even quicker to more people in more places.

Radio reporters must be able to multitask, says Minnesota Public Radio news director Bill Wareham. "We're past the age where we can hold off delivering critical information until the next drive time—we have so much competition, primarily on the web, that we have to get it out fast." In the 1990s, reporters were expected to deliver a four-minute story plus a couple of newscast cuts (actualities) daily. "Now they're expected to take photos and post their text to the website, provide extra audio or other content," says Wareham. Some maintain blogs, others produce podcasts.

MPR correspondent Mark Zdechlik, a twenty-year veteran, says deadlines are getting tighter and pressures are increasing with the additional responsibility of producing material for MPR's website. He traveled to Washington, D.C., to cover Minnesota's new senator and representative at their swearing-in ceremonies. After recording the audio and taking photos, Zdechlik rushed back to his hotel room. Back in Minnesota, online editors were pressing him to send the pictures electronically as soon as possible. Zdechlik had little more than an hour to send his photos back, then write the seven-minute story, pull the sound and edit it, and upload it to MPR in time for the broadcast. He occasionally finds himself interviewing a news source holding a mic in one hand and a digital camera in the other, simultaneously taking photos and recording sound.

More advanced technology, such as a satellite phone, is needed when a foreign correspondent travels to inaccessible or war-torn locations. In the spring of 2003, when it became apparent that war was imminent, National Public Radio's Anne Garrels was the only broadcast journalist who remained in Baghdad. She relied heavily on a satellite phone to report around the clock as American soldiers approached, then attacked Baghdad. Wartime tests the resourcefulness of radio reporters. **Garrels broadcast naked from her hotel room, hoping that the few extra minutes she would need to dress would allow her to hide her illegal satellite phone if security knocked on her door.** It worked. Satellite phones performed heroically in reporting Hurricane Katrina as well. The storm knocked out telephone lines and limited cell phone service, making satellite phones a must for reporters covering the devastating storm in August 2005.

Radio's Laptop Reporter

As more and more municipalities offer citywide wireless Internet access, known as Wi-Fi, reporters are among the beneficiaries. Sitting in a car, coffee shop, or library within a designated wireless service area, today's reporter can accomplish a variety of tasks that once required returning to the station to use a production studio. Using a laptop computer with special software, the reporter can speak into a laptop mic and send audio via the Internet back to the station and directly on the air. A quick connection to a digital camera and an audio recorder allows the reporter to dump still photos and audio into the laptop. The pictures can be sent off immediately. And, after some speedy editing, the audio files soon follow.

For the first time, says Byman, radio reporters have to think visually. Byman sees the changes in technology as liberating. "New technology really frees radio reporters to disseminate news even faster." The newest cell phones called smart phones make use of touch screens instead of tiny buttons. With Wi-Fi capability, users can access the Internet, choosing to listen to a streaming radio newscast, view the headlines, or click on the traffic report. Radio stations have found podcasting a valuable addition to their programming delivery options. Reporters blog, making online journal-style entries, take still photos, produce podcasts of special news reports, and add breaking news alerts to the station's website. Listeners in many markets can sign up for breaking news emails. Podcasts allow listeners to follow the news when it's convenient for them.

Digital technology requires radio reporters to adapt to new equipment on a regular basis. Palm-sized digital video camcorders can be used to shoot video, still photos, or record audio. Satellite phones, once bulky, have shrunk to a size comparable to cell phones, and cell phones have been made even more useful. Third-generation cell phones, available in Europe, have American journalists dreaming of the day a 3G network covers the United States. The super phone is the ultimate all-in-one field reporting device. Basically, it's a miniature computer, capable of word processing and Internet access. Plus, it shoots high-quality still photographs and digital video and records digital audio. Add a built-in FM radio and the ability to attach a portable keyboard, and a reporter has the equivalent of a bag full of equipment in his coat pocket. And, to top it all off, the super phone has Wi-Fi capability.

Although the technology associated with radio news has changed in recent years, the traditional aspects remain unaltered. Reporters must be flexible, able to work independently or in teams. Multitasking continues to be an invaluable skill, along with the willingness to learn new techniques. Time pressure and deadlines, always factors in the news business, continue to challenge reporters. With new technology offering the capability of providing news nearly instantaneously to a wide audience, it's more important than ever before that reporters exercise judgment over speed and clear-headed analysis over action. **Getting the story right is always more important than getting it first.**

Creating a Broadcast Sound

BRUCE J. EVENSEN

At the close of World War II, the Three Stooges paid homage to radio, America's favorite form of mass communication. An opening scene in the 1945 short *Micro-phonies* places Moe, Larry, and Curly in a radio studio.

"Oh, a microphonie," says Moe, trying out some overripe tones for his first broadcast.

"Yea, and a phony at the mic," Curly tells him.

Don't be like Moe. Don't try to sound like a broadcaster by trying to sound like a broadcaster. It will only make you sound like you're trying.

Ever find yourself driving through some small town and listening to the radio? Ever wonder what makes the small-town newscaster sound small town? The trouble is often style and substance. After a little listening you may come to the conclusion that the newscaster is trying to sound authoritative about something he or she knows nothing about. A mispronounced name said emphatically is a bad audition for someone who wants to be taken seriously. Misplaced emphasis is enough to not be taken seriously.

In life, people are seen as credible if they seem to know what they're talking about. It's no different for someone on the air. So, know what you're talking about. Study the issues. Know the major players. Know how to pronounce their names.

Listeners will come to one of two conclusions. You know what you're talking about or you don't. Job security and prospects are limited for newscasters who have been found out by the audience. **The best way to seem authoritative on the air is to actually know what you're talking about.** Then you won't have to appear confident because you'll *be* confident. At the end of the newscast, either the script will have been your master, or you will have mastered your script. Knowing your material is the first step in exercising control over your copy, while indicating competence to your audience.

Always keep the audience in mind. You are speaking to one person. So stop shouting. Don't project to the back row of the theater. Don't preach to the back bench of the congregation. Keep it conversational. Imagine that you are sitting across the table from a friend. You're interested in the story you're telling, and you want your friend to be interested as well. That's the tone to take into a studio. You may be talking to ten thousand people or 10 million, but you're talking to them one at a time. Keep that in mind.

Your success on the air comes before you go on the air. Edison observed that the key to invention is 1 percent inspiration and 99 percent perspiration. The same is true when you're constructing a newscast. Think of anything you've ever been successful in. It's likely that preparation, hard work, and repetition was at the heart of that success. That's the way it is with broadcasting. Millions of Americans read the news. What raises your reading above theirs is what you know about what you're reading.

In the 1970s, George Carlin's "hippy-dippy weatherman" was a clever caricature of the individual who's too cool on the air to be credible. The cool customer doing news drives too fast for conditions. **Speed kills.** In this case, the news reader's credibility is killed. Consonants become transposed as the tongue clumsily plays catch-up with the over-eager achiever. This is particularly a problem for beginning broadcasters. They start to sound like disc jockeys in a patter so fake that if you were to hear it in casual conversation you'd think the other person had completely lost his mind. The more nervous beginning broadcasters get, the faster they tend to go. When they make their inevitable mistakes, they feel the obligation to make up for it by going even faster. The unhappy result is even greater failure. An occasional mistake in reading a story is to be expected. Don't draw attention to it by speeding up or apologizing. Beginning journalists are often their own worst critics. Audiences are much more forgiving. We make mistakes in casual conversation all the time. An occasional slip on the air is not a capital crime. Plan for success by accepting occasional failure. Correct the mistake if necessary and keep going.

Occasionally, beginning broadcasters don't suffer from speed skating but give you the appearance of the person going out onto the ice for the first time. They seem to fear that every reluctant stride could be their last. They have the impression that the ice below is thin and about to give way. As a result they move too slowly through their story and read…each…word…as…if…were…a…monument…to…itself. They need to pick up the pace and aim at a more conversational reading, one that will preferably keep audiences awake. Time yourself. Casual conversation proceeds at about 125 to 135 words a minute. If you're a lot faster, you may be a train heading off a track. If you're much slower, you may be stuck in the depot. Find a consistent pace that conveys enthusiasm for the story you're telling without sounding affected or forced. Do the same reading at difference speeds. Record yourself. Play it back. Which reading seems most conversational? Ask friends for their evaluation. You will likely find that there is broad agreement on the pacing that's right for you.

Keep your voice clear, not too high and not too low, by bringing your voice up through the diaphragm. Don't simply start at the throat. It's a way of bringing your body into the news read in a very natural way. Singers and public performers create voice depth by bringing the sound up from the gut and getting their upper body in on the act. To help you do this, be sure you're not crouched down over your copy. Pull your shoulders back, put that chest out, and look the viewer straight in the eye. Don't appear or sound as if you've anything to hide. Going on the air is a performance that requires the concentration of an actor who has authority and presence. You can't have either if you're not squared up to the mic, shoulders back, chin forward. There should be no marbles in your mouth. Spit them out. Listeners shouldn't wonder what you've said after you've said it. **Be definite. Be decisive. Be honest.**

Practice pause points and emphasis keys. Indicate them in your script. In normal conversation notice how we speed up and slow down. We do this around certain inflective keys that appear naturally in the sentences we say. Every seven to ten words you can hear these choices clearly. Strong verbs almost always get emphasis and come at a brief pause point. The same is true for adjectives and adverbs. These words are qualifiers and reveal opinions and attitudes. Proper names often get similar treatment, numbers do too, and so do prepositional phrases. Pause points and emphasis keys tend to go together. A word worth emphasizing is generally also worth pausing over. Beginning broadcasters who ignore pause points and emphasis keys run the risk of respiratory arrest. A half-second pause every seven to ten words lets you take a breath and resume the pace. It also allows you to untie your tongue and reload for the reading of the next sentence segment.

Avoid predictability in your reading cadence. Some beginning broadcasters develop a sing-song sound that emphasizes every third or fourth word. Up and down they go. Up and down. Up and down. It's enough to make the listener seasick. Let the content of your copy dictate pause points and emphasis keys. Be careful not to let your voice come up to signal the end of the sentence. You'll make the sentence sound like a question if you do.

Spencer Tracy was widely considered the greatest actor of the first hundred years of American movies. When asked how he did it he answered, "Don't let them catch you trying." The key to great acting was to not appear as if you were acting at all. Naturalness came through practice. Practice makes the performance seem like a lived experience. In the case of the beginning broadcaster, practice helps make the news read a conversation between two friends.

Remember how comfortable it is to be with friends. Keep that mindset as you go into the studio. You know something that others need to know. For the responsible reporter, the broadcast is all about what is being broadcast and not the broadcaster. Do all you can to make your content understood, and listeners will like you.

12

Writing and Reporting Television News

DAVID MARSHALL[*]

If you cover breaking news as a broadcast journalist long enough you will be faced by some circumstances that are more horrible than you can imagine. The question is, What does a responsible reporter do then? Let me give you a terrifying example of what I mean. You arrive with police and paramedics at a home in a fashionable part of your city. There, you are shocked by what you see and find out. The lifeless body of an eight-year-old girl, clad in her pajamas, is found in an upstairs washroom. She's been stabbed, strangled, and drowned. Police question the father in the case. He tells authorities he became convinced in a family card game that his daughter was the devil and that he was on a holy mission to kill her and save the world. Police ask what made him think so, and he answers that she "delighted" in drawing three sixes. These numbers, he was convinced, signaled that she was the anti-Christ.

Neighbors describe the father as "loving" and "caring." They tell you that he was often seen playing with his daughter in their yard. The man's employer says he was their "most talented" software salesman. The man's church says he was a Sunday-school teacher. The man's wife, a nurse, is being counseled by a psychotherapist, as you prepare to write and shoot your story for the nightly news.

With your deadline quickly descending, you must professionally think through how you will present a story that involves an inconceivable family tragedy. You consider how

---

[*]   Bruce Evensen contributed to this chapter.

you can balance the family's right to privacy with the public's right to know. Prosecutors tell you the father will be charged with first-degree murder. If convicted, he is eligible for the death penalty. The man's attorney tells you his client is not guilty by reason of insanity.

Now, what do you say and what do you show as you do your stand-up in front of the family home at the open of your nightly newscast? You write an intro for the studio anchor that leads with the charges that have been filed in the murder of the girl. You've obtained a mug shot of the suspect, taken when he was charged at police headquarters. That is the image the story's viewers see. The anchor reports that the father will plead not guilty by reason of insanity. The anchor then throws you the story, and you set the scene. It was a family card game, you explain, that persuaded the father, "a successful software salesman," that "his daughter was a devil." A cut of an investigating detective confirms that authorities have a videotaped confession in the case. Your interview with a neighbor describes "a normal, caring" family man. An exterior shot of the family's church is followed by a scene of people praying inside the church. The family's pastor in an interview says that "the church is grieving over this senseless family tragedy" and that church members are "doing all they can to assist the mother." A brief follow-up with a psychotherapist, not involved in this particular case, tells viewers that "at times like this it is very important for survivors to know they are not alone in their grief and pain." This observation is followed by your stand-up closer indicating that the mother of the victim is "safe" and is "receiving care."

Your coverage of the story gives citizens information that is critical to the case while respecting the privacy of the mother. It stops short of making a spectacle of the lurid details surrounding the daughter's death, while capturing a sense of the communal grief and compassion that followed it. What responsible reporters realize in such circumstances is that tragedies are not isolated to the people they directly affect. As far as the community is concerned, crimes of great consequence diminish us all, and often elicit our need to know not only what has happened but what others are doing about it. This is a profoundly important thing for reporters to find out and citizens to know if we are to live in a more civil society.

The Reporter as Detective

The work of reporters and detectives is sometimes somewhat similar. Each is in the business of knocking on a lot of doors before one opens. One of the stories I covered that shows this was my attempt in 2002 to interview O.J. Simpson, the retired football star and actor who was tried and acquitted of murdering his ex-wife Nicole and her friend Ron Goldman. Some three years after the "trial of the century," O.J. made a visit to Trenton, New Jersey, to promote a documentary about his life after the trial. Simpson and his production team were traveling to different U.S. cities to drum up interest for the project. I was a reporter for the WB affiliate in neighboring Philadelphia and got assigned to the story.

When I arrived at work for my evening shift that Saturday between two and eleven, I saw on the Associated Press news wire that Simpson was to appear at a local nightclub that night around eleven. The news producers thought it was a great story, given the lingering controversy after the trial. However, there were two problems. First, our news aired at ten o'clock, one hour before Simpson was set to arrive at the club. Secondly, no one had any information about where Simpson was staying in the Philadelphia area in order to get a one-on-one interview with him. Even though there was the potential that I would be standing outside a nightclub at ten o'clock saying that Simpson would be here in an hour, the producers thought it was a good story and sent me out to see if we could chase Simpson down. I was reluctant. If we didn't find Simpson, where's the story? Finding him in a metropolitan area of 6 million people under deadline was daunting. I had one clue. A local battered women's shelter was holding a march and rally to protest Simpson's visit. The protestors were offended that Simpson was coming to Trenton to profit from the case. While acquitted of murder at the criminal trial, Simpson was found liable in a civil trial for the deaths of Brown and Goldman and had been ordered to pay a $33.5-million-dollar settlement.

My photographer and I left the station at about 2:35 and drove to Trenton, about forty-five minutes away. During the trip we brainstormed. Whom do we know who might know where O.J. would be? We called all of our usual celebrity sources, to no avail. We called the nightclub, but at three in the afternoon nobody answered. When we arrived at the nightclub the doors were locked and the parking lot was empty. A sign on the back door said in case of emergencies, please call a certain number. We dialed that number but it was an answering service. The operator claimed to have no direct contact information with the owners of the nightclub, only a pager number, which they could not release. By this time it was close to 4:30 and we had nothing on the story.

The protest march and rally was at 5:30. So we headed over to a local park to cover it. There we talked to a spokesperson for various battered women's groups. We also interviewed a woman who told us that her daughter was killed by an abusive boyfriend. These interviews were powerful indictments of Simpson's visit, but they were not Simpson. At 6:15, we went back to the nightclub. We began knocking on the doors of nearby houses and businesses, hoping that someone would lead us to the owners or managers of the club. If we could not find Simpson, at least we could talk to the club owners about why they were hosting such a controversial public figure. More than an hour went by and we struck out. It was now 7:30, less than two hours to go before our deadline. My photographer and I were a bit panicky. Amazingly, our hard work was about to pay off. A teenager knew the janitor of the nightclub and offered to take us to his house three blocks away.

We got the janitor to call the club owner. He agreed to grant us an interview and have our live shot from inside the club at ten instead of outside, where our competitors would be. We asked the owner if he knew where Simpson was staying, and he gave us the number to Simpson's road manager. Simpson's manager arranged for us to get fifteen minutes with Simpson, but stipulated that we had to come alone! Are you kidding? Of course we would!

This was an exclusive we had worked hard to get. The interview was scheduled for 8:30, leaving us less than forty-five minutes to write the story and get the script approved and edited. Keep in mind the photographer also had to set up the live shot, which included running cables and setting up lights. It was going to be a tight fit.

We went to Simpson's location and conducted the interview. We asked very tough questions about the public's perception that he had gotten away with murder. We asked how he felt about those who called him a "murderer," "woman beater," and "scum." Simpson said he didn't care about his detractors He was traveling around the country to meet his supporters. The video documentary's goal was to show that Simpson had a wide base of support, which rejected the notion that he could have ever committed a double murder.

By the time we got out of the interview it was nearly nine, which left only a few minutes to get the story together. I wrote the story and read it over the phone to a producer, who approved it. I led with Simpson's claim that he was oblivious to those who were certain he'd killed two people and incensed that he should come to Trenton to personally profit from what he had done. I gave protesters and the club manager their say too. The story was edited and ready to go by 9:25. That left us about thirty minutes to set up for the live shot inside the club. By this time, phone calls were coming into our newsroom from other news organizations who had heard that we had landed an exclusive interview with Simpson. We did share the video with other WB affiliates, but only after our exclusive lead story had aired. Other stations in the market eventually did catch up with Simpson, but it was during a 12:30 A.M. news conference at the club, long after their 11:00 P.M. newscasts were off the air. Their stories ran Sunday morning. Ours ran Saturday night. I had placed forty-eight telephone calls and knocked on twenty-eight doors before getting the information I needed. You may need to do that and more to scoop the competition. But that's only part of the story. For the responsible reporter, the harder part is making sure that all points of view, including Simpson's, are carefully balanced in the piece. **The story is not about what you think, but about what Simpson and the others think.** Let viewers draw their own conclusions.

Reporting on Deadline

Broadcast journalists are always chasing deadlines. Often we feel as if deadlines were chasing us. A couple of years ago, a competing Philadelphia news station reported that a pipe bomb had been found at a local church. Viewers were told that the station had a crew on the scene and would report details at 11:00 P.M. Police sources confirmed that a pipe bomb had been found and detonated. By the time a cameraman and I could get to the scene we were already behind. The bomb squad had exploded the device twenty minutes earlier. Another station had captured the explosion on video. All we had was video of the sand and debris from the detonation. Police had whisked away the church's pastor to a remote part of the church. Bomb experts were interviewing him to see what he knew. By 8:40 I was able to interview him.

The way to make this story distinctive in the limited time we had to produce it was to capture the anxiety and anger of those threatened by the incident. That would be my angle. At 8:40, we recorded the minister's firsthand account of how he found the device and what he did once he found it. Parishioners said that they would not be terrorized by the attacker. I had barely enough time to have federal agents confirm on camera that the device had been disabled before anyone was hurt. We reported on where the investigation would go next. Looking back, I'm proud of the work we did that night under a tight deadline, but not altogether content. Philadelphia is a diverse community, but our story wasn't. Unfortunately, it couldn't be helped. Only white males appeared in the story. As a beginning television reporter you will often be reminded of how important it is to make your stories reflect the communities it represents. Sometimes deadlines prevent you from doing that in a single story. That's why the second-day story should report what the first-day story left out.

Remember that your viewers have likely seen hundreds of stories before yours. They have no obligation to watch a story that is not done well. The problem you face is telling a story in less than two minutes in a way that engages citizens without trivializing the story or ignoring its complexity. Viewers look for memorable moments in the stories they see. Part of thinking through a television news story is seizing upon such moments in producing your story, while appreciating the limits of what you can show and tell on the air.

Challenges to Responsible Reporting

Television news need not tease in order to serve. "There's a dangerous milk formula that could hurt your baby" is one news promo that comes to mind. "What product is this, and why should you throw it away immediately? It's a report no mother can afford to miss, tonight at eleven." A station might run this tease several times between the 6:00 and the 11:00 news. The obvious question is, If the station really cared about babies, why not give parents the information they need immediately? Responsible reporters should go beyond the endless tease of promising big and delivering small. Instead, they should seek news worth knowing that often goes unexplored within communities. You will find that there are stations that work hard to give a good balance to the news, but the competition is so intense that station managers often first ask, "What will audiences watch?" instead of "What stories are worth doing?"

The scheduling pressures of television journalism make it imperative that you have a firm foundation in the values of responsible reporting. Know your community. Know its concerns. At daily story meetings have an original story idea. Don't be chained to the morning newspaper. Be observant. Maybe you noticed that city road crews in your neighborhood are not working and suggest to the news director that you follow them to see if streets in the area are being repaired. Perhaps you overheard a conversation at your neigh-borhood grocery store about an auto repair shop that may be ripping off customers. Start asking around to find out if others feel the same way and might have a story to tell. Temple University journalism professor Karen Turner routinely makes her students ride the subway in Philadelphia to find out what people are talking about. This exercise is an attempt to help students develop the skills of cultivating story ideas by interacting with people in the community. This is essential. Keep in mind, ideas are the fuel of a competitive news sta-tion. Your ability to have a sense of what is captivating people in your community is essential to becoming a successful reporter. Although you may have a great look and a wonderful voice, you may be very aggressive and outstanding with a camera, your real value comes in communicating information that may be of real value to your viewers.

It may surprise you to know that good writing is at the heart of being a television journalist. Reporters are often required to submit several versions of their stories for dif-ferent anchors for different times of the day. This means that the television news journalist must not only be a good writer, but a quick one. Journalism students who can shoot, write, and edit a package in less than ninety minutes are poised for success in landing their first job. If you are capable of writing three or four stories within an hour, that is a good pre-dictor of whether as a beginning journalist you can keep up in a fast-paced newsroom.

One of the thrilling parts of the job is not knowing from day to day, and sometimes hour to hour, what you'll be called upon to do. A television reporter might cover a big fire during one part of a shift and then be in the middle of a very high-profile and complicated trial later that day. I know. It's happened to me. If you become a television reporter, it'll happen to you. Think about it! You walk into a courtroom at 2:00 not knowing who the defense attorneys are, who the prosecutors are, who the important defense witnesses are, or who the grieving family members are, and by 5:00 you may have to give a live report? This is possible only if you have a solid sense of how responsible reporters approach any assignment. It starts with having a good understanding of your community, and what it needs and expects in news. It also requires you to be mentally engaged and intellectually flexible so that you can become a quick study on any assignment suddenly thrown your way.

A television reporter often begins his or her day around 9:00 A.M. with a morning story meeting. In these meetings the news team sets the coverage goals for the day and decides who will report what stories. It is fairly standard that a reporter may have completed three or four different stories by the noon newscast. It is 9:30 by the time the news director assigns your main story for the midday newscast. You then have less than two and a half hours to get some background research done on your story, call and set up interviews, travel across town, interview people for your story, write your story, get it approved for legal and editorial content by a producer, edit your story, and be standing in front of a camera for a live shot ready to go by 11:50. Keep in mind that you may have to gather and write two additional unrelated stories for the noon newscast as well.

For the 5:00 or 6:00 newscast, you may have to write two more variations of the story you reported at noon. It is likely that the court case you did a live report on at noon has been replaced by some sort of major breaking news in the afternoon. Frequently, a reporter on a day shift may write one or two different packages and two or three additional voice-overs and stand-ups unrelated to their package. In breaking news situations, you may likely be required to abandon a story that you originally started and go the scene of a fire, for example. In this case, **you may have as little as ten minutes after arriving on the scene before you have to file a live report.**

There is always a great temptation to report information that you have not thoroughly checked. Reporters sometimes feel it is safe because they have heard a competing station report the information. Absolutely avoid this! You are responsible for the information you pass along to viewers. Even the most credible newscast will have trouble repairing its credibility if the station passes along information that does not check out. Former network news anchor Dan Rather used to say, "It's better to be second and right on a story than to be first to report it and wrong!" Rather's eventual failure to verify information from a source led to his forced departure from CBS News.

At a fire, for example, a broadcast journalist will probe how it started, who has been hurt, what is the damage, how many firefighters are on the scene, and what the future impact may be. It does not matter that you arrived there at 5:55. When the newscast begins at 6:00, the station is counting on you to deliver something of real relevance to viewers. Initially, for your first live shot you may have very sketchy information. You will then have to be able to tell what you know for that one live shot at 6:02 and then quickly gather more information before the station comes back to you for another live report at 6:10. This means you have to have the ability to get information quickly and get it to your viewers just as rapidly.

Deadline Pressures in Television News

Television news reporters from two or three other stations in your market are doing exactly what you are doing. At no point do you want them to scoop you by getting on the air first with more information than you have or to report information that you have but have not confirmed with an official source. When interviewing a politician about why he or she supports a particular bill, deadline pressures may prevent a conscientious reporter from doing research to see if the politician's stand is consistent with campaign promises he or she made a year ago or if the politician may get some personal benefit from the proposed legislation. On the surface, the reporter may have done a passable story about the bill, but deadline pressures in this example have prevented the reporter from doing a basic part of a reporter's job—holding people in authority accountable for their actions.

Field reporters are often required to watch and observe what is going on in the field while simultaneously taking note of where interviews and compelling shots are on their tapes. Economics for the most part still prevent many television stations from equipping all of their reporters with laptops in the field, so many reporters may have to write the stories out on reporter's notebooks, while working with a photographer on finding shots.

Except for the largest markets, **video satellite phones** remain a luxury. Television news reporters are more likely to use cell phones to file stories from far-away places if there is no satellite availability. It is not uncommon for the audience to see a map or a picture of the reporter as they talk with anchors by phone. Even with all of the available technology and new media, the phone still remains one of the television journalist's biggest tools. Responsible reporters develop the ability to pick up the phone and find someone with information worth knowing. Reporters should cultivate connections with interesting and important people to ensure a wide range of perspectives on the news of the day.

The Watchdog Role of the Reporter

Most television reporters I've known are serious journalists who care about helping communities by providing them good information quickly so that those citizens may in turn meet their civic responsibilities. The watchdog function of television news journalists is alive and well, despite the criticism television news deserves for not doing its job well enough often enough. However, there can be little doubt that when the news means the most, as on September 11, 2001, citizens rely on television journalists to give them news they need to know. In the weeks after that terrible day, more than half of all viewers told researchers they were "addicted" to the coverage. Television news on that day and afterward helped unify and heal the nation. While print reporting may have greater ability to deeply explore important events, television remains the go-to medium in bringing powerful images to millions. Simultaneous viewing allows reporters and audiences to share experiences and learn of events together. In the aftermath of Hurricane Katrina, the visual images of what was happening in New Orleans provided a framework for the nation to ask tough questions about our government and its responsibility to take care of its citizens. The visual images of conditions in New Orleans and elsewhere along the Gulf Coast motivated Americans from all over the country to help those who had been devastated by the storm.

Some say local television news is on its last legs because audiences are being drawn to the web. Historically, as new technologies emerge, existing media have found ways to reinvent themselves or coexist with new technologies. Just a few years ago, I recall attending a training seminar where we learned how important it was that new stations have a web presence. It was thought then that consumers would soon be turning away from watching news. This was a failed prediction. Several years ago, tech-savvy consultants were showing how a station's website should look and what types of stories should be on them. Most television news reporters had little Internet presence. In fact, very few reporters even had an email address! Instead, the station's website was left to a webmaster, who was expected to write a few paragraph briefs on various stories reporters were working on and the station would use a picture frozen from a clip of video.

By the first decade of the twenty-first century, you can hardly find a station that does not have a website. Their web pages are filled with video and interactive links and weather satellites. Many stations now have reporters write Internet versions of their on-air stories, insist they return viewer email, and submit blog entries about the steps reporters took behind the scenes to bring that story to air. In some cities, reporters will stay after a newscast and chat with viewers via instant messaging and email about the stories they prepared that day. Some reporters further extend their relationship with audiences with **MySpace** pages. Audiences are increasingly being invited to share online their accounts of news of the day and in some cases submit pictures or video for airing. A decade ago, when a viewer captured news events on video and submitted that video to the news station for review, it was likely called "amateur" and seen as a novelty. Now audience content in newscasts seems to be omnipresent. Viewers are referred to in some markets as coverage "partners."

Stations are now experimenting with podcasting, a type of on-demand technology with which audiences can download audio and video prepared by the station to some sort of digital media player or iPod. This is a big change in the delivery of news. Not too long ago, local television news audiences had to wait until a specific time to watch news. Web-based technologies allow digital and cable channels to produce and air local news virtually nonstop. The news audience appears to be responding to delivery systems and news stations that give them news when they want it. Some stations are taking advantage of this trend, positioning themselves as the **"online, on-demand"** choice in their market as audiences now have greater flexibility to get their news from the Internet, a BlackBerry, a cell phone, or an iPod.

The Future of Television News

Technology makes news consumption more convenient and heavily influences the news-gathering process. Reporters in a growing number of markets are being required to gather more news for multiple delivery options. There is even greater pressure to generate more content in less time for more news venues. Critics say this delivery model erodes journalistic credibility by emphasizing speed over certainty in satisfying the news-on-demand audience. These reporters are often asked to find news that fits viewer appetites instead of news that matters most.

The traditional model of news had members of a mass audience simultaneously watching the news. In a newly emerging model, consumers are being groomed to choose not only when they want their news, but also the type of news they want. Critics are concerned that this delivery model empowers audiences to ignore news that isn't easily accessible. **Responsible reporting not only gives audiences what they want, but the information they need.** An uninformed electorate inhibits the possibility of democratic governance.

The twenty-first-century television news journalist will be intimately involved in the new technology of storytelling. However, the responsible reporter should always remember that while the tools of journalism may change, the principles of good reporting do not. New tools will not alter the obligation of the responsible reporter to make sure reports are fair, accurate, and balanced. News should represent a range of ideas in a community. News should affirm the good in communities. Viewers deserve more than just a diet of bad or negative news. News delivered to an audience's desktops, cell phones, and digital devices certainly will emphasize brevity. However, good television reporters understand the importance of making citizens aware of what happened and how those events may impact their lives. Ultimately, the responsible television reporter is the individual committed to journalism's job of making self-government possible by giving citizens news they need to know.

Creating a Broadcast Style

BRUCE J. EVENSEN

Ever turn the dial at the top of the hour and miss the beginning of a newscast by a few seconds? The radio announcer is saying, "He was one of the greatest actors of his generation. He was an Oscar winner. Critics claim he will be remembered in history as . . ." The news reader goes on and on. "He" this and "he" that. By the end of the story you're angry and frustrated because you never learned who "he" was.

In broadcast journalism, personal pronouns…he, she, it, they, them…are your mortal enemy. Don't use them. Repeat the proper name. If you're reading a story in a newspaper, magazine, or online, you can go over the paragraph a second time or look elsewhere in the story to find out who "he" or "she" is. Listeners can't. Responsible broadcast journalists should always try to create copy with their audience in mind. Stories that are worth saying and written in such a way that they're easily understood are stories that meet the social responsibility of broadcast journalists.

The backbone of broadcast journalism is the simple declarative sentence, one that flows from left to right across the page with a subject acting on a verb and often ending in a direct object. "The president issued orders." "The suspect is charged with killing four policemen." "The tornado devastated the neighborhood." There may well be a prepositional phrase or two thrown into the mix, and perhaps an adjective and an adverb, but essentially this is the thrill ride of broadcast journalism. It's exciting, safe, and gets you where you're going. Cognitive psychologists say that simple declarative sentences are the easiest sentences to understand. Beginning journalists will tell you they're not the easiest sentences to write. We're so used to sticking prepositional phrases at the beginning of sentences that indicate "where" or "when" that we tend to forget that the most important thing about a story is almost always "what" happened and "why" it happened. It's particularly important to keep this in mind when you're writing broadcast style. Three in four listeners won't stay through the end of your story. The majority of these bail at the first sentence. They're not interested because you haven't made it interesting. Their time is short, and you may be wasting it. That's why you need to hook them with a simple declarative sentence that captures the most recent relevant detail of the story.

For broadcast journalists **the most recent relevant detail of the story is that part of the story that has the greatest impact on the greatest number**. When listeners search for significance in a story that is what they are searching for. And since they've likely searched thousands of stories before getting to yours, listeners have a pretty good idea of what they're listening for. You frustrate the legitimate expectation of your listener at your peril. That is why the broadcast journalist has the immediate obligation to give the audience the news it most needs to know and to give the listener the "who," "what," "when," "where," "why," and "how" of every story in the first two sentences of that story. Your sentences should be no more than twenty to twenty-five words long. Your paragraphs should be brief. Three or four sentences are generally enough on one idea before you turn to another. That means your first paragraph, of two sentences, no more than fifty words, should let listeners know "who," "what," "when," "where," "why," and "how" of the story. To make sure you've done this, consider creating a little checklist for every story you write. Check off the "who" and the "what" and the "when" and the "where" and the "why" and the "how" to make sure you've covered them all.

Broadcast copy is conversational. Write simply. Avoid compound or complex sentences, which are usually linked by words like "and" or "but" or a similar conjunction. Every sentence should have one idea in it, not two, not three. That sentence should be easy to understand. If it sounds great and can't be easily understood it's a failure.

Your copy will be full of opinions, but the opinions shouldn't be yours. That's why you need to rely on attribution. Broadcast journalism is built on attribution. Say who says so. Any time you see an adjective or adverb that characterizes something or someone, you absolutely, positively must have attribution. "It was a rotten speech." "It was a great speech." These claims cry out for clarity. So, say who says so.

Always **be as specific as you can be**. Don't say "sources say." Who the heck are they? When you say "sources say," your listener will think you're saying it, and often they'll be right. Many news organizations have banned inexact and anonymous sourcing and require two sources to be on the record. "Informed sources" doesn't get you any closer to a specific, verifiable source that your audience can trust. "Sources close to the president" is nearly as weak. If your news group allows anonymous sourcing to protect the confidentiality of sources or for some other compelling reason, then the obligation of the responsible reporter is to verify the information from more than a single source. A second obligation is to give your listener as much information as possible about who is making the claim and what that person's competence is in making the claim.

When you say what the source is saying, don't say "according to." That's an old newspaper phrase. You wouldn't say "according to" if you were speaking in casual conversation, so why say it when you're on the air? **The simplest way to say something directly is almost always best.** This goes for words and phrases that lawmakers might use, or police might use, or educators might use, that most of us would never use. Police claim to "apprehend" suspects when they arrest them. Lawmakers talk of "torts" when they mean laws. Educators hold "seminars" when they really mean meetings.

Although broadcast journalism relies on conversational English, don't write the first thing that comes into your mind. The first thing that comes into your mind has often made several stops before getting there. **Avoid banality.** Clichés are not to your credit. Listeners will take you less seriously. Stating the obvious in an obvious way needlessly antagonizes the serious listener. It immediately suggests that there is little reward in staying with you or your story. In an age of digital media, many alternatives await the anxious, the annoyed, or the simply bored. They will drill down elsewhere. Your relevancy depends on your ability to write in a crisp, clean way the news others need to know. If you don't deliver, you will be found out and ignored. That's why, at the heart of a solid broadcast style, one finds substance. It is substance achieved through years of careful preparation and thoughtful repetition. At the heart of graceful broadcast writing is the art of invention. Every sentence of every paragraph should be seen as an exercise in discovery. You may be composing a sentence you've never written before and no one has ever written. That makes each story an odyssey into the unknown. You are in a place you've never been in exactly before, and you are bringing the listener to that place as well. You have a template that serves as a guide to you both. The most recent, relevant detail will be found first. The "who," "what," "when," "where," "why," and "how" will appear before the first two sentences have run their course. By that time, as a responsible reporter you will be well on your way to telling a story worth knowing and will have the satisfaction of knowing that the public accompanies you on this journey and relies on you as its guide every step of the way.

13

Feature Writing

SONNY RHODES[*]

The feature story allows a journalist to show the reader the world in ways generally avoided in hard news stories. The news story will continue to tell readers the facts about the world on the surface. The feature story will continue to go below the surface, showing readers the significance of these events. **Feature stories capture the "so-what" that deadline-driven hard news so often misses.** Their stories put a human face to homelessness, crime, and poverty. Feature writers interview the famous and the anonymous. They write about holidays, historic homes, gourmet dishes, and exotic locales.

Feature writers are storytellers. They can construct a story so that it goes full circle, tying the end back to the beginning. They can use foreshadowing and flashbacks. They can provide rich descriptions of the subjects and their surroundings. They have the opportunity to use rhetorical devices such as alliteration, metaphor, and onomatopoeia. They may use quotes that give readers insights into their interviewees' psyches, quotes a city desk editor would banish if they appeared in a news story. Like news stories, feature stories have no room for creativity with the facts—feature stories must be factual. The road to journalistic perdition is lined with the broken careers of poor souls who were creative with the facts. The creativity is in how the facts are presented.

---

[*]   William David Sloan and Bruce Evensen contributed to this chapter.

Good feature writers are enterprising. A reporter who covers a fire caused by faulty Christmas tree lights may get the basics for a routine news story on a weekday, then follow up by gathering information for a human-interest story on Sunday, showing readers how a family tries to cope with the loss of their home and belongings just before Christmas.

Qualities of Good Feature Stories

John Arwood, an assistant metro editor with North Carolina's *Charlotte Observer*, advises, "If you're on the schools beat, write about what teachers are doing, what students are doing, and what the bureaucrats are doing. Probe deeply in your reporting. Find the revealing detail, and make the people come alive. You can do the same on government beats: a story about a rezoning, for example, is always, in the end, a story about people, and what kind of community they want to have." Mitch McKenny, features editor for the *Beacon Journal,* says a good feature writer should be observant, persistent, curious, and have a good sense of humor. Besides such traits, McKenny says, a good feature writer must have a highly important skill: "You must know your way around the language."

"Feature writing is the act of taking a fact and expounding on it, taking that which is black and white and adding color to it; it is taking the reader beyond an introduction and inviting him to sit and have a full-length, full-disclosure discussion with the subject," says Angela Thomas, editor of *AY Magazine,* a Little Rock, Arkansas–based publication. "A good feature is important because it adds depth and texture to the fabric of a person, adds the answers to the who, what, when, where, why, and how in a way that hard news cannot." Kyle Massey, an assistant editor for the *New York Times,* observes, "Features are stories about people, problems, shifting attitudes or ways of life, and novelties, rather than accounts of news events like plane crashes, coups, car bombings, or tornadoes." Massey says feature stories often give readers a glimpse into how people live through the challenges, triumphs, and joys. The stories range from one about how a navy medic handles the physical and emotional strains of digging bullets out of marines in Iraq to how some people surf in Cleveland in the brown, waste-filled waters of Lake Erie. One of Massey's most famous stories recalls a family's struggle to live day to day with a mentally ill child. Its headline was "Living with Love, Chaos and Haley." The feature told the tale of a ten-year-old, Haley Abaspour, living in a Boston suburb with her parents and older sister. The child was diagnosed with a combination of bipolar disorder, obsessive-compulsive disorder, generalized anxiety disorder, and Tourette's syndrome. The story noted that her illness "dominates every moment, every relationship, every decision" involved in her family's life. Holly Tabor, of the Elizabethtown *News-Enterprise,* believes feature writing, at its best, "introduces your community to itself one piece at a time. From profiling a man with a terminal illness to following a marching band through a season in a series, I've found the best stories aren't just about the subject, but about some shared aspect of human nature.

Features can be emotional and revealing and remind us of things we may have forgotten about ourselves."

Award-Winning Feature Writing

Pulitzer Prize–winning feature writer for the *Orlando Sentinel* Jeff Kunerth says, "Feature writing is the way to bring the drama, excitement, humor, tragedy, triumph, sadness, disappointment, conflict, exaltation that is life into the pages of the newspaper." The genesis of his four-part "Anatomy of an Accident" series was a simple one, about events that happen every day, Kunerth says. "People in car crashes die. And most of the time we write those stories to answer two questions—what happened and who's to blame. I had the opportunity to go back, bring the dead to life, examine the aftermath of tragedy on the survivors, and to bring the reader along for the ride."

In preparing to write the series, in which he reconstructed events and dialogue from more than two years earlier, Kunerth interviewed the victims' families and neighbors; survivors of the four-vehicle crash; highway patrol, sheriff's office, and fire department personnel; county road officials; and a pharmacologist who analyzed autopsy reports of two of the victims. He pored over court records, investigation reports, and other documents. The painstaking research led to a vivid and dramatic account that began this way:

> "Three died. Three emerged scarred forever. In the memories of the survivors and the grief of the families, the accident on Poinciana Boulevard just after 6 A.M. on April 7, 2002, was the beginning of a day that never ended."

The third paragraph plainly states the reason for the series:

> "This is the story of one accident worth telling not because it is more significant than any other. But by considering the causes and consequences of one fatal crash, then multiplying its power and tragedy by all the others like it, we can begin to comprehend the true human toll of the carnage on our roads."

Two of the dead were Tommy Allen, twenty, and Brian Smith, seventeen, who had left an all-night party shortly before the fatal crash. Allen was driving. "Tommy's bloodstream was a pharmaceutical sewer of painkillers, barbiturates, antibiotics and tranquilizers," Kunerth reported. "He had enough alcohol in his blood to make two people drunk." Consider how anemic that last sentence would have been if Kunerth had simply used the boilerplate news story description and written that Allen's blood-alcohol level was twice the legal limit.

The *Arkansas Democrat-Gazette*'s Ron Wolfe, a feature writer and columnist who has also authored several books of fiction, says that fiction-writing techniques have helped with his feature writing. "Fiction helps enormously with features. For one thing, it teaches us to use all five senses. The ones used the least in newspaper writing—taste, touch, and smell—can be the most evocative. If you take the typical newspaper story based on a telephone interview, it's like a flat voice in a dark room. Describe the voice, and you've got a character. Describe the room, and you've turned on the lights. The more senses, the more vivid." The story structure of feature writing, Wolfe says, can be thought of as a circle. "It's the hero's quest. The hero leaves home, has adventures, and finally comes back where he started. This is Frodo's story, and Luke Skywalker's. It's also the story of anyone in the news who has faced some kind of problem, gone in search of an answer, and come back to share what he's learned."

Tools and Techniques of Feature Writers

Feature writers collect information in many ways—face-to-face interviews, telephone interviews, the Internet, books, periodicals, government documents, and faxes. Kunerth points out that it requires "collecting details, descriptions, and using the five senses as a routine part of your note-taking. You can't go back and get that stuff. You have to collect it while you are there. And you can't do it from your desk." The Internet is invaluable when a feature reporter gathers background and statistical information, but it has its limits. Rhonda Owen, editor for the *Arkansas Democrat-Gazette*, says, "When we get a topic, we Google it. That gives us a starting point and also can lead us to sources we wouldn't find elsewhere. The Internet saves us a lot of research time because we can access library databases, document databases, and all kinds of publications." The downside of using the Internet, Owen says, is that it "nurtures a tendency to over-research and get bogged down with too many extraneous facts and figures, resulting in lost or fractured focus."

The unlimited space of the Internet is creating a golden age for feature writing. Arwood says his newspaper is increasingly using the Internet to enhance the impact of its features. "I think you'll see feature writers everywhere do that more and more. Some of the most popular features of our website, charlotte.com, are the photo slideshows that accompany the feature stories." Arwood's paper published a six-part series in October 2006 on under-age drinking. Each installment tried to convey the impact of teen drinking by focusing on a different individual: a teen who tried to help a friend stop drinking, a young man trying to abstain amid increasing peer pressure, a trooper who investigates alcohol-related traffic accidents and has to knock on doors and inform families that their loved ones are dead. "The words on the printed page were quite powerful, but the impact of the series was heightened by the audio interviews with the profile subjects that we posted online," Arwood says. "It's powerful to read a trooper's comments about the anguish of informing a family they've lost a loved one to a drunk teenage driver. It's powerful, in a different way, to go online and hear that trooper talk about that experience."

While only a few years ago a reporter needed only a notepad, a pen, and perhaps a still camera, today he or she may need to take along a video camera. Digital photography is utilized to give added value to feature stories appearing online. "Just in my seven years at the *Times*," Massey says, "I have seen a remarkable transformation in the way features are told. In the old days, journalists talked to people, studied data, went out and saw things for ourselves. Now things are different." Audio-visual presentations strengthen the emotional power of what the feature reporter has written, giving readers and viewers more ways to experience the story. Kunerth notes that online storytelling allows feature writers to "expand on what is in the paper, to augment the newsprint version, or add another level to the story."

A Case Study in Feature Writing

An editor at the *Arkansas Democrat-Gazette* recently asked me to write a profile of Ken Smith, executive director of Audubon Arkansas, an organization celebrating its fifth year of environmental education in our state. It began with a search on Lexis-Nexis for "Ken Smith" and "Audubon Arkansas." More than two hundred articles appeared. Scanning the headlines revealed twenty articles that provided a good sampling of the organization's goals and activities. An interview with Smith followed. He recounted how he realized as a college undergraduate that he wanted a career in conservation biology rather than medicine. He talked of how he wished he could have seen Arkansas when it was largely in its wilderness state, before the area was settled and some of its species driven to extinction. The interview ended with names and phone numbers of several people Smith had worked with in thirty years of public life. Phone calls followed.

The first draft of the story began with Smith's epiphany of what he wanted his life's work to be. The lead read: "Ken Smith remembers where he was and what he was doing the day he realized he wanted to be a conservation biologist." I decided that lead would not work because the story would next have to go back and explain who Smith was and why his work mattered. So, the information was saved for later in the story. In a subsequent draft, I developed a descriptive lead, hoping to hook the reader's imagination with a brief chronicling of Arkansas' past and present and how they are connected with Smith's work. The other half of the story told how Smith became interested in conservation biology and the difference his work had made to the state and its citizens.

That published story begins:

> Try to picture the Natural State when the Spanish conquistadors crossed the Father of Waters in 1541 and clambered onto the river's west bank in search of gold. Led by Hernando De Soto, the plunderers were as unsuccessful in finding riches west of the Mississippi River as they had been in the two previous years of meandering through the lands to the east. Had they not been so obsessed with finding gold, the conquistadors might have appreciated another type of wealth: the plants and wildlife surrounding them. What would become designated as the Mississippi River Alluvial Plain, better

known as the Delta, contained millions of acres of bottomland forests. To the west lay millions more acres of prairies and mountains. Elk and bison roamed the prairies. Red wolves stalked the woods for prey. Passenger pigeons and colorful Carolina parakeets arose in such enormous flocks they cast shadows upon the land.

The story then recounts how by the early 1800s "commercial hunting and trapping had begun to take a toll on some species, but those fertile fields and forests still supported wildlife in amazing numbers." By the 1960s, however, "kids roamed the forests and fields" because "their parents have told them to get outside and entertain themselves. So, they play football or baseball in a well-worn pasture, or hide-and-seek among the brush piles and woods just beyond the subdivision fences. Some of them fish and swim in muddy Delta bayous or clear Ouachita streams, catching minnows, crawdads and tadpoles. Others stalk rabbits and squirrels. The kids play until dark and then head home for supper. The bison, elk and red wolves," the story continues, "are long gone from these parts. The passenger pigeons, once thought to be the most populous bird species in North America, also are gone," replaced by "urban sprawl, logging and farming. Forests were cut, swamps drained, prairies plowed." At this point in the piece I introduce "Ken Smith of Bryant who wishes he could visit Arkansas in the 1700s. Smith would love to see prairies full of elk and bison," its skies "clouded by pigeons and parakeets. At 55," the story goes on, "Smith is troubled that many of today's children don't know nature the way kids did when he was a youngster. Even some small-town youths are intimidated by the outdoors, being more comfortable with the virtual worlds offered on computer and television screens." On the first Earth Day on April 22, 1970, Smith remembers "taking an environmental issues class." He decided that he "wanted to be a conservation biologist. 'This is what I want to be,' he recalls thinking. 'That is what I want to do.'" For Smith, "protecting the environment became a commitment that has spanned more than a third of a century.

The story concludes with Smith's estimate that Audubon Arkansas has worked with 5,500 students in five years, hoping "to create the next generation of stewards." The kicker for him is when "they get so fired up about science. To be on a field trip with children, even adults, who have had little exposure to the outdoors and to see them become excited about nature" feels, Smith said, smiling, that they've been "reborn."

Learning How to Look and Listen

A dozen years ago, in the first edition of *The Responsible Reporter*, Tom Berner, a veteran feature writer, wrote that the best feature writers "learn how to look and learn how to listen." He observed that a good feature story is not about the feature writer but "the people in the story." The good feature story, Berner remarked, "calls attention to the people in the story, and not the way the story is written." Those observations are no less true today. John Hersey noted that **"journalism allows its readers to witness history"** and that the very best feature writing "gives the readers an opportunity to live it." This happens when the feature writer captures the lived detail that brings to life his or her story and the people in it. If you do this, there is a strong chance your story will be remembered long after the reader finishes it. Ernest Hemingway, a successful reporter before he became a bestselling author, put it this way: "Watch what happens. If we get into a fish, see exactly what it is that gives you the emotion. Whether it is the rising of the line from the water and the way it tightens like a fiddle string until drops start from it, or the way the fish smashes and throws water when he jumps. Remember what the noises are. Find what gives you the excitement. Then write it down, making it clear so the reader will see it too and have the same feeling that you had."

Remember the sounds and smells of the scene you're writing about. William Bolitho famously wrote on the death of actress Sarah Bernhardt that "the air was steady and bright the day they buried Sarah Bernhardt. The crowd heard the wheels creaking as she passed and smelled the loads of costly roses like heavy incense in their faces. Even those at the back, who could see nothing, had this satisfaction: they grumbled less than is usual at so great a show." The story of another death is equally compelling. Royce Brier of the *San Francisco Chronicle* won a Pulitzer Prize for his November 1933 account of mob justice. "Lynch law wrote the last grim chapter in the Brooke Hart kidnapping here tonight," he famously began. "Twelve hours after the mutilated body of the son of Alex J. Hart, wealthy San Jose merchant, was recovered from San Francisco Bay, a mob of ten thousand infuriated men and women stormed the Santa Clara Jail, dragged John M. Holmes and Thomas H. Thurmond from their cells, and hanged them in historic St. James Park. Swift and terrible to behold," Brier wrote, "was the retribution meted out to the confessed killers and slayers. As the pair were drawn up, threshing in the throes of death, a mob of thousands of men and women and children screamed anathemas at them. Great cheers from the crowd of onlookers accompanied the hoisting of the two slayers. Old women with graying hair and benign faces expressed satisfaction at the quick end of the murderers. King Mob was in the saddle and he was an inexorable ruler."

Wonderful feature writing can be compelling when the character it reveals is like someone the reader knows or can easily imagine knowing. Margo Huston of the *Milwaukee Journal* won a Pulitzer Prize for a spirited piece about a wily old lady confined to a wheel-chair. "At 91, her blue eyes still twinkle," Huston wrote. "Her smile beckons, and she manages, ever so slowly, to raise her saggy arms and motion, come here, with her fingertips. Her stringy hair matted, she cocks her head coyly and, smiling like a contented but shriveling babe, softly pleads to this stranger, 'Come here, lady, and give Bertha a little kiss.'"

Many of your best feature writers have a love affair with language. Lafcadio Hearn, long ago a writer for the *New Orleans Item* and the town's *Times-Democrat*, put it prettily. "See the color of words, the tints of words," he advised a young reporter, "the secret ghostly motions of words. Hear the whispering of words, the rustling of the procession of letters, the weeping, the raging and racketing and rioting of words, sense the fragrance of words, the tenderness or hardness, the dryness or juiciness of words." Donald C. Drake, an award-winning feature writer on the *Philadelphia Inquirer,* urged beginning feature writers to be patient. "It's so easy to lose faith in yourself," he warns, "when attempting something so difficult. It requires detailed reporting, beautiful writing, and hard work, and it's worth the effort." He points out, "If you're not good, you've got nothing." But if you are good, you'll be giving your reader everything he or she needs to enter the life and circumstances you are writing about.

Remember, if you plan on becoming a successful feature writer, be spare. Be alert to the detail that captures the lived experience. Do this through acute observation of the people you report on. Offer insight by searching for significance. If some detail arrests your attention, remember why, and share that sentiment with your reader. At its best, excellent feature writing enlarges our imagination and connects readers to those being written about.

Commentary and Column Writing

SAM G. RILEY

"In March 2003, Pat Robertson tried to give President Bush some advice about the coming invasion of Iraq," begins Leonard Pitts, Jr., in his syndicated column that appeared in newspapers across the nation on the eve of the 2004 election. "Robertson, founder of the Christian Coalition," Pitts continued, "supports the president. But he told CNN on Wednesday that he advised Bush to prepare the nation for the likelihood of casualties. Bush's reply? 'We're not going to have any casualties.' That was 9,100 casualties ago."

Pitts is a Teddy Roosevelt Rough Rider, directly attacking his foe. Using an anecdote lead, he dramatizes what he considers the naïve ineptitude with which President Bush and his advisers invaded another country that posed the United States no direct threat. While news reporters must stick to objectively reporting the content of the administration's latest press releases and its other pronouncements, Pitts and his fellow opinion columnists are free to take a jaundiced view of those pronouncements, and of the president himself. Like many of the best opinion writers, Pitts pulls no punches.

Reporters' words must march calmly and deliberately across the page. Columnists and commentary writers' words are free to dance or caper or stomp across the page. Reporters must tackle a topic head on; writers of commentary, if they wish, can sneak up on their topic from an oblique angle. The reporter must concentrate on informing via rational presentation of fact. The editorial writer does the same, with persuasion added. **Columnists are able to give attention not just to informing, but to entertaining while also persuading their readers.** A large measure of emotion can make its appearance in a column, while expression of the writer's own emotions would be out of place in a news story. Such is the freedom of approach and of technique of people who write columns or commentary—a short-essay journalistic form that, along with editorials and reviews, make up the parts of a newspaper in which writers can express their opinions.

Any newspaper's heart is its reporting; its soul is in its editorials; but a large part of its personality resides in the work of its columnists and commentators. And the best columnists are often among the best reporters and information gatherers. Celebrated Chicago columnist Mike Royko saw himself as "a sworn enemy of every slum owner who made a buck off the small and weak" and of every building inspector "who took a wad from a slum owner to make it all possible." He developed a devoted readership in 7,500 columns over four decades and became their representative in insisting that city leaders do their duty. He could write in the rough, unlettered language of the street, and at times he made his point through an intermediary, a skinny, hard-bitten tenement kid named

"Slats Grobnik." Through Slats, Royko mined the oblique angle. "The subject of criminal rehabilitation was debated recently in City Hall," Royko remarked. "It's an appropriate place for this kind of discussion because the city has always employed so many ex-cons and future cons." A long line of columnists similarly saw themselves as being about the people's business. Columnist Don Marquis used "Clem Hawley" (the Old Soak), to ridicule Prohibition; "Hermione" (and her Little Group of Serious Thinkers), to satirize well-to-do but flighty do-gooders; and even a literary cockroach, "Archy," who lampooned the literary life. Chicago's Finley Peter Dunne had his fictitious bartender, "Mr. Dooley"; Philander Johnson his "Senator Sorghum"; Bill Vaughan his "Congressman Sludgepump," "Sam Sausage, the Good Rumor Man," and "Westbrook Normal, well-known average man."

Dave Barry, a highly skilled Pulitzer Prize—winning humorist, needled a radio genre in a famous 1988 column that recalls an early-morning commute into the infinite blandness of easy-listening radio. "Monday morning," Barry begins, the traffic is bad and what's on the radio is little better. It opens with a plea to "send Bill Doberman to Congress. Because Bill Doberman agrees with us. Bill Doberman. It's a name we can trust. Bill Doberman. It's a name we can remember. Let's write it down. Bill . . ." A competing station claims the listener has "just heard 19 uninterrupted classic hits," while at another, a disclaimer breathlessly erupts: "…followingisbasedonan800yearleaseanddoesnotincludetaxtags-insuranceoranacualcarwegetyourhouseandyourchildrenandyourkidneys." Those wanting a car are harangued: "NINE THOUSAND DOLLARS!!! BUD LOOTER CHEVROLET OPEL ISUZU FORD RENAULT JEEP CHRYSLER TOYOTA STUDEBAKER TUCKER HONDA WANTS TO GIVE YOU, FOR NO GOOD REASON . . ."

Barry's odyssey into the brainless and bizarre world of '80s radio returns the reader to an announcer's assertion that "…Bill Doberman. He'll work for you. He'll FIGHT for you. If people are rude to you, Bill Doberman will KILL them. Because Bill Doberman . . ." And a competing call-in show, which starts, "…listening audience. Hello?…Go ahead…Steve?…This is Steve…Go ahead…Am I on?… Yes…Go ahead…Is this Steve?" As the column swirls to its conclusion Bill Doberman returns again and again, asking and then pleading for your vote. Radio evangelists make guest appearances, as does breaking news, and uninterrupted "classics" reaching into the thousands. The beleaguered Barry, as our Everyman, finds little satisfaction. His skillful indictment of the sad state of radio content demonstrates the freedom of approach that is granted to the columnist, and most of all to the columnist who deals in satire. It is a column, but it was not written in standard essay format. Freedom in format-ting is what helps make Barry's column so devastating.

Columnists approach their subjects from all angles, using many voices. Russell Baker of the *New York Times* is urbane; Walter Winchell was the father of slang. H. L. Mencken sought to "comfort the afflicted and afflict the comfortable." Oklahoma cowboy columnist Will Rogers never met a man he didn't like. New York's Damon Runyon chronicled the underside of life in the big city. Art Buchwald amused himself at the expense of official Washington. Erma Bombeck was the queen of around-the-house humor.

Most successful political columnists make use of wit yet write about serious subjects. Maureen Dowd became known for her snide, slashing attacks on presidents Clinton and Bush. Ann Coulter views all liberals as the spawn of Satan. Columnists Drew Pearson and Jack Anderson led investigative crusades exposing corruption. Westbrook Pegler took public figures to task so frequently and brilliantly, it was said that those individuals had been "Peglerized." Perhaps the patron saint of all columnists everywhere is Ernie Pyle, much beloved for his World War II columns from the front that gave the point of view not of the generals, but of the privates. Pyle was embedded the old-fashioned way—in a foxhole. That's a good place for a columnist to be.

Sports Reporting

MIKE CONKLIN

The CEO of a Major League Baseball franchise once told me two things he doesn't like to hear when interviewing prospective employees: (1) they know a lot about sports and (2) having a job in sports seems like a lot of fun. Working for a team should never be confused with being a sportswriter *covering* a team, but his observation is applicable both on and off the field of play.

For one thing, it does not take long as a sportswriter to learn that someone always knows more than you do, whether it's a referee citing rules, coaches explaining strategy, someone sitting next to you in the press box, or simply a fan with encyclopedic knowledge. That's OK. Your job is to learn something new and relay it to an audience.

And "fun" is not a word you hear much when toiling in press boxes long after everyone else has left to attend post-game parties. The hours can be late, typically you work nights and weekends, and there's constant pressure to accurately handle many facts and numbers while meeting deadlines.

But the job, while not necessarily fun in a traditional sense, can be as satisfying as anything in journalism. Assignments can take you to exciting and dramatic events, where you may interview high-profile figures and write with a creative freedom not always allowable in other sections of the paper or newscast. You almost always are guaranteed an eager, attentive audience.

In the end, what really separates sports writers from everyone else following sports is simple: access.

The job means you get to ask questions of principals involved in a story, whether it's getting reactions from athletes immediately following an event, talking to a university official about candidates for a coaching vacancy, or interviewing the top draft choice of a National Basketball Association team. Use it. The more news you provide, the more your audience depends on you as a source.

In this clip-and-paste era, one in which speculation often passes for news, the role of the reporter with access has become even more important. He or she provides fresh information for the ongoing dialogue, whether it is for fans discussing high school football over coffee or radio talk show hosts who almost never go into locker rooms and often seek reporters as guests. Your own columnists may base their opinions on your articles.

It is easy to get swept up by the excitement and chatter that surround sports, but the professionals stick to the same fundamentals and techniques discussed throughout this book. On the other hand, it would be naïve to say that covering sports is like covering any other topic. With that in mind, here are ten tips, some obvious, some not so obvious, to help you navigate this world.

1. The score. Put the final score in your game story, certainly no lower than the third paragraph. Don't make readers search. Seems simple enough, but you'd be surprised how easy it is to get so absorbed in an event you've witnessed that basic facts, such as the score, significant statistics, location, and star performers for both sides, are forgotten in the reporting.

   It's happened to the best of them. If you're working for a reputable, daily newspaper, undoubtedly there will be an alert, professional copy editor to cover the oversight. The best way to avoid omissions, of course, is to **make a checklist of the event's important facts before starting to write.**

2. Nut graph. It gets drilled into you almost from day one in Journalism 101, but a paragraph or two devoted to setting the stage, whether it's a feature or a gamer, remains as important in sports as it would be covering a school board meeting.

   Unless you are writing a sidebar placed next to the main story, you simply cannot assume everyone knows the background of what you are reporting. Every sports fan in town may know the storyline, but not every reader or viewer may be a sports fan. Don't get too consumed and forget that segment of the audience.

3. No homers, please. How many times have you seen a community newspaper account of a game in which the local heroes got slaughtered, but it is almost impossible to tell they lost by a lopsided score when reading about it? Sadly, it happens too often and it is an insult to audiences owed a journalistically sound explanation of why a team lost.

   Reporting a story from the viewpoint of a local team is perfectly acceptable, but blindly accepting inadequate, cliché excuses from participants after a bad loss is not OK. Fans deserve—and expect—objective explanations, which includes talking to the other team and including its significant statistics too.

4. Don't sweat it. At some point, you may encounter a condescending coach or athlete who'll say you can't know much unless you played the sport. Bulletin: you're there to report the game, not play it, and that requires an entirely different set of skills.

   The quick reply is this: Could they do your job? Other replies could be: You don't have to be a legislator to report about a vote in Congress. You don't have to own Google stock to know when to sell it. You don't have to be run over by an automobile to learn it hurts.

5. Forget loyalties. You're a native of Nebraska, grew up rooting for Cornhusker football teams, graduated from the University of Nebraska in Lincoln in journalism, and you're offered a job by a daily newspaper in Oklahoma to cover the Oklahoma Sooners in football.

   Could you do it? If not, better find another profession. Your ability to shift perspectives is called professionalism, and it adds context to your understanding of sports in general. This, in turn, enhances skills, knowledge, and job prospects. Or, to put it another way: How objective could you really be staying in Nebraska and covering the Cornhuskers?

6. Fore! The first tennis match I covered was the U.S. Open in New York City. The first downhill skiing I covered was in France during the Olympics. Within one week on a trip east, I

covered boxing in Madison Square Garden, Yale-Harvard football, and the annual Hall of Fame college basketball game in Springfield, Massachusetts.

Your ability—and willingness—to apply basic journalism techniques to any sport is important and can lead to great assignments. You may have a favorite sport, but cover as many as possible. This versatility makes you more valuable to audiences and, in turn, to editors.

7. Show me the money. Sports no longer is simply fun and games. It is a billion-dollar industry reaching into grammar schools. As a result, today's reporters occasionally find themselves covering contract holdouts, NCAA recruiting violations, steroid abuse, criminal court proceedings, and teenagers with agents.

It would be nice to avoid this, but you can't. Become well versed in the terminology, meaning, rules, and implications surrounding news that has nothing to do with winners and losers on the field. Don't be afraid to ask the simplest questions if you don't understand something. Above all, be open-minded: the bad guys aren't always bad and the good guys aren't always good.

8. Stay aggressive. Don't wait for the tip-off to become familiar with what you're covering. Do your homework in advance and learn about players on both sides. This makes it easier to understand noteworthy developments as they occur—the ball-handling guard uncharacteristically scoring fifteen points in the first half or the singles-hitting shortstop with two home runs in his first two at-bats.

The athletic director for the university you cover may call a press conference for tomorrow, but that doesn't mean you have to wait with everyone else to learn what will be announced. Start poking around to get the news in advance. Nothing impresses editors and sports directors at the next level more than someone who beats the competition.

9. Shhh. Jerome Holtzman, a former *Chicago Tribune* sportswriter and a member of baseball's Hall of Fame, once wrote a book entitled "No Cheering in the Press Box." It was a collection of job-related experiences from some of the nation's most famous sports writers. He borrowed this title from one of the most sacred, but unwritten, rules among professionals.

For starters, cheering can be disruptive for the person on a tight deadline. This occurs a lot in college football press boxes, and it is a sign that your loyalty to a particular team is stronger than your objectivity. This, in turn, signals that you put being a fan ahead of your job as a journalist. This is also not helpful for job prospects if the sports editor of a larger, more professional newspaper you admire is in the vicinity.

10. Read. Read a lot. Read *Sports Illustrated,* especially the shorter "Scorecard" items in the front of the magazine. Read *Sporting News, USA Today,* and *ESPN.* Also, read the great variety of sports websites, including those produced by professional teams. The more up-to-date you are on events, the more knowledgeable and meaningful you can make your stories.

Always read someone else's story about the same event you covered. In fact, there is no single, best way to write any article. It is easy to fall into familiar patterns, and eventually readers pick up on your predictability, which is not good. By reading a lot, you learn new techniques to add to your approaches.

Writing the Obituary

JANICE HUME

Chances are, when you first dreamed of becoming a journalist, writing obituaries wasn't what you had in mind. After all, most obits don't make the front page. They don't call for social reform, expose corruption, or identify trends in popular culture. An obit simply reports a death. It's a period, the final punctuation marking the end of someone's life—a dead end.

So why do readers love obits? Why do some people bookmark the "obituaries" link at the online *New York Times,* or buy a subscription to the tiny *Guntersville Advertiser-Gleam* when they don't live within range of its north Alabama circulation? The answer: they have discovered a secret. **Obits do more than report deaths. They are all about life.** Done well, they paint fascinating little portraits of our neighbors, people who influenced our world, interesting strangers. They are personality profiles that share what we want to remember about people we've lost, and that celebrate what we value about ourselves.

Covering the death beat can be interesting and challenging, especially if you are lucky enough to work at a newspaper that takes obituaries seriously. The job might surprise you. For example, as an obit writer you might actually interview the deceased! Some obituaries, particularly for famous people, are anticipated, the reporting done ahead of time. Information from these interviews is held until after the subject's death.

However, most obits are breaking news stories about people who are not famous. The reporter must quickly pull together salient facts about the deceased, double check for accuracy, and then write in a way that compels readers to pay attention. It's a difficult job, but one that can be extraordinarily rewarding. *New York Times* writer Margalit Fox, in the *Times'* online feature "Talk to the Newsroom," said this about obituary writing: "On the days when it works well, inhaling a stranger's life through intensive study and exhaling it again onto the page—rapidly, accurately and, if one is very lucky, elegantly—is the most exhilarating feeling, and one of the greatest privileges in the world."

Reporting the obit is like working on any other kind of deadline news story. You need to answer some basic questions. Who died? Where? What was the cause of death? When did it happen? How did it happen? Beyond these basics, an obituary includes information about the funeral and the burial, visitation, and the names of survivors. You'll need to gather details about the deceased, including his age (verified by a birthday), where he worked, and club and organization memberships. If you are writing for a large daily, you might explain why his life was newsworthy, understanding that "celebrity" and "newsworthy" are not the same thing. What impact did she make on our world? If you work for a small newspaper, you might write about his passion for fishing or college football, or that he lived within walking distance of his grandchildren. Obituaries at small papers reveal people with strong ties to place, family, church, and neighbors. They contribute to the community's vitality and help the newspaper perform its mission not only to report the news, but also to connect readers.

Be extra careful to get the facts right. Few errors cause as much pain, and anger, as an incorrect obituary. Your credibility and your publication's reputation are on the line. The first fact to double check: Is the person really dead? My own newspaper prematurely reported the death of one of its columnists when a family member gave us incorrect information. A quick confirmation call to the mortuary would have saved much embarrassment for the paper, and grief for the family.

Make sure every detail is checked, and rechecked, including the spellings of names, the funeral arrangements, and any religious terms you might include. It's great to use the Internet to research your subject, but only if the information you uncover is about the right person and can be verified. **Families cherish obituaries and pass them down for generations.** It's important, and honorable, to make sure they are complete, fair, and accurate.

It's also honorable to be inclusive. For my book *Obituaries in American Culture,* I read more than eight thousand obits from 1818 to 1930. One of the things I noticed was that not everybody who died got an obit. The deaths of many African Americans, Native Americans, and women weren't considered worthy of reporting. And even if included, their lives were reported in different ways. For example, men in the nineteenth century were noted for being gallant, honest, bold, patriotic, and industrious. Women, on the other hand, were patient, resigned, obedient, pious, gentle, and virtuous. Were men and women so different, or were those simply the characteristics that society, and the newspapers, valued? The scant few people of color were remembered for getting along with white people, for adhering to the social order. If they had been interviewed, would they have emphasized those qualities? How sad to think of so many interesting lives not shared.

Unfortunately, most large newspapers today simply cannot include a news obituary for everyone. That would take too many reporters, and too much space. So the most newsworthy people are profiled, and others left out unless families purchase obituaries through the advertising department. Paid obituaries are different from news obits in that the family member decides what content is important enough to include, and what should be left out. They pay by the word or line for publication. News obituaries are written with the same ethical and reporting guidelines as news stories. No money is exchanged for a news obit.

Many newspapers, like the *Atlanta Journal-Constitution,* try to single out interesting "regular" people for news obituaries. Small-town papers, like the *Guntersville Advertiser-Gleam,* have the luxury of publishing an obituary for everyone who dies. This newspaper has made a name for itself by treating everyone the same, whether rich or poor, black or white, man or woman. In death, the newspaper finds something interesting to remember about each one.

As newspapers move online, the potential for the death beat is boundless. **Online obits include guest books for readers to share memories.** They can be multimedia, including audio and video of the deceased. And like their print predecessors, they are more than simple reports of death. They are vibrant and exciting, not a "dead end" but a celebration of life.

14

Writing for Magazines

JAMES MARTIN

The 1907 Nobel Prize for literature winner, Rudyard Kipling, started his writing career in 1882 as a newspaper journalist, but soon began freelancing as a magazine writer and poet. He became immensely popular and one of the highest paid authors of his day. According to one story, which may well be apocryphal, a London newspaper reported that Kipling was making the unheard-of sum of ten shillings a word for everything he wrote. Some university students were not impressed and sent Kipling an irreverent note: "We read in the newspaper that you are now making ten shillings a word. Enclosed are ten shillings. Will you please send us one of your best words?" Kipling's one-word reply was simply, "Thanks!"

Magazine article writers today are often paid by the word, but very, very few come anywhere close to Kipling's success. In fact, it is extremely difficult to make a living as a freelance magazine writer. Most freelancers hold down other jobs while they are trying to break into the magazine field.

One of Kipling's often-quoted poems celebrates the five Ws and one H of journalism. Four lines from *Just So Stories* have been repeated so many times they have become stock:

> *I keep six honest serving-men*
> *(They taught me all I knew);*
> *Their names are What and Why and When*
> *And How and Where and Who.*

These six interrogatives are easily worth a thousand times whatever Kipling was first paid for them. Although a little shop-worn, they continue to serve well as a convenient way to organize material. This chapter will answer some of the five *W*s and the *H* of magazine article writing.

The Market for Magazine Writers

There are around two thousand consumer magazine titles sold on newsstands each month. About three fourths of these are listed by Standard Rate & Data Service, the monthly listing service of magazines. About a fourth choose not to be listed by SRDS because they do not sell advertising. On the other hand, advertising dollars are so crucial to another fourth that they have audited circulations. This means that they have their circulation numbers verified twice a year by the Audit Bureau of Circulation. They are known in the trade as ABC magazines. At the end of 2005, the top ten ABC magazines were: *AARP The Magazine*, *AARP Bulletin, Reader's Digest, TV Guide, Better Homes and Gardens, National Geographic, Good Housekeeping, Family Circle, Ladies' Home Journal*, and *Woman's Day*. Other titles in the top one hundred include *Sports Illustrated* at number fifteen, *Guideposts* at number twenty, *Ebony* at number fifty-five, and *Forbes* at number one hundred.

The multitude of consumer titles can be divided into two groups: general-interest magazines and specialized publications. General-interest magazines like *Reader's Digest, TV Guide*, and *National Geographic* are directed to a broad audience with wide-ranging interests, while specialized magazines, as the designation implies, target readers with specific interests. The *Writer's Market*, an annual directory that lists hundreds of magazines that buy freelance articles, classifies specialized magazines under about fifty headings, including "Automotive and Motorcycle," "Aviation," "Disabilities," "Hobby and Craft," "Home and Garden," "Photography," "Religious," "Science," and "Sports." But these are broad categories. Most specialized publications are far more focused. For example, under "Sports" are magazines that concentrate on archery and bow hunting, bicycling, hiking and backpacking, hunting and fishing, martial arts, and running. Under fishing, some of the titles are *Game and Fish, Alabama Game and Fish*, and *California Game and Fish*. Even more specialized are *Bassmaster Magazine, Fly Fisherman Magazine*, and *Sport Fishing Magazine*. Then there's *Flyfishing & Tying Journal, Salt Water Sportsman Magazine*, and *Marlin*. In addition to the two thousand consumer titles sold on newsstands, there are at least twice that many more sold by subscription only. Some of these are listed in *Writer's Market*; many are not.

Yet another category of magazines is business or trade publications. *Writer's Market* calls them "**trade journals.**" These magazines target business, industry, and the various professions. They go to "insiders" and are not normally sold on newsstands. They are read by doctors and lawyers, brickmasons and truck drivers, butchers and bakers and candy makers. Titles range from *Pizza Today* and *Convenience Store Decisions*, to *Recycled*

Paper News and *Portable Restroom Operator;* from *Limousine Digest* and *Dermatology Insights,* to *Biotechnology Healthcare* and the *Pennsylvania Lawyer.* Many trade journals are sent to members of a particular occupation or profession on what is called a controlled circulation basis. That is, they are sent free to everyone who can be identified as having a legitimate interest in the occupation. The goal is to deliver to advertisers as many members of the trade as possible. The 2006 *Writer's Market* advises freelancers, "Writers who have discovered trade journals have found a market that offers the chance to publish regularly in subject areas they find interesting, editors who are typically more accessible than their commercial counterparts, and pay rates that rival those of the big-time magazines." But there is also a warning: "Trade magazine editors tell us their audience is made up of knowledgeable and highly interested readers. Writers for trade magazines have to either possess knowledge about the field in question or be able to report it accurately from interviews with those who do." Still, "Writers who have or can develop a good grasp of a specialized body of knowledge will find trade magazine editors are eager to hear from them."

In addition to consumer magazines and trade publications, there are also hundreds of technical and scholarly journals published each year. These all add up to well over ten thousand titles. They all need articles. As a brief look at the *Writer's Market* will quickly confirm, most consumer magazines and trade journals use some combination of staff-written and freelance-written articles. Some magazines are almost entirely staff produced and some are 80 to 90 percent freelance written. Who writes for all these magazines? Trained journalists and English majors. Novice authors and untrained beginners. Students and teachers. Physicians and preachers and printers and politicians. Dog owners and cat lovers. Helicopter pilots and cross-country skiers. Nosey neighbors and stay-at-home moms. **People from all walks of life can write for magazines if they have two qualities: the ability to write well and the ability to market themselves and their work.** Well, make that three. A little luck doesn't hurt.

Leads in Magazine Writing

As opposed to straight news, most magazine articles are feature stories. They may make us laugh or cry. They intrigue us. Their value is not in timeliness or proximity, but in human interest. They are written as much to entertain as to inform. Magazine articles differ from hard news in form. They are not written in the inverted pyramid style, but, like nonfiction short stories, have a well-crafted beginning, middle, and end. They have a definite organizational structure or plan, but content determines form, so structure varies from story to story. Many articles are written using the familiar chronological storytelling technique. Others use an hourglass structure or a problem-then-solution construction. Some use a question-and-answer format and some are structured more like essays.

Whatever form the article takes, the lead is a very important part of it, maybe the most important part. Feature leads differ from hard news leads. As opposed to the newspaper direct lead of thirty words or less that summarizes the story in a sentence, magazine article leads (or introductions) often run several paragraphs, sometimes several pages. They lure readers into the story, taking forms that most newspaper editors would not allow in a hard news story. Some of the more common are:

Narrative Lead	Uses chronological storytelling techniques to start the article with enough dramatic action that readers feel they are watching the event unfold.
Descriptive Lead	Sets a scene or creates an atmosphere using sensory details and vivid description to place readers at the scene; describes a person, place, or event.
First-Person Lead	Uses "I" or "we."
Direct Address Lead	The writer pulls readers into the story by speaking to them directly using "you."
Contrast Lead	Informs the reader by contrasting then and now, cause and effect, or the known with the unknown.
Anecdotal Lead	Entertains readers with a little story, usually personal, that illustrates some problem or reveals a subject's character or personality.
Quotation Lead	Begins the story by offering the reader something particularly well said, or words uttered by someone famous or infamous.
Cliché Lead	Puts a new twist on an old saying; agrees with, disputes, or illustrates an adage, proverb, or maxim.
Question Lead	Poses a question to the reader.
Teaser/Mystery Lead	Uses the element of surprise to lure the reader into the story; encourages readers to read on by arousing their curiosity; hints at, but does not reveal, what is to come.
Shocker Lead	Grabs the reader's attention by relating a startling fact, statistic, or statement.
Combination Lead	Just like the pizza—two or more types of leads are combined for one amazing result.

Look at the leads from these two magazine articles, both award-winning science and nature pieces.

BRAISED SHANK OF FREE-RANGE POSSUM?

By Burkhard Bilger
Outside, July 2001

"What we have here is a radial pattern of wild meats," Jeff Jackson says, pointing his spatula at a cast-iron skillet. Four small mounds of mangled protein, each a different shade and texture, lie in a perfect parabola, like tissue samples from a crime lab. "First you'll eat them," Jackson says. "Then I'll tell you what they are."

Lifting my fork, I probe a mushroom cap brimming with a gray, speckled, liverish substance. To my right, Jackson's wife, Phyllis, picks at her salad and watches. "Back before we were married, we spent a whole summer living off roadkill," she says. "I remember one time, we ate a mink."

THE MOST IMPORTANT FISH IN THE SEA

By H. Bruce Franklin
Discover, September 2001

First you see the birds—gulls, terns, cormorants, and ospreys wheeling overhead, then swooping down into a wide expanse of water dimpled as though by large raindrops. Silvery flashes and splashes erupt from thousands of small herring-like fish called menhaden. More birds arrive, and the air rings with shrill cries. The birds alert nearby anglers that a massive school of menhaden is under attack by bluefish....

Before long, two boats have trapped the entire school… These kibble of the sea fetch only about ten cents a pound at the dock, but they can be ground up, dried, and formed into another kind of kibble for land animals, a high-protein feed for chickens, pigs and cattle. Pop some barbequed wings into your mouth, and at least part of what you're eating was once menhaden.

The body of a magazine article will have a theme—one main point that can be summed up in a single sentence. This middle part of the story will have background information and explanation. It will have examples and illustrations. It will have quotations and context. It may well touch on many different aspects of the story, but each aspect will help develop the theme.

Closers in Magazine Writing

Hard news stories often give the facts in descending order of importance. These stories stop when there is nothing left to report. But a magazine article needs a well-thought-out ending. If the lead is the most important part of the article, the close may be the most memorable. Some possibilities for ending the feature story are:

The Kicker Quote   Ends the story with a striking or memorable quotation. It may be funny or unexpected, authoritative or convincing, but it should have a sense of finality.

The Full Circle	Ends the story by restating or echoing the lead. It may duplicate or amplify the lead's theme or it may simply allude to the story's beginning.
The Proximity Close	Uses material immediately preceding the final paragraph as a foundation for the close. This ending is sometimes an "add-on" close that uses the article's last paragraph or two to make a point that has not been made before.
The Restatement or Summary	Reminds the reader of the article's theme by restating or summarizing it, or tries to tie up loose ends by reviewing and refining the story's main points.
The Anecdote	Ends with an entertaining snippet that illustrates or exemplifies the story's focus. Sometimes the anecdote is started in the lead or body of the story but not finished until the close.
The Editorial Assessment	Ends the article with a closing thought from the author, usually an opinion as to relative worth or moral value. The author tells why he or she thinks the subject is right or wrong, a good idea or bad idea, worthy or unworthy.
The Call to Action	The close is used to motivate readers to act by encouraging or discouraging a specific behavior.
The Last Word	Gives the reader one final admonition, word of warning, or piece of advice.
The Stinger	Closes with a surprise ending that startles, shocks, or astounds the reader. This ending sneaks up on readers so they don't even see it coming.

The theme of "The Most Important Fish in the Sea" is that the overfishing of menhaden threatens the entire food chain up and down the Eastern Seaboard. This story ends with a kicker quote:

"Bill Matuszeski, former director of the EPA's Chesapeake Bay Program, says: 'We need to start managing menhaden for their role in the overall ecological system. If this problem isn't taken care of, the EPA will have to get into the decision making.' Matuszeski believes estuaries like the Chesapeake Bay should be put off limits to menhaden fishing immediately. 'That would be inconvenient for the industry, but it would be inconvenient to the species to be extinct.'"

"Braised Shank of Free-Range Possum?" explores why the idea of eating some wild foods is distasteful to so many people. This article ends with an anecdote and editorial assessment:

"A few years ago my father-in-law was driving to Nebraska to visit his ninety-year-old mother…when something hit the windshield with a terrible crash. There, lying in the road, was a wild turkey…. He picked it up and threw it in the trunk. No sense letting a thing like that go to waste.

"When he arrived, he handed the bird over to his mother. That night when he was dressing the bird, he found a surprise. Reaching inside like a magician, he pulled out an egg the size of his fist, still intact.

"'What about that?' she asked him.

"'Fry that up for breakfast,' he said.

"An egg, eaten without prejudice, is like any other under the sun. But an egg with a story behind it—that egg tastes like nothing you've ever imagined."

Techniques in Magazine Writing

Magazine articles differ from hard news in technique. They are more likely to be written using literary and creative writing techniques such as:

1. Scene-setting
2. Sensory detail
3. Description
4. Suspense
5. Flashbacks
6. Plotting
7. Dialogue
8. Logical development
9. Storytelling
10. Perspective

Magazine writing offers more opportunity for flexibility and artistic creativity than straight news reporting. Writing in the first person is allowed, even encouraged. Voice is important; style and structure are crucial. Authors are permitted, and often expected, to express a point of view. Feature writing is subjective rather than objective.

In *America's Best Newspaper Writing*, editors Roy Peter Clark and Christopher Scanlan let Richard Zahler of the *Seattle Times* make the distinction between writing to inform and writing to engage. Zahler explains that in feature writing the *who* becomes *characters* and *characterization*. *What* becomes *plot*. *When* is *chronology* and *where* is *setting*. *Why* is *motive* and *how* is *under what circumstances*. But although magazine article writers are not bound by the same standards of objectivity as are newspaper reporters, and even though some of the techniques are borrowed from fiction writing, socially responsible magazine writers remember that they are journalists, not novelists. They cannot make things up. They cannot invent characters or create composite characters. They cannot change settings or rearrange the order of events. They cannot make up quotes or dialogue. They cannot add to a story things that never happened. They cannot—that is—do these things and still keep faith with readers who expect journalists to get at and report the truth.

Magazine articles differ from hard news stories in purpose. They are written to entertain as well as to inform. They are optional reading. Readers choose them because they want to read them, not because they have to. Timeliness is not a dominant news value. A magazine article can be read tomorrow or next week; it will likely be just as good next month or the next. Many articles reprinted in *Reader's Digest* are more than a year old before they are published, and nearly all magazines require holiday or seasonal stories to be written months in advance. Since magazine writing is more likely to be non-deadline writing, the extra preparation time allows for more thorough research and a more polished finished product. Magazine articles are usually longer than straight news stories and explore their topics in greater depth. But they also have more discerning readers with higher expectations.

The Focus of Magazine Writing

Magazine articles differ from hard news stories in focus. They focus on people rather than events. They have more description and more quotations. They use anecdotes to reveal how people think and act. They help us see the human condition—our shared hopes, fears, dreams, and desires. Hard news stories focus on *who* and *what*. Feature stories provide insight on *how* and *why*.

In his classic *On Writing Well*, William Zinsser quotes Chic Young, creator of the popular comic strip *Blondie*. Young had been writing and drawing *Blondie* for nearly half a century, and Zinsser asked him what made the strip so enduring.

"It's durable because it's simple," Young told Zinsser. "It's based on four things that everybody does: sleeping, eating, raising a family and making money."

Like Young's humor, most magazine articles are about the same basic issues—health, family, work, and play. Month after month, issue after issue, in different styles and in various formats, magazines run articles covering the same handful of topics:

}   diet and exercise
}   health and medicine
}   love and sex
}   marriage and children
}   making and saving money
}   government and politics
}   travel and adventure
}   arts and entertainment
}   sports and hobbies
}   houses and vehicles
}   animals and pets
}   business and social relationships
}   celebrities and achievers
}   science and technology

} business and industry
} fashion and appearance
} history
} humor

Of the 25,000 to 30,000 magazine articles published each month, most of them cover these same twenty-five or thirty topics in one way or another.

Zinsser observes, "The professional must establish a daily schedule and stick to it." Novelist and award-winning short story writer James Brown agrees. "I used to think that it was talent that made me a writer, but over the years I've come to believe that it has mostly to do with discipline and a certain urgency, a certain need to tell a story honestly and well."

Successful magazine writers set goals and deadlines. Keep records. Log your progress. Set deadlines for yourself. Let people know you have them, and don't let other things distract you. Manage your writing time. Ask yourself if what you are doing is important, productive. If not, move on to something that is. You will need time for reading, for reflection, for planning, and for research.

Many beginning magazine writers are greatly surprised to find that it is often much easier to sell an article *before it is written* than after it is finished. Most editors don't have time to read through what they call the "slush pile" of unsolicited manuscripts. Instead of a finished article, they want a tightly written query letter that pitches the story idea in just a few paragraphs. A query is a one-page sales pitch that a freelancer uses to try to interest an editor in a story. Actually the writer is trying to sell the editor on two things: the story idea itself, and his or her ability as a writer to deliver it. A talent for writing is not enough to get an author published. Freelancers must successfully market both their work and themselves. The query letter is the most critical step in the process.

The Query Letter

The query sets one writer apart from hundreds of others. Many editors feel that the query is a better gauge of a writer's ability than published clips. It makes a first impression. It should be absolutely letter perfect—no white-outs or penciled-in corrections. There must be no grammatical mistakes or typos. There certainly can be no coffee stains or grease spots, and the letter shouldn't smell of cigarette smoke when the editor pulls it from the envelope. It should be addressed to the editor by name. No "Dear Editor" or "To Whom It May Concern." And it should be addressed to the correct person. Many editors are more than a little annoyed at letters addressed to their predecessors.

Beyond the first impression, the query lets the editor assess the writer's craft. It should grab the editor's attention. It should sparkle. It should let the editor hear the writer's voice. And it should contain enough information to convince the editor that the writer knows what he or she is talking about. The query letter gives the editor an opportunity to respond to the *idea* and to offer the writer suggestions before the article is too far along. Editors may want to turn the story in a slightly different direction or recommend another focus altogether.

Query letters also help writers. They keep freelancers from wasting valuable research and writing time on articles for which there are no buyers. They allow writers to market their ideas in volume, slanting the pitch to multiple magazines with very little extra work. They force authors to refine and refocus their ideas, to come up with an angle for the story. So the query letter saves the editor time, and it saves the writer time and trouble.

Before making the pitch, the writer must know whom to pitch it to. One very good way to look for promising outlets is to use the *Writer's Market*. This annual volume lists literally thousands of consumer magazines and trade journals, all potential buyers. Entries vary in length, but all of them contain much valuable information. From a typical entry in *Writer's Market,* the freelancer can learn:

- } The publication's name, address, phone number, fax number, website, and email address. (Some two thousand magazines are arranged by topic and indexed.)
- } The names and titles of editors. (Editors come and go quickly. Before you send a letter, double check names by looking at the masthead of the magazine's most recent issue or calling the switchboard.)
- } The magazine's circulation numbers, frequency of publication, and how long it has been in existence.
- } The percentage of the average issue that is freelance written and how many manuscripts are purchased each year.
- } The pay rate, when payment is made, and what rights the magazine wants to purchase. Many entries also note whether the magazine pays a kill fee (a percentage of the negotiated payment if the editors decide not to use the article), and whether the author gets a byline.
- } The magazine's focus and its target audience, the kinds of articles the editors are looking for, and any topics of special interest.
- } Response time, lead time, and whether the magazine accepts simultaneous submissions and will consider previously published material.
- } If photos are desired or required, and if there is extra payment made for them.

In addition, most entries have a paragraph or two of "Tips," the editor's particular expectations, likes, and dislikes.

A Formula for Magazine Writing

Writer's Market can help you find outlets for your magazine writing that you never knew existed. But this guide is just a starting place. **To successfully sell your work, you will have** to get a feel for the publication's style and the kinds of articles it runs and doesn't run. Unless you read at least six months of back issues before writing your query, you are shooting in the dark and probably wasting your time.

A well-crafted query is both striking and polished. It must address routine questions and still manage to stand out. One formula calls for a letter of five paragraphs. On letterhead, following the inside address and salutation (addressed to the proper editor by name and title), the letter is typed single space with an extra space between paragraphs. The paragraphs are short, two or three sentences each, and follow this pattern:

Par 1—The Pitch. This paragraph is the hook. It must grab the editor's attention and keep him or her reading, else all is lost. One way to do this is to start with a sentence or paragraph that could eventually be used as a lead for the article itself. This is your audition. Most editors will be able to tell from the first few notes if you can sing, or at least if they like your style.

Par 2—The Angle. The second paragraph tells the editor how you propose to handle the story. There is a big difference between a topic and an angle. Most stories have been written dozens of times before. What makes this one different? What's your slant? Why will this story appeal to the magazine's readers? Let the editor know directly your planned approach and focus—that you know where you want to go with this piece. Name your sources and include enough facts and statistics from your research to let the editor see that you know what you are talking about.

Par 3—Credentials. In a sentence or two sell yourself to the editor as a professional writer who can deliver the goods. If you have several publications to your credit, mention the best ones and include clips (or offer to send clips later). If you don't have clips, sell yourself in some other way—special access to a source, expertise, or even a unique perspective. Let the editor know that you are *the* right person for this story.

Par 4—Business Basics. Use this paragraph to wrap up loose ends by listing any other information the editor should have, such as when you can have the article finished, the estimated length, and whether you can supply extras such as photos, illustrations, or sidebars. Don't offer to send the article "on spec." This might be the best deal you can get, and that's fine, but don't show your hand. The editor might have already decided to accept the piece. But you're offering to let him or her look at it for free. Let the editor make that proposal.

Par 5—The Request. How about it? Close by asking directly, "May I send you the article?" You might want to close with a thank you to the editor for considering your idea, and a mention of the enclosed self-addressed stamped envelope.

Proofread the letter carefully for typos, grammatical mistakes, and logical lapses. Then sign it, mail it, and forget it for at least a month. It will likely be longer than that before you get a response. And the response may not be what you want to hear. Sad to say, a good idea, great talent, and a sparkling query letter are not always enough to make a sale. Even the professionals get far more rejection slips than acceptance letters. Timing and luck are a big part of the freelance process. If at first you don't make the sale, find another potential market, revise your query, and try again...and again.

The Future of Magazine Writing

Most magazines these days have some kind of presence on the World Wide Web. Many of them have an online edition quite different in both content and form from the print version. This comes in response to direct competition from electronic magazines (called online magazines, webzines, or e-zines). Advances in technology have helped some of these become major forces in the magazine industry. But many more are shoestring operations, poorly written and poorly maintained. They come and go overnight. Electronic publishing is rapidly evolving, however, and Internet magazines are providing more and more outlets for freelance writers. At this point, most of them pay far less than their print counterparts, and many do not pay at all. *Writer's Market* does not yet have a special section for online publications, but in light of their spectacular growth this is sure to change.

The Internet has brought about one change that *is* reflected in *Writer's Market*: a growing willingness of editors to accept email queries. The rules are pretty much the same as for standard query letters. Email queries should be well thought out and mistake-free. Many magazines, however, even those with a web presence, still do not accept them.

Some writers say they *have* to write, that they are *driven* to write, that even before they started turning in stories to grammar school teachers, they knew that all they ever wanted to do is write.

Some say they write for emotional release and self-fulfillment.

Some talk about the satisfaction that seeing their work in print brings.

Some writers are so passionate about a cause or conviction that they want to go tell it on the mountain.

Some write for recognition and the hope of glory.

Some do it for the money.

But whether they do it as a passion or a profession, a joy or a job, magazine writers today give voice to a variety of viewpoints. Jewelers and mail carriers and musicians and nurses speak, and millions listen. That is one reason freelancers are so important. The First Amendment makes the American press the freest on earth. Magazine writers amuse and entertain; they inform and enlighten; they charm and persuade. They change minds and lives.

According to one biographer, 1890 was a banner year for Rudyard Kipling. That year he published or republished, in America and England, at least eighty magazine articles and short stories, besides a number of poems and one novel. Some years later, he told a group of doctors: "I am, by calling, a dealer in words, and words are, of course, the most powerful drug used by mankind."

Literary Journalism

JOHN J. PAULY

The term "literary journalism" today describes the stylish long-form reporting published in magazines, Sunday supplements, and books rather than in the daily newspaper. Literary journalists use techniques such as plot, characterization, point of view, symbolism, and scene-by-scene construction—in other words, the devices traditionally found in novels, plays, and films—in the service of factual stories. The recent practitioners of such work have included a long line of *New Yorker* journalists, from Joseph Mitchell, Lillian Ross, and John Hersey to John McPhee and Jane Kramer; the New Journalists of the 1960s such as Tom Wolfe, Norman Mailer, Joan Didion, Hunter Thompson, and Michael Herr; and contemporary writers such as Madeline Blais, Susan Orlean, Ted Conover, Tracy Kidder, and Adrian LeBlanc.

Actually, however, elements of literary journalism have long been present in some of the best writing found in newspapers. Before he became a Broadway playwright, George Ade wrote more than eighteen hundred scenes of street life in Chicago during the 1890s that appeared in the pages of the *Chicago Record.* His vignettes capture the essence of working-class life in a rapidly industrializing city where citizens are often strangers to one another. He found his subjects at sidewalk stands, small shops, and farmers' markets, and on trolley cars, in dime museums, police courts, tugboats, and on the vaudeville circuit. He fashions portraits of anonymous people in vulnerable situations. One back-room resident Ade writes about reluctantly admits he leaves his boarding room late each night to work as a chiropodist in a Turkish bath. In February 1894, a terrified medical student is chased around an insane asylum only to be tagged and told, "You're it." Ade attacks class distinctions in his much-praised March 1896 piece called "Effie Whittlesley," about a woman who puts on airs in hiring a family servant, only to find that the maid and the employer's husband grew up as best friends in the same small town and can't help calling one another by their first names.

Damon Runyon, the nation's best known news columnist of the 1920s and '30s, was also a forerunner of modern literary journalists. Runyon entered the profession with a sixth-grade education at the age of twelve. An active listener and unsurpassed scene setter, his work was nationally syndicated by William Randolph Hearst and through many Jazz Age magazines. His capacities in characterization have been the envy of nearly every writer ever since. Waldo Winchester, Miss Missouri Martin, "The Brain," "Regret," and "Bookie Bob" were based on real-life characters Runyon encountered on lower Broadway. They're famously on display at the fine funeral of waiter Harry Tibbetts, a fan favorite at Jack Dunstan's all-night, all-you-can-eat restaurant. "Actors and actresses" came to

Dunstan's, Runyon writes, and "polo players, song writers, newspapermen, authors, artists, pamphle-teers, poets, prizefighters, ball players, promoters, grifters, hotel keepers, jockeys, billiard players, horse owners, chorus girls, gunmen, and gamblers." To be "Runyonesque" is to colorfully capture the romance and corruption of modern men and women on the make.

At first glance, the work by Ade and Runyon may not seem journalistic in the usual sense. Work like it does not always abide by daily deadlines and, done today, literary journalism may require months or years of research. In their day, Ade and Runyon did not often focus on the political topics regularly covered by the daily newspaper. And that is true of literary journalists today. Their work not only probes the familiar world of elections, legislation, and policy. It also borrows heavily from the spirit of the feature story, exploring the human dimension of the front-page story and celebrating the lives of ordinary people.

Some contemporary advocates of literary journalism have argued for its political as well as aesthetic significance. Mark Kramer believes that the intimate, authentic voice of the literary journalist offers a humane alternative to the "august authority" of the experts and institutions whose bureaucratic voices dominate daily news stories. Robert Boynton has argued that contemporary literary journalism amounts to a "New New Journalism," a blend of the stylistic innovations and depth reporting of the 1960s with older traditions of muckraking. Though both these arguments remain open to debate—Kramer may exaggerate the political power of the individual authorial voice, and Boynton may under-estimate the 1960s New Journalists' interests in politics and social class—both writers nonetheless raise an important question: What does literary journalism contribute to public life? If everyday journal-ism claims that it provides citizens with the information they need for self-governance, what does literary journalism claim to offer them?

The deceptively simple answer is this: stories. **Literary journalists write stories that are long, deeply researched, complex, and subtle, in the conviction that readers yearn to make sense of the world.** An interest in storytelling is nothing new in the history of journalism, of course. For more than a century, news reporters have described their work in such terms. What is different today is the importance that philosophers, theologians, literary critics, historians, and social scientists now attribute to all forms of storytelling. Many describe it as a fundamental communication practice, one of the characteristic ways by which humans come to understand their experience, imagine themselves, and dramatize their relations with one another. As Joan Didion puts it, "We tell ourselves stories in order to live."

Seen from this perspective, the storytelling of journalists always implies a political struggle over whose version of reality will be celebrated in print. Daily news reporting manages that struggle by adopting a conscious policy of impartiality, setting strict rules to govern its storytelling practices. News reporters typically allow events to drive coverage, write from a third-person point of view, balance opposing opinions, and maintain emotional neutrality in their writing style. Literary journalists some-times employ these same techniques, but they also allow themselves more leeway in choosing how to tell each story. They may search for significance in everyday routines rather than in momentous events, or write in first person, or allow a character to express strong opinions without contradiction, or acknowledge their own role in their stories.

Literary journalists pursue topics that do not easily fit within the standard categories of daily news. For example, in his forty-year career John McPhee has published thirty books, on topics ranging from the construction of birch-bark canoes to oranges, the life of a small Scottish island called Colonsay, the geology of the United States, the psychology of tennis, the politics of environmentalism, the history of nuclear energy, the Swiss army, Alaska, and shad fishing. McPhee often approaches his stories as biographical profiles, allowing his expert informants a key role but also adding layer after layer of technical, historical, and cultural evidence.

Many writers consider McPhee a model literary journalist, not merely for the range of his intellectual interests or for his remarkable productivity, but also for his command of virtually every literary technique available in long-form nonfiction. His 1975 book *Encounters with the Archdruid* admirably demonstrates the depth of his mastery. The archdruid of the title is David Brower, longtime executive director of the Sierra Club and the most prominent conservationist of his age. Although McPhee's book can be read as a typical *New Yorker* profile, it also embodies a larger purpose. McPhee uses Brower's encounters with his opponents to dramatize the politics of environmentalism—the social policies it proposes, the mythic enemies it conjures, the arguments each side invokes.

Encounters features three long "chapters," each of which originally appeared as a stand-alone piece in the *New Yorker.* McPhee wrote the separate parts with the whole story in mind. Each chapter focuses on a different site of environmental conflict—mining in the Cascade Mountains, real estate development on the Georgia coast, dams along the Colorado River. Each features a different antagonist— a mining engineer, a developer, a government official. In each section, McPhee has organized a trip into the wilderness—a climb into the mountains, a tour of a sparsely inhabited island, a rafting expedition—in the hopes of creating verbal conflict that he will be able to report. The plotting of the stories is intricate and sophisticated. McPhee's book includes massive amounts of background information—biographies of each major character; meticulous descriptions of flora, fauna, and geology; social histories of each region; the politics of the environmental movement—but he introduces such details gradually, at apt moments in the narrative. For example, Brower's attempt to warm a butterfly chilled by the mountain air leads to a digression upon his expert knowledge of that creature. McPhee withholds a detailed account of Brower's dismissal as Sierra Club director until well into the book, in order to allow readers to see Brower in action without prematurely coloring their impression of him. When documenting the arguments between Brower and mining engineer Charles Park on their hike through the Cascades, McPhee simulates the back and forth of discussion by juxtaposing scenes in which first one character, then the other, is given the last word.

McPhee threads together the three stories with recurring symbolic motifs. In each section of *Encounters,* a bulldozer appears as a symbol of the forces of development. On their way out of the Cascades, the hiking party encounters a bulldozer plowing at will across a mountain river. On the island, the developer Charles Fraser suggests the need for a bulldozer to clear a junk heap. And the U.S. commissioner of reclamation, the most dangerous environmental enemy of all, the man in charge of damming rivers across the West, has a model bulldozer sitting prominently on the shelf behind his desk. (McPhee uses the grizzly bear in an analogous way, as a symbol of the Alaskan wilderness, in all three sections of his best-selling book *Coming into the Country.*) McPhee documents idiosyncratic personal habits in order to reveal character. Park taps one rock after another with his hammer, restlessly testing each for the possibility of ore. Floyd Dominy, the reclamation commissioner, constantly puffs on his cigar, even through the worst Colorado River rapids. And Brower travels everywhere with his Sierra Club cup, eating all his food from it, dipping it into a wild stream for water, and filling it with wild blueberries that he offers his fellow travelers.

This combination of aesthetic polish and meticulous research has made literary journalism particularly attractive to educated, upscale readers of books and of magazines such as the *New Yorker, Esquire, New York, Harper's,* and *Vanity Fair.* It costs money to sponsor such work, and great intellectual and literary skill to conduct it. Nonetheless, literary journalists' commitment to storytelling makes their work accessible to many readers. And **in a society that depends upon specialized technical, scientific, and business expertise, literary journalism often makes difficult issues intelligible for a general audience**, offering more complex forms of storytelling than most newspapers can manage and attending more closely to public issues than many essayists want to. In particular, literary journalism often explores the human consequences of social problems and political policies. For example, Conover's book on correction officers in Sing-Sing penitentiary has documented the human costs of imprisonment, for both convicts and guards. Writers such as Walt Harrington, Leon Dash, and Alex Kotlowitz have confronted the legacy of racism. Thomas Bass has traced the fate of Vietnamese who worked with American troops then fled to the United States following the fall of Saigon. And Jane Kramer's "Letters from Europe," published in the *New Yorker* for more than thirty years, have explored contentious debates over immigration, ethnicity, and national identity.

Literary journalists write for the future as much as for the present. Because they take the long view, they help readers discern the political, social, and historical forces moving beneath the surfaces of daily events. Their work can be read and consulted over many years without diminishing either its literary pleasure or its relevance. Literary journalism ultimately affirms and extends the journalism profession's traditions, demonstrating the imaginative possibilities of fact-based writing and the political importance of deeply researched reporting.

15

Re-writing and Editing

DAVID COPELAND*

Every writer needs an editor. Thomas Jefferson was a wonderful writer, but Benjamin Franklin was just as good an editor. The most famous phrase in the Declaration of Independence owes much to both men. "We hold these truths to be self-evident, that all men are created equal," Jefferson's rough draft read. "They are endowed by their creator with certain inalienable rights" and "among these are life, liberty, and property." The line read well to Jefferson, a slave holder. Franklin, however, was the better editor, preferring "life, liberty, and pursuit of happiness," a happy compromise between an editor and writer that became one of the most stirring sentiments in our nation's history.

The Continental Congress gave Jefferson, Franklin, and John Adams two and a half weeks to work on their declaration. Today's news reporters and editors, however, work under much shorter time constraints. Daily deadlines mean that reporters must gather information, organize it into a coherent story, and do rewrites often within a matter of hours. Copy editors have even less time to read the story, ask questions about the content, verify facts, fix grammatical and style errors, and put the story into the proper presentation format for public consumption.

---

*   Bruce Evensen contributed to this chapter.

The Role of the Editor

Despite the pressure of the deadline, the public expects accuracy, fairness, and error-free information from the media. People do not really care that producing the news is pressure-packed for those doing it. They want information, and they expect it to be available continually, something made possible in the twenty-first century by satellite broadcasting and the Internet. People want the who, what, when, where, and how questions answered. This is the reporter's job, but **editors give the story its final shape and make decisions that affect the information that is presented to the public.** Reporters are the experts on the information in a story, but editors format its presentation for the audience. Just like Thomas Jefferson, every reporter needs an editor, even if the reporter does not believe it.

Throughout history there have been many extraordinary events that were poorly reported and would have benefited immensely at the hands of a good editor. Good editing has been an acquired skill in American press history. No blue pencils were out when dispatches from Washington reported the shocking news of Abraham Lincoln's assassination. Four hours after Lincoln was shot in Washington's Ford Theatre on the evening of April 14, 1865, Secretary of War Edwin M. Stanton sent the story of the assassination attempt to newspapers across the country. "This evening at about 9:30 P.M. at Ford's Theatre," the War Department bulletin began, "the President, while sitting in his private box with Mrs. Lincoln, Mr. Harris, and Major Rathburn, was shot by an assassin, who suddenly entered the box and appeared behind the President. The assassin then leaped upon the stage, brandishing a large dagger or knife, and made his escape in the rear of the theatre." Later in the story readers learn that Lincoln was shot in the back of the head, is still alive, but that doctors fear he will not survive his wound. These details are obviously more important than the fact he went to a play that night, with whom he went and when he was shot. Stanton can be forgiven this lapse. As war secretary he was used to controlling what readers read. But he was a better military man than a journalist. He was retelling one of the most important events of the nineteenth century as if it were a bedtime story with a beginning and a middle and an end. A good editor would have recognized that in this case, the end is the beginning. The fact that Lincoln may die from a bullet wound to the head needs to appear at the beginning of the story, not in the third paragraph. That is what satisfies the citizen's search for significance.

Custer suffered the same fate as Lincoln and was just as badly treated in the press. He could have used more men and a good editor. First reports on July 6, 1876, sent nationwide by the Helena, Montana, *Herald* indicated that "Muggins Taylor, a scout for Gen. Gibbons got to Helena last night from the Little Big Horn River." The report states that "Gen. Custer found the Indian camp of about 2,000 lodges on the Little Horn, and immediately attacked the camp. Nothing is known of the operations of this detachment, only as they trace it by the dead. Major Reno commanded the other seven companies, and attacked the lower portion of the camp. The Indians poured in a murderous fire from all directions." The correspondent from the *Herald* goes on, "The greater portion fought on horseback. Custer, his two brothers, a nephew, and a brother-in-law, were all killed, and not one of his detachment escaped." Obviously, in historical hindsight the killing of Custer and his entire 264-man command is infinitely more important than the fact that a scout for Gen. Gibbons got to Helena several days after the fighting. It is the editor's job to ensure that the writer immediately states the significance of what happened.

For many years, reporters on both sides of the Atlantic wasted readers' time by beating around the bush. The *London Globe* on June 9, 1870, reported, "Charles Dickens had been seized with paralysis, and was lying insensible at his residence at Gad's Hill, near Rochester, in Kent. The news spread rapidly," readers were told, "and created the most profound regret; but the worst was still to come. Telegrams have since been received announcing the death of the great novelist, at a quarter past six in the evening." Clearly, the death of one of Britain's great writers is bigger news than the fact that he had been "seized with paralysis" prior to his death. And although his "lying insensible" understandably filled the writer with "the most profound regret," his editor needed to make sure that readers were aware that the greatest living writer in English had passed. **Dickens was an excellent editor who would have understood the importance of reporting his death at the outset of the story.** Every editor remembers the famous nursery rhyme that begins, "Jack and Jill went up a hill to fetch a pail of water. Jack fell down and broke his crown, and Jill came tumbling after." The lead of this sad story, editors will tell you, is not that Jack and Jill went up a hill. The fact that two kids went up a hill is not particularly newsworthy even on a light news day. But that Jack broke his head and that Jill sustained serious injuries is something the community might need to know. That's why editors will insist that reporters mention the condition of the kids first.

The first thing that Connie Chung thought to report for CBS News when a federal building was blown up in Oklahoma City on April 19, 1995, was that "it is apparently the deadliest single terror attack on U.S. soil ever." Chung, reporting from the scene, said, "here in Oklahoma City today a car bomb demolished a federal office building with hundreds of people trapped inside. The attack came without warning...according to a U.S. government source, who told CBS News that 'it has Middle East terrorism written all over it.'" We now know that it wasn't Middle East terrorists but homegrown anti-government militiamen who attacked the Murrah Federal Building that day. Timothy McVeigh, a Gulf War veteran, was arrested ninety minutes after the 9 A.M. incident, and if Chung didn't know that when she went on the air seven hours later, she was aware that hundreds had been killed and injured, yet she's strangely silent on these facts. She could have used a good editor. One hundred sixty-nine people, including nineteen children, were killed in the attack, and more than eight hundred were injured and treated for shock. Twelve thousand individuals participated in relief and recovery efforts. Three hundred buildings were damaged. Hundreds were made homeless. Viewers had a right to know these extraordinary details. A good editor will insist that they be told.

"President Lincoln is near death following an assassination attempt." "General George Armstrong Custer and his command of 264 men have been killed fighting Indians at the Little Big Horn." "Noted author Charles Dickens died tonight at his home from a stroke." "One hundred sixty-nine people have been killed and more than eight hundred injured following an explosion at a federal office building in Oklahoma City, Oklahoma." Almost always editors recognize that "what" is the most important element in breaking news. That's why "One hundred sixty-nine people" leads the Oklahoma City bombing story. When a person is well known—Lincoln, Custer, Dickens—"who" will take precedence. Editors realize that almost never are the "when" and "where" parts of a story so essential that they are the first thing a reporter is obligated to state at the very start of the story. "Why" becomes increasingly important as an explanation for "what" happened. So, 169 deaths and 800 injuries leads the Oklahoma City bombing story. The criminal investigation of "who" was responsible for the attack and "why" the attack took place takes on increasing importance in the hours and days after the attack. Editors repeat this pattern in all disaster coverage, when cars, planes, or trains crash, when storms strike, or bombs fall.

Searching for Significance

Editors understand that the best writing searches for significance through specificity. Lincoln is assassinated with a bullet fired at the back of his brain. That is more precise than a "head wound." The "deadliest terror attack on U.S. soil ever" could be many things. A veteran editor will object that it is difficult for readers to see any specific thing in such a wide-ranging lead. Specificity helps them enormously. "One hundred sixty-nine killed and more than 800 injured" is precisely what most matters when a bomb goes off in a federal building in Oklahoma City. Timothy McVeigh was not executed on June 11, 2001, for bombing a building. He was given a lethal injection because the bombing was murder. Many bombings leave no death tolls. This bombing killed 169 people. That's why editors will insist that their reporters search for significance through specificity. They know that this greatly aids the reader and is the job of responsible reporters and editors.

Let me illustrate this point by telling you a story. One afternoon, an excited managing editor rushed into a newsroom after learning there had been a school bus accident in his community. Several students had been injured, some, perhaps, critically. The managing editor looked around the newsroom. All of the reporters were out, either on their beats or on assignment. One was on the scene of the accident. That's how the paper learned of the wreck. The news editor and city editor had stepped out for their lunch. The only reporter left in the newsroom was a sports writer, who had only been on the job for two weeks. Time was of the essence, and the managing editor needed someone at the hospital's emergency room to cover the arrival of ambulances. His only option was the new reporter. Hurriedly, he stepped into the sports department and began briefing the reporter.

"The accident involved a school bus and a car carrying students," the editor told him. "The car tried to pass the bus but couldn't. The car flipped, and the bus hit a tree. The students on the bus are okay, our reporter says, but the kids in the car aren't. There may be fatalities. I need you to go to the emergency room. We need a story on this end of this tragedy."

The sports reporter wasn't so sure he was the man for the job. "I don't really know much about covering things other than sports," he told the editor. "Can't you find someone else?"

"No, you're the only person available," the managing editor answered. "Go, now."

The sports writer knew how to write other stories, but he'd always concentrated on the nuances of sports. He knew he couldn't use the action verbs of sports stories in an accident story, involving fatalities. The story required careful writing. He felt out of his league.

The reporter arrived at the ER about five minutes before the first ambulance.

"I'm not sure, but I don't think this one's going to make it," the ER attendant told him, when he heard how seriously injured the victim was.

When the ambulance arrived, the reticent reporter asked a few questions, fearing he was being too intrusive. When he learned the name of the victim, a sister of a friend, he felt even worse. Painfully, he pushed on, asking more questions of authorities and grieving family members, as well as critical care workers. Two more ambulances arrived—two fatalities and one student who would survive. The reporter listened and asked a few more questions. He then left and returned to the newspaper office.

Back in the newsroom, the reporter began to write. No other story, he was certain, could be harder to write. Nothing had prepared him for this assignment. He wanted to be sure that he didn't offend the families of the victims, especially since he knew one of them so well. So he kept the story, focusing it on the basics taught in every news writing class——the who, what, when, where, why, and how of the story. He gave his copy to the managing editor, who read it carefully.

After a few minutes, the editor called the reporter back to his office.

"You've got the facts," he told him. "You told us the five *W*s and the *H*, but we already know these things. Where are your quotes?"

"I didn't put them in," the reporter said. "It just seems too offensive to quote grieving parents in a situation like this."

"Every story needs a quote," the editor explained, "especially stories like this one. Where's your notebook? Let me have it."

The managing editor took the notebook and sent the reporter away. About an hour later, the story showed up on the computer of the news editor, who called the reporter to the news editor's office. He complimented the reporter on the story, on its compassion, on the good judgment in refraining from using quotes purely to elicit a response from readers, and for letting the quotes show compassion, despite the agony of the situation, without pandering to the typical tragedy-story responses.

The reporter explained that it was the managing editor, not he, who had made the story so good. The news editor didn't care who wrote the quotes into the story, only that the story had them. A tragic story was given a human face through good editing.

In the next paper, the story of the wreck and the fatalities was the lead story. Running with it was the sidebar about the experiences in the emergency room. About a week later, the paper received a letter from the family of one of the victims thanking the paper for such a caring and accurate account of the horrors of the emergency room.

The managing editor saved what would have been a throw-away story by using his experience to teach the young reporter that there are ways to cover any event accurately and with compassion. The reporter discovered that day what good editors know to be true. Quotes are vital if stories are to become more than a list of unadorned facts. In this case, good editing retained the basic who, what, when, where, why, and how of the story, but enlarged the story by taking readers inside the emergency room to describe the extraordinary efforts to keep critically injured accident victims alive. That managing editor understood what experienced editors well understand: the careful development of the specific circumstances of an accident story can transport it into a lived experience for attentive readers. In this case, it introduced readers to the enduring consequences of what had happened that day. Editing created a better story.

The Importance of Editors

Editors are the people who review, rewrite, and edit the work of reporters. They assign stories to reporters and create opinion pieces. Often, media outlets have multiple editors with varied responsibilities. The larger the outlet, the more layers of editors one finds. All media have multiple divisions like advertising, business, production, and news-editorial. Newspapers pioneered the position of editor in the early 1800s. Editorial jobs in print journalism begin with the executive editor or editor in chief. Under this person are two editors, the managing editor and the editorial-page editor. Their areas within the news-editorial division are totally separate. The editorial-page editor is responsible for opinion, while the managing editor takes care of all other news that the outlet presents. Reporters may influence the editorial stance of the media outlet, but they are rarely allowed to write editorials. They deal exclusively with managing editors and those who work under them.

Under the managing editor, one finds another layer of editors. They might carry titles such as assistant managing editor for news or assistant managing editor for features. More likely, though, you will find titles such as news editor, sports editor, city editor, business editor, features editor, photo editor, and so on. The next layer of editors, the copy editors, generally work with editors and reporters in all areas. In broadcast, many of these positions also exist, but the job titles are not always the same. News directors, producers, assignment editors, and video editors are the most common names for those who do the editing jobs in broadcast. Online media would have a combination of print and broadcast editorial positions, since online encompasses presentation methods of print and broadcast.

The executive editor is responsible for all news-editorial content of a publication. For newspapers, budget meetings are held daily to determine major stories to include, especially on the front page. While editors from all areas attend the budget meeting, the executive editor would be the person to make the final call on anything controversial. A good example of this would be the work of Ben Bradlee at the *Washington Post* during the Watergate era. As executive editor, it was ultimately Bradlee's call to run the stories of Bob Woodward and Carl Bernstein and the other *Post* reporters as they uncovered information about the break-in at the Democratic National Headquarters in 1972 and the subsequent cover-up that led ultimately to the resignation of President Richard Nixon. Often, the *Post*'s stories were based upon anonymous sources and information that could not always be verified by more than one source. Bradlee had to make the decision to run the story. If the stories had proved to be inaccurate, it would have been Bradlee who would have been held accountable.

Within the editorial structure, the copy editor might be considered the foot soldier. While there is one city editor and one sports editor, there are usually several copy editors at work in a newsroom. Copy editors read stories to make sure that they make sense. They correct grammar and style mistakes. They verify facts. Though publications sometimes use names such as design or layout editor for the people who lay out pages, this job is still in the purview of the copy editor. Copy editors also write headlines for stories. While the job of editing for mistakes, laying out pages, and writing headlines might fall to different people at some outlets, at others, especially smaller publications, the same copy editor might proof the story, write its head, and lay out the page on which the story appears.

The broadcast newsroom operates in a similar way, though with different names and some variance in job responsibility. A news director at a television station would be comparable to the executive editor and managing editor of a large newspaper. The news director is responsible for developing the news-editorial product of the station, hiring employees, formulating budgets, and making other major decisions. Assignment editors at television stations do some of the same things their print counterparts do. They create the daily schedule for reporters and photographers. Because broadcast has multiple deadlines daily for news shows, the assignment editors must stay in contact with employees in the field to make sure that they will be able to put their package together in time for its scheduled slot in a newscast. Video editors work with the products created in the field. They put the stories together, though in smaller markets this is often the responsibility of reporters.

The Social Responsibility of Editors

Meetings among editors on how to handle the day's news can be controversial. At a morning meeting of editors at the Detroit *Free Press* there was a heated discussion about the paper's decision to run a picture of a missing seven-month-old girl. The baby's body was found in a vacant lot after her father admitted to killing the child and then leading police to where he'd hastily buried his daughter. What raised the public's anger was not the story, but the large, color photograph of a medical examiner carrying the tiny child's body away in a plastic bag. Immediately, people began calling the paper to complain. The decision to use the photograph had been made in an editors' meeting. The next day, its editors explained they had weighed public opposition against the paper's responsibility to "tell our readers about a horrific story that took place in our community."

The public outcry over its coverage required the paper's editorial-page editor to deal with the backlash. He ran an editorial on the child's death, pointing out how the death could have been prevented since abuse of the child had been reported to the proper protective agencies at least two months earlier. Public reaction to the paper's continuing coverage filled two thirds of the editorial page and included the same photograph that had so enflamed readers, only this time the photo was in black and white and about one column by three inches. The episode points up how the decisions of editors matter every day in every publication where editors work. In the Detroit example, one reader on September 19, 2000, wrote, "If it takes a photograph like the one you published on Sept. 15 to awaken people to the pain and suffering being inflicted on children each and every day, then so be it."

The U.S. Department of Labor, Bureau of Labor Statistics, in its *Occupational Outlook Handbook,* predicts that editorial jobs in print journalism and jobs as producers in broadcast will increase between 9 and 17 percent from current numbers through 2014. The Bureau of Labor Statistics estimated that in 2004 there were approximately 28,000 employees within broadcast and cinema who worked with video or film footage. Of those workers, more than 62 percent were editors. With the expanding broadcast field in cable and satellite, the government predicts growth in this area of editing comparable to that of print editors and producers through 2014.

In the early 1990s, few media outlets had a web presence. Today, it is almost impossible to find a television or radio station, or a newspaper or magazine, that does not have a website. Online editing jobs will continue to be a source of employment for people with editing skills. So, wherever you look in communications, editing jobs exist, and there are hundreds of independent editing companies that freelance for and subcontract work from major publishers.

With more information available than can be shared with the public, someone must choose which stories to pass on to the public and which stories not to use. This process, called gatekeeping, is central to the work of the editor. While reporters are responsible for generating news through their contacts and ideas, news editors, city editors, and specialty area editors also have ideas about what is newsworthy and assign stories to reporters. **At the heart of gatekeeping is the editors' understanding of what is newsworthy,** and fundamental to what makes information newsworthy is knowing the audience your media outlet serves. So, in some ways, editors "edit" before reporters ever write the stories by focusing upon issues that affect the greatest number of people within the audience of the media outlet and letting other stories become secondary or not presented to the readership or viewership.

A Case Study in Editing

You are the news editor for a daily newspaper that serves a population of around 150,000 people. Your constituency is comprised of people who have mostly worked in textile mills and agriculture, but those jobs are rapidly being lost to the move of manufacturing overseas and to shrinking farm profits. The readership tends to be conservative, but, increasingly, people are moving into your area who work in a research and technological business center about thirty minutes away. You have five stories from which to choose to fill three nonlocal spots in the next paper. Your wire editor tells you that these are the stories: Chinese exports to the United States top $800 billion; Midwest snows may reduce grain crops by two thirds; scientists say the Arctic ice cap is shrinking three inches a year; new federal rules will create more delays at airports; and a pregnant woman is missing in California, presumed murdered by her husband.

Now imagine that you are the news editor who must decide which of these stories makes it into your paper or onto your news website. You push the Chinese exports story, and no one argues. You also decide to run the story on airport delays. You say that the influx of technology workers who fly from two international airports within easy commute of your city means the story will be of value to readers. Some people in the meeting say that the grain reduction story is more important and should fill this slot, but you win the debate. The airport story runs.

Your final choice is the story of the missing California woman, and no one disagrees. In fact, other editors begin calling reporters and giving them assignments related to the story. What the editors know is that a local, pregnant woman disappeared nearly three months earlier, and her husband is the suspect, though the woman has yet to be found.

Your editorial staff chose these stories based on their understanding of news values. The choice to use one story but not another is central to editorial work. Knowing the audience is foremost in making this judgment. But other factors come into play. Timeliness is important. So is proximity. With two airports within forty-five minutes of the city and an increasing readership that flies often, this story made sense to run. Prominence is important, too. Though none of the stories these editors considered dealt with a prominent person like the president or a local leader or personality, had one of them done so, the editorial choices might have changed.

Editors look at stories to find relevance for the audience. The Chinese export story was relevant because hundreds of local jobs have been lost to foreign manufacturers. This would not be a pleasant story, but it is one that would matter locally. The story about the missing California woman was timely. It offered the paper the opportunity to localize the story by tying it back to the missing local woman. Because the story was one of suspected domestic violence, conflict existed, and it involved human interest.

The Future of Editing

In most twenty-first-century newsrooms, editors work digitally. Editors nowadays need to know the basics of web design. Editors of websites for print and broadcast outlets will need to be familiar with video and how to upload it. As media outlets expand their online offerings, they are requesting more interaction with their audiences. They are asking members of the audience to send in photos to be uploaded, and they are setting up web logs and online chats. Here, according to Lea Donosky, interactive editor for the *Atlanta Journal-Constitution*, editors need to be particularly vigilant, policing the language of those who write in. Some people who participate online, Dave Larimer, of floridatoday.com, agrees, are rude and crude. Catching, changing, or eliminating real-time postings will be challenging for future editors who will have multiple blogs and chats to oversee in addition to posting more traditional news stories, images, and videos. Automated computer programs can now search online news outlets for the day's major stories. It pairs them with video and still photos taken from sites found through Google image searches and from YouTube.

However the technology improves, it is difficult to see a time in which there will not be great demand for intellectually engaged editors who have a deep understanding of their audience and its need for news. Digital-age editors may work with different tools but will need the same intuitive skills they have used since the nineteenth century, when Joseph Pulitzer warned reporters and editors that **"accuracy, accuracy, accuracy"** needed to be their highest priority. Since then, Associated Press managing editors have advised that the ability to "think analytically" and "write concisely," now joined to "an ability to present information visually," are key qualities of the best editors. That's why the look of modern newsrooms may change but the values that make for socially responsible reporting won't. Behind those flat-screen monitors labor reporters and editors, working cooperatively to provide citizens and our democracy with news worth knowing.

Health and Medicine Reporting

HOLLY SHREVE GILBERT

Ritalin took quite a public beating during the 1980s and '90s when the press and publishing industry overwhelmingly characterized it as a menace to society. The stimulant was purported to cause cancer, provoke suicide, and incite homicidal behavior. Despite this, millions of American children and adults diagnosed with attention deficit hyperactivity disorder were taking one or more of the pills every day. A project involving James Shaya, James Windell, and me got started because we were interested in connecting these extremely disparate dots.

We began our research with a broad analysis of the press on Ritalin. Most of it was generated by a dozen or so cases in which the drug had been implicated in a patient's addiction, death, or psychosis; understandably most of the news was bad. Not so easy to understand, however, was the fact that the media coverage of Ritalin was almost exclusively based on anecdotal evidence. The press and the publishing industry had, for the most part, neglected to provide the public with any significant objective analysis of the drug.

We realized then that we had more than a story; it would take a book to fill this information gap. Within a few months Bantam had bought the idea for what became *What You Know about Ritalin,* and we found ourselves with a direction, a deadline, and a daunting task.

Although my colleagues were medical and mental health-care professionals, we agreed that in order to avoid the pitfall of being too limited, we would not base the book solely on their opinions and expertise. I was the appointed skeptic and given a mandate to challenge every claim and conclusion brought to the table until it was thoroughly fact-checked. Ritalin was extremely controversial, and we wanted our research, first and foremost, to be grounded in certainty.

We dived into the story by starting with the science, and within several weeks we'd amassed a mountain of research on methylphenidate, the generic name for Ritalin. The Internet was enormously helpful in this task, but in 1998 and 1999, when we were doing our research, the web was nowhere near as fertile as it is today. Major databases, such as the National Institutes of Health, the American Medical Association, and the Department of Education were digitized to a moderate degree, but we still had to resort to phone calls and written requests to obtain the bulk of the data.

Newspaper archives were crucial to our book as well, but, again, most of the stories were not available online. We had to track down stories like "Ritalin Linked to Bludgeoning Death of Teenager" and "Parents Blame Son's Suicide on Ritalin" the old-fashioned way, by going to the library and taking extended trips on the microfilm reader. These excursions were particularly annoying for me, as I have never spent more than ten minutes in front of one these contraptions without succumbing to a serious bout of motion sickness.

Obviously, having a doctor and a psychotherapist as colleagues was invaluable when it came to interpreting articles from medical journals with scary names like "Child and Adolescent Psychopharmacology" and "Diagnosis in Psychopathology." To actually be able to write the book so that the layperson could understand it, however, it was essential that I arm myself with a substantive understanding of the related science. In essence, I did what any journalist does when he or she is writing a story; I researched and I studied.

We also found it necessary to embark on a crash course in government policy. Because Ritalin was, and remains, a controlled substance, agencies like the Food and Drug Administration, the Drug Enforcement Administration, and the Department of Education became main characters in our book. Deciphering their roles, untangling their policies, and interpreting their applications to our material became one of the most challenging tasks of the entire project.

No research was more beneficial, in the end, than that conducted in the kitchens and living rooms of parents and children who had stories to tell about Ritalin.

It is, of course, the human element that transforms a piece of journalism from a mere report into a compelling story, and we had plenty of it for the book. We spent hours with fathers and mothers and middle-school students who shared horror stories as well as happy endings. At that time, the stigma of psychotherapy, psychostimulants, or, really, psycho anything, was much more pervasive than it is today. One father whose young daughter's life was positively affected by the drug told me through tears that he still couldn't bear to admit to his friends and family that her treatment program required visits to "a shrink." Conversely, the mother of a young boy who was prescribed Ritalin by a pediatrician who "barely made eye contact with him" shivered as she recalled the zombie effect the drug had on her child.

Our "aha" moment, rather than being monumental and cathartic, was instead a budding realization that the interviews with patients and parents would provide the foundation of our book. The painful and poignant stories of success and failure with Ritalin exemplified what we would say: Ritalin was neither entirely curse nor cure, but when prescribed properly it could be exceptionally therapeutic. As a journalist I was somewhat disappointed that the proverbial nut graph or so-what factor of our work wasn't going to be something more provocative. But **I took enormous satisfaction in knowing that what we were writing was truth.**

The storytelling, incidentally, was perhaps one of our greatest challenges. Three voices and one story present an obvious problem; who, in the end, is the voice? To overcome this obstacle we worked in layers; as each chapter was written, it was processed by the psychotherapist, the pediatrician, and the journalist—in that order. The final edit, a group project in which the three of us huddled around a computer monitor in my living room and read each word out loud, might have been unceremonious, but it got the job done and, most importantly, the stories told.

"Millions of children and adults begin each day by swallowing a little yellow pill."

This was Jim Windell's original lead for our book and I thought it was a gem. Concise and visual, it set the stage for what we wanted to write. I'd do that lead over in a heartbeat if we were to write this story for a newspaper or magazine article. In the second paragraph, though, I'd immediately introduce the reader to the conflicted father, because he sincerely and emotionally exemplified the plight of our audience. Instead, in the book the entire first chapter is void of human experience and serves to explain, in depth, the chemistry and efficacy of Ritalin. That call was made by our capable but oh so pragmatic editor (she also insisted that Windell's lead be changed, a directive that grieves me to this day).

Given the lack of shock value in our book, and the fact that its pages do not contain the "silver bullet" so often pandered by self-help gurus, it didn't surprise us that it never appeared on a bestseller list. Even so, it did sell respectably and garnered overwhelmingly positive reviews by those whom we most wanted to enlighten—parents and patients. It continues to sell around the world today, several years after its publication. A reader in Australia recently posted that our research removed "the cliches and media distortions about ADHD and the use of Ritalin. Dr Shaya (et al.) carefully annotates every fact with the source of that fact. As a parent of an ADHD teenager, this book has provided me with a strategy to manage the ADHD situation."

A little gratification goes a long way, especially when you've spent five years working on a story. Longer lasting, however, is the lesson I learned about using expert sources. Far too often in our profession we interpret this as a mandate to fill our copy with quotes from authorities, and, as a result, our writing comes off as arrogant, stuffy, and irrelevant. There is, in the end, a priceless and genuine expertise provided by the perspective of the people on the other side of the equation—the laypeople. These are the experts whose experiences resonate with readers, and nowhere has this become more evident than in the citizen journalism that is flourishing on the Internet today. For the fledgling journalist, this is a cautionary tale worth repeating: don't fail your readers by under-representing them in your writing. They are, after all, why journalism exists.

Weekly Reporting

SHAWN MURPHY

"Passion Proves Fatal."

This was the headline over a front-page cop beat story that I wrote in the late 1980s while a reporter for the *Island Sun,* a weekly newspaper on Florida's Anna Maria Island, about a man who had died while having intercourse with his next-door mistress—both identified by name and address. They were eighty years old—the unique twist that I thought defined its newsworthiness.

This close-knit island community along the Gulf Coast was, and still is, a retirement haven. Most of the winter residents were themselves senior citizens. Perhaps needless to say, these readers were displeased by this story in their *Island Sun,* a paper distributed free to their doorsteps, including the doorsteps of the mistress and her deceased lover's now-widowed wife.

Angry phone calls to our newsroom, including a death threat directed at me, began the morning the paper hit the streets. As the week passed, dozens of readers canceled mailed subscriptions to their summer homes and threatened to file a littering complaint with the police department should the *Sun* get tossed into their driveway again. And they wrote letters: letters to the editor renaming the paper "the *Island Enquirer*" and letters to our advertisers asking that they discontinue running ads in our paper, many of which did. By week's end my editor asked me, "Are you sure we did the right thing?" By this point, I was having my doubts.

All of this changed, however, when the widow stopped by the *Sun*'s newsroom. I will never forget watching her pull up in front of our office, slowly step out of her car, casually walk through the newsroom door, and gently answer the receptionist's offer to assist her by saying, "Yes, dear, I would like to renew my subscription to the *Island Sun.*"

Those words echo in my head to this day. Expecting tears, sobs, and a tongue-lashing, we got grace, dignity, and kindness. At that moment I could have crawled under my newsroom desk. Instead, I watched her write the check for the subscription, thank the receptionist, and drive away. From that point forward I heard nothing from her, the true victim in this story.

Years later, I can reflect. As a reporter fresh out of college, I pushed for the story when my editor's first instinct was to hold it. My editor thought that perhaps we ought to wait until the police investigation into the tampered body had concluded. He noted that the police report, the main source of information for the story acquired on deadline, had stated that it appeared there was no criminal foul play. But I was young and green. I saw comedy in the tragedy; I saw sweet irony in the generational Peyton Place scenario.

Today I know I saw it the wrong way. Years ago I did not clearly see the impact that news about sensitive issues in a weekly newspaper in a small community can have on real people and their three-dimensional lives.

Jim Pumarlo's book *Bad News and Good Judgment: A Guide to Reporting on Sensitive Issues in a Small-Town Newspaper* addresses coverage of controversial and sensitive stories such as suicides, rapes, and student-athlete suspensions. It discusses the appropriateness of running gory photos of fatal accident scenes, and whether it is necessary to name names of those charged with, but not convicted of, crimes, as noted in police reports. It concludes with adaptable sample newsroom policies that teeter on the parapet between ethics and realism, what is considered "right" by readers versus what is deemed "just" by reporters. While it does not specifically address what to do if faced with a story about a heart-attack death caused by an adulterous affair conducted by two octogenarians in a small town of retirees, it is nonetheless a helpful resource for both reporters and editors at community newspapers.

The stories about which I am most proud are the ones I wrote for weekly newspapers from Florida to Maine that have helped real people in very real ways. These stories, initially overlooked by daily newspapers, included the following:

} When the nearby chain-owned daily declined coverage about a fundraiser for an uninsured lifeguard in need of cancer surgery because it saw the story as an inconsequential small-town matter, my story for a weekly paper proved to be a catalyst for fundraising that led to his operation being fully covered.

} When a city daily opted not to go beyond the spot news brief about a fire leveling a house, my story for a weekly examined the human impact of the fire on a family's home. And follow-up stories ensured that donations of shelter, food, and clothing came to the parents and children displaced by the blaze.

} When a mixed-race couple and their children moved into a very Waspy New Hampshire small town and were greeted by ignorance and racism, which was of little interest to the big-city daily paper, my story for a weekly paper told their story and shined the journalistic spotlight on the scurrying racist rats.

Unfortunately, the result from a slew of media mergers and chains gobbling up community newspapers, both weeklies and small dailies, in recent years has been somewhat of a local news disconnect. Community news—the type that affects the average American in real ways—has been sacrificed. Consequently, city neighborhoods and small towns without papers have limited access to the news that impacts them the most. These newspapers are essential, since they serve as crusaders for their communities and as powerful tools to effect change.

Weekly newspaper editors and reporters should accept that their media cannot compete with daily papers, television, radio, or the Internet for the news of the day. Instead, weeklies should concede the limitations of their timeliness and opt instead for depth and breadth of coverage. The luxury that weeklies have that dailies do not is time, which is used to work a story into a news feature with a fresh development and unique angle instead of an inverted-pyramid, "just the facts" formulaic news story.

SIDEBAR

Weeklies can expend the resources necessary to repeatedly cover a story in-depth from beginning to end—exploring causes, examining outcomes, finding solutions—whereas a nearby TV network news crew or large daily newspaper will parachute in to report only on the breaking spot news story with little chance of a follow-up, giving its audience a Polaroid snapshot rather than a landscape portrait. Because weeklies are concerned with news on a micro level rather than a macro level, they are capable of scooping the dailies and local TV stations because these larger mediums overlook the small towns or city neighborhoods except to report on odd stories or horrific acts.

In short, weeklies can demonstrate compassion for their communities and the people living within them—despite what a certain Florida newspaper did more than a decade and a half ago.

Further Readings

American Society of Newspaper Editors. "Examining Our Credibility." http://www.asne.org/kiosk/reports/99reports/1999examiningourcredibilityindex.html.

Aucoin, James. "The Media and Reform, 1900–1917." In *The Media in America: A History,* edited by William David Sloan. 6th ed. Northport, AL: Vision Press, 2005.

Bass, Frank. *The Associated Press Guide to Internet Research and Reporting.* New York: Basic Books, 2002.

Bates, Stephen. *Realigning Journalism with Democracy: The Hutchins Commission, Its Times, and Ours.* Washington, D.C.: The Annenberg Washington Program in Communications Policy Studies, 1995.

Beam, Randal A. "Journalism Professionalism as an Organizational Level Concept." *Journalism Monographs* 121 (June 1990).

Bishop, Ronald. "To Protect and Serve: The Guard Dog Function of Journalism in Coverage of the Japanese-American Internment." *Journalism & Communication Monographs* 2, no. 2 (2000): 65–103.

Bruns, Axel. *Gatewatching: Collaborative Online News Production.* New York: Peter Lang Publishing, 2005.

Bybee, Carl. "Can Democracy Survive in the Post-Factual Age? A Return to the Lippmann-Dewey Debate about the Politics of News." *Journalism & Communication Monographs* 1, no. 1 (1999).

Cunningham, Brent. "Re-Thinking Objectivity." *Columbia Journalism Review* 42, no. 2 (2003): 24–32.

Dimmick, John, Yan Chen, and Zhan Li. "Competition Between the Internet and Traditional News Media: The Gratification-Opportunities Niche Dimension." *The Journal of media Economics* 17 (2004): 19–33.

Ehrlich, Matthew C. "The Journalism of Outrageousness: Tabloid Television News vs. Investigative News." *Journalism & Mass Communication Monographs* 155 (February 1996).

Evensen, Bruce J. "Progressivism, Muckraking, and Objectivity." In *Fair & Balanced: A History of Journalistic Objectivity*, edited by Steven R. Knowlton and Karen L. Freeman. Northport, AL: Vision Press, 2005.

Fredin, Eric S. "Rethinking the News Story for the Internet: Hyperstory Prototypes and a Model of the User." *Journalism & Mass Communication Monographs* 163, September 1997.

Gans, Herbert J. *Democracy and the News.* New York: Oxford University Press, 2004.

Gibbs, Cheryl J., and Tom Warhover. *Getting the Whole Story: Reporting and Writing the News.* New York: The Guilford Press, 2002.

Gillmor, Dan. "Moving Toward Participatory Journalism." *Nieman Reports* 57, no. 3, (2003): 79–80.

Grossman, Lawrence K. *The Electronic Republic: Reshaping Democracy in the Information Age.* New York: Viking Press, 1995.

Haynes, Charles C., Sam Chaltain, and Susan M. Glisson. *First Freedoms: A Documentary History of First American Rights in America.* New York: Oxford University Press, 2006.

Hewitt, Hugh. *Understanding the Information Revolution That's Changing Your World.* Nashville: Nelson Books, 2005.

Howe, Jeff P. "The New (Investigative) Journalism." *Crowd Sourcing: Tracking the Rise* (November 4, 2006), http://crowdsourcing.typepad.com/cs/2006/11_the_new-investi.html.

Johnson, Thomas, and Barbara Kaye. "Webelievability: A Path Model Examining How Convention and Reliance Predict Online Credibility." *Journalism & Mass Communication Quarterly* 79, no. 3 (2002): 619–42.

Kovach, Bill. "The Roots of Our Responsibility." *Nieman Reports* 53, no. 4 (1999).

Kovach, Bill, and Tom Rosenstiel. *The Elements of Journalism: What Newspeople Should Know and the Public Should Expect.* New York: Three Rivers Press, 2007.

Kurprius, David D. "Sources and Civic Journalism: Changing Patterns of Reporting," *Journalism & Mass Communication Quarterly* 79, no. 4 (2002): 853–66.

Lasica, J. D. "Weblogs: A New Source of News." *Online Journalism Review,* April 18, 2002.

Lippmann, Walter. *Public Opinion.* 1922. Reprint, New York: Free Press, 1997.

Lowrey, Wilson. "Mapping the Journalism-Blogging Relationship." *Journalism* 7, no. 4 (2006): 477–500.

Lowery, Wilson, and William Anderson. "The Journalism behind the Curtain: Participatory Functions on the Internet and Their Impact on Perceptions of the Work of Journalism." *Journal of Computer-Mediated Communication* 10, no. 3 (2005): article 13.

Manoff, Robert Karl, and Michael Schudson, eds. *Reading the News.* New York: Pantheon Books, 1986.

Matheson, Donald. "Weblogs and the Epistemology of the News: Some Trends in Online Journalism." *New Media and Society* 6, no. 4 (August 2004): 443–68.

Newhagen, John E., and Mark R. Levy. *The Future of Journalism in a Distributed Communication Architecture.* Mahwah, NJ: Lawrence Erlbaum, 1997.

Niles, Robert. "A Journalist's Guide to Crowd Sourcing." *Online Journalism Review,* July 31, 2007, http://www.ojr.org/gr/stories/07073/niles.

Palser, Barb. "Is It Journalism? Yahoo! News Attracts a Large Audience But Does No Original Reporting." *American Journalism Review* 24, no. 5 (2002): 62.

Paterson, Chris, and David Domingo, eds. *Making Online News: The Ethnography of New Media Production.* New York: Peter Lang Publishing, 2008.

Paul, Nora, and Kathleen A. Hansen. "Newsroom Information Practices: Results of a National Survey, Implications for News Organizations." Paper presented at the Conference on Dynamics of Converging Media, Columbia, SC, November 7, 2002.

The Pew Center for the People and the Press. "Pew Internet & American Life Project." 2000–2008.

Reston, James. *Deadline: A Memoir.* New York: Random House, 1991.

Rosenstiel, Thomas, and Amy S. Mitchell, eds. *Thinking Clearly: Case Studies in Journalistic Decision-Making.* New York: Columbia University Press, 2003.

Schiller, Dan. "An Historical Approach to Objectivity and Professionalism in American News Reporting." *Journal of Communication* 29, no. 4 (1979): 46–57.

Schwarzlose, Richard A. "The Marketplace of Ideas: A Measure of Free Expression." *Journalism Monographs* 118, December 1989.

Shaw, Donald L., Maxwell McCombs, and Gerry Klein, *Advanced Reporting: Discovering Patterns in News Events.* 2nd ed. Prospect Heights, IL: Vision Press, 1997.

Singer, Jane B. "The Metro Wide Web: Changes in Newspapers' Gatekeeping Role Online." *Journalism & Mass Communication Quarterly* 78 (2001: 65–80.

Sloan, Wm. David, and Cheryl S. Wray, eds., *Masterpieces of Reporting.* Northport, AL: Vision Press, 1997.

Smolkin, Rachel. "The Expanding Blogosphere." *American Journalism Review,* June 2004, 38–43.

Society of Professional Journalists. "Code of Ethics." 1996, www.spj.org/ethics_code.asp

Sperber, A. M. *Murrow: His Life and Times.* New York: Freundlich Books, 1986.

Stevens, John D. *Shaping the First Amendment: The Development of Free Expression.* Beverly Hills: Sage, 1982.

Storm, E. Jordan. "The Endurance of Gatekeeping in an Evolving Newsroom: A Multi-Method Study of Web-Generated User Content." Paper presented at the International Communication Association Meeting in San Francisco, May 23, 2007.

Thussu, Daya Kishan, and Des Freedman, eds. *War and the Media: Reporting Conflict 24/7.* New York: Free Press, 2003.

Tobin, James. *Ernie Pyle's War: America's Eyewitness to World War II.* New York: The Free Press, 1997.

Williams, Bruce A., and Michael X. Deli Carpini. "Unchained Reaction: The Collapse of Media Gatekeeping and the Clinton-Lewinsky Scandal." *Journalism* 1, no. 1 (2000): 61–85.

Witt, Leonard. "Is Public Journalism Morphing into the Public's Journalism?" *National Civic Review* 93 (Fall 2004): 49–57.

Contributors

BRUCE EVENSEN was a broadcast journalist for eleven years and a network news bureau chief in Washington, D.C., and Jerusalem. He has written many books and articles on journalism history and the social responsibility of the press. Evensen has a doctoral degree from the University of Wisconsin-Madison and is graduate director of the master of arts in journalism program at DePaul University.

JAMES L. AUCOIN is the author of *The Evolution of American Investigative Journalism*, published by the University of Missouri Press. He is a professor of communication at the University of South Alabama and received his doctorate from the University of Missouri School of Journalism. He has spent fourteen years reporting and editing newspapers.

FREDERICK R. BLEVENS is a professor in the School of Journalism and Mass Communication at Florida International University. For nearly twenty years, he was a journalist at metropolitan newspapers in Florida, New Jersey, Pennsylvania, and Texas. He is past president of the American Journalism Historians Association. In 2001, he was recognized as a national Teacher of the Year by the Freedom Forum.

CAROLYN S. CARLSON has a doctorate from Georgia State University, where she is a lecturer in the communications department. She is a longtime reporter for the Associated Press as well as a reporter for the *Orlando Sentinel* and the *Augusta*

Chronicle. She is co-chair of the Society of Professional Journalists Freedom of Information Committee Subcommittee on Campus Crime.

CATHERINE CASSARA-JEMAI is an associate professor of journalism at Bowling Green State University in Bowling Green, Ohio, where she teaches undergraduate courses in news writing, public affairs reporting, editing, the international press, and media history, as well as graduate courses in news framing. She is the author of several articles and book chapters on human rights and American newspaper coverage of international news.

MIKE CONKLIN is journalist-in-residence at DePaul University in Chicago. For thirty-five years he was a reporter, feature writer, and daily columnist for the *Chicago Tribune.* He has been a correspondent for several television and radio stations and continues to do freelance work for newspapers and magazines.

DAVID COPELAND is a former editor and reporter and currently the A. J. Fletcher and Distinguished University Professor in the School of Communications at Elon University. He is the author or editor of ten books, including *The Idea of a Free Press: The Enlightenment and Its Unruly Legacy.* He is past president of the American Journalism Historians Association and received his doctorate from the University of North Carolina.

DAVID R. DAVIES, a former reporter for the *Arkansas Gazette* in Little Rock, is the dean of the Honors College and professor of mass communication and journalism at the University of Southern Mississippi. The author of two books, he has written extensively about the Southern press and the civil rights movement.

SANDRA ELLIS teaches at the University of Wisconsin–River Falls, where she supervises the news operation of the campus radio station and TV cable channel. Ellis worked for radio, newspaper, and television stations in Virginia, Tennessee, and North Carolina.

ART GOLAB has worked for the City News Bureau in Chicago, Reuters Business Wire, and, since 1994, the *Chicago Sun-Times.* He has been doing database reporting since 2003, reporting racial profiling by Illinois police departments as well as abuses in Chicago's Hired Trucks and Worker's Compensation programs.

ARI L. GOLDMAN is a professor at the Columbia University Graduate School in Journalism, where he is the director of the Scripps Howard Program on Religion and Journalism. He is a former *New York Times* reporter who now writes the "On Religion" column for the *New York Daily News.*

JANAN HANNA is a graduate of the Loyola University School of Law and a former reporter for the *Chicago Tribune.* She has been a passionate advocate for reporters' access rights. She teaches journalism skills courses at Northwestern University and media law at DePaul University.

JANICE HUME is an associate professor at the Grady College of Journalism and Mass Communication at the University of Georgia. She's a former lifestyle and arts editor at the *Mobile Register* and the author of *Obituaries in American Culture,* published in 2000, and the co-author of *Journalism in a Culture of Grief,* published in 2008.

EDMUND LAWLER teaches journalism at DePaul University. For fifteen years, Ed was a reporter and editor for several newspapers and the Associated Press. He received his master's degree from the University of Notre Dame and is the author of five business books.

DAVID MARSHALL is a professor of communication at Shaw University. He spent over fifteen years as a television news anchor, reporter, and writer in Atlanta, New York City, Philadelphia, and Baltimore. He holds a doctoral degree from Temple University.

JAMES MARTIN is an associate professor of journalism at the University of North Alabama and editor of *American Journalism,* the journal of the American Journalism Historians Association. He is the former publisher of a weekly newspaper and a national religious monthly. He received his doctorate from the Southern Illinois University at Carbondale.

SHAWN MURPHY is chair of the Department of Journalism and co-director of the Center for Communication and Journalism at the State University of New York at Plattsburgh. Murphy worked as a reporter, editor, and photographer for several newspapers and magazines throughout New England and in Florida.

ANN O'DATA LAWSON is the director of forensics and an instructor in communication arts at Malone College in Canton, Ohio. She worked for thirteen years in corporate public relations, winning several awards for her community service. She has a master of business administration degree from Youngstown State University.

JOHN J. PAULY is the William R. Burleigh and E. W. Scripps professor and dean of the Diederich College of Communication at Marquette University. His research focuses on the history and sociology of journalism and the theory and practice of literary journalism. He is currently completing a book on the origins, influence, and legacy of the New Journalism of the 1960s.

LISA PECOT-HEBERT is an assistant professor at DePaul University, specializing in broadcast journalism, who received her doctoral degree from the University of Georgia. She has produced a health-based television program called *Urban Pediatrics* and has also reported for the *Dallas Morning News* and the *New Orleans Tribune.*

SCOTT L. POWERS joined the *Chicago Tribune* in 2000 and was named entertainment editor in 2002. He oversees the Sunday Arts and Entertainment section as well as daily arts and entertainment coverage. He has a master's degree from Kent State University, where he wrote his thesis on arts criticism. He has taught arts reporting and online journalism at Northwestern University and DePaul University.

TRACE REGAN is a journalism professor at Ohio Wesleyan University in Delaware, Ohio. His research interest is journalism ethics. Trace was a television news reporter for nine years at KWWL-TV in Waterloo, Iowa, and has also worked at the *Dallas Morning News*, the *Charlotte Observer*, and KOMO-TV in Seattle, Washington.

SONNY RHODES is an associate professor of journalism at the University of Arkansas at Little Rock. He has worked for newspapers for twenty-five years, including service as chief of the copy desk at the *Arkansas Democrat-Gazette*. Rhodes also writes a nature column for that newspaper.

SAM G. RILEY is a professor of communication at Virginia Tech University. He received his doctorate degree from the University of North Carolina and has written eleven books on the history of the magazine industry as well as published works on African Americans in the mainstream news media and columnists and their work.

AMY SCHMITZ Weiss is a doctoral candidate in journalism at the University of Texas at Austin. She has worked at *Chicago Tribune Online* and the *Indianapolis Star News Online*, where she produced and wrote news packages. Her research interests include online journalism, media sociology, news production, and multimedia journalism.

DEBRA A. SCHWARTZ is a veteran freelance reporter for many news outlets, including Reuters, the *Chicago Tribune*, and the *New York Times*. She received a doctorate degree in journalism and public communication from the University of Maryland in 2004. Her book *Writing Green: Advocacy and Investigative Reporting about the Environment in the Early 21st Century* was published in 2007.

HOLLY SHREVE GILBERT is an adjunct instructor of journalism at Oakland University in Rochester, Michigan. She has written for newspapers and magazines, and in 1999 co-authored the mass market paperback *What You Need to Know about Ritalin*.

LES SILLARS received his doctoral degree from the University of Texas at Austin in 2004 and is associate professor of journalism at Patrick Henry College in Purcellville, Virginia. He is an editor at *World* magazine, a contributing editor at *Salvo* magazine, and an instructor in the World Journalism Institute. His byline has appeared in the *Washington Times*.

STEVE SMITH is a lecturer at Appalachian State University in Boone, North Carolina, and has been teaching courses in electronic media and broadcasting since 1997. Steve began his radio career in 1968, and has worked at nine radio stations from North Carolina to Hawaii.

BRUCE C. SWAFFIELD is the founder and director of the Worldwide Forum on Education and Culture. He teaches writing, literature, and journalism courses at Regent University in Virginia Beach and writes a monthly commentary on international issues for *Quill* magazine, published by the Society of Professional Journalists.

SHAYLA THIEL-STERN is an assistant professor in the School of Journalism and Mass Communication at the University of Minnesota. Earlier in her career, she worked for Washington Post/Newsweek Interactive and was a contributor to CNN.com and brittanica.com. Her book *Instant Identity: Adolescent Girls and the World of Instant Messaging* was published by Peter Lang in 2007.

Index